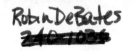

D0485067

Powerful Praise for *Girl Power*

"AN ENLIGHTENING READ—LIKE TAKING A PEEK AT THE COLLECTIVE DIARY OF TODAY'S AMERICAN TEENAGE GIRLS. GIRL POWER will be a comforting and vital revelation: whether a cowgirl in Nevada, a homegirl in L.A., or a sorority girl in South Carolina, all girls coming of age wrestle with the same issues and share what Hillary Carlip calls 'the universal desire for love, acceptance, and a sense of belonging.'"
   —Jacqueline Shannon, author of *Why It's Great to Be a Girl*

"STIRRING. . . WE ALL NEED SOMEONE TO HEAR US WHEN WE SHOUT, TO ENCOURAGE US WHEN WE SING. What is remarkable about GIRL POWER is not only the fierce music of many voices but the way in which Hillary Carlip creates a place of trust and love in which they can resonate."
   —Francesca Lia Block, author of *Weetzie Bat* and *Witch Baby*

"THIS BOOK GIVES US A CHANCE TO HEAR THE VOICES OF GIRLS WHO ALL TOO OFTEN LIVE THEIR LIVES ON THE REMOTEST CORNERS OF THE MINDS."
       —Judy Mann, author of *The Difference: Growing Up Female in America*

more . . .

"STUNNING... A DEEPLY MOVING AND OFTEN HAUNTING ACCOUNT OF ADOLESCENCE."
—Connie Glaser, co-author of *Swim with the Dolphins*

"WHAT A MAGNIFICENT AND IMPORTANT BOOK FOR WOMEN AND MEN ALIKE. There are very few opportunities to get an intimate view into the minds and hearts of today's young women. I discovered a clearer awareness of myself, and deeper appreciation for all women, with the turn of each page of GIRL POWER."
—Jennifer Aniston, actress, *Friends*

"HILLARY CARLIP REACHES INTO THE AWKWARD TIME OF A GIRL'S LIFE AND BARES IT ALL, UNEDITED. No longer hushed and behind closed doors, she gives young women from all walks of life an opportunity to speak about dreams, joys, the sadness and horrors of their worlds. This book is sure to be a beacon in the darkness for those who feel that they are alone."
—Melissa Etheridge

Girl Power

Hillary Carlip

with photographs by Nicola Goode

WARNER BOOKS

A Time Warner Company

If you purchase this book without a cover you should be aware that this book may have been stolen property and reported as "unsold and destroyed" to the publisher. In such case neither the author nor the publisher has received any payment for this "stripped book."

Copyright © 1995 by Hillary Carlip
All rights reserved.

Grateful acknowledgment is made to Red Crane Books for permission to reprint an excerpt from the previously published "Working in the Dark: Reflection of a Poet of the Barrio" © 1992 by Jimmy Santiago Baca.

Warner Books, Inc., 1271 Avenue of the Americas, New York, NY 10020

W A Time Warner Company

Printed in the United States of America
First Printing: July 1995
10 9 8 7 6 5 4 3

Library of Congress Cataloging-in-Publication Data
Carlip, Hillary.
    Girl Power: Young women speak out! / Hillary Carlip.
        p.   cm.
    ISBN 0-446-67021-9
    1. Teenage girls—United States—Attitudes. I. Title.
HQ798.C274   1995
305.23'5—dc20   94-41718
                                                              CIP

Book design by Wilderbeast Grafiks
Cover photography by Nicola Goode
Cover design by Julia Kushnirsky

ATTENTION: SCHOOLS AND CORPORATIONS
WARNER books are available at quantity discounts with bulk purchase for educational, business, or sales promotional use. For information, please write to: SPECIAL SALES DEPARTMENT, WARNER BOOKS, 1271 AVENUE OF THE AMERICAS, NEW YORK, N.Y. 10020

ARE THERE WARNER BOOKS
YOU WANT BUT CANNOT FIND IN YOUR LOCAL STORES?
You can get any WARNER BOOKS title in print. Simply send title and retail price, plus 95¢ per order and 95¢ per copy to cover mailing and handling costs for each book desired. New York State and California residents add applicable sales tax. Enclose check or money order only, no cash please, to: WARNER BOOKS, P.O. BOX 690, NEW YORK, N.Y. 10019

To Fanny

ACKNOWLEDGMENTS

A zillion thanks to my loved ones whose endless support I cherish, and whose contributions to my life, in so many ways, have helped me to realize this book, especially Miriam and Bob (wish you were here!) Carlip and Maxine Lapiduss.

A trillion thanks to Nanielle Devereaux for all her assistance—her brilliant offerings, insight and input.

Also to my circle of amazing muses and angels, all incredibly talented and inspiring in their own art. Their presence and/or feedback has contributed much to *Girl Power*—Katie Ford, Miriam Eichler Rivas, Danielle Eskinazi, Francesca Lia Block, Leni Schwendinger, Jessie "Cookie" Nelson, Wendy Melvoin, Lisa Coleman and Leigh-Kilton Smith (assistant, researcher and schemestress extraordinaire!).

A bazillion thanks to my editor Anne Hamilton, whose belief in *Girl Power*, ongoing encouragement, and input were invaluable.

A billion thanks to my agents Julie Fallowfield and Louise Quayle for their faith in me from the start, and their constantly inspired ideas.

A million thanks to all those who especially went out of their way to help make it happen: Sam Christensen, Ken Cortland, Howard Carlip, Sally Lapiduss, Jackie Nadler, Libby Applebaum, Teresa Jordan, Ann Block, Diane Krausz, Jaime Hubbard, Kristin Hahn, Bobbie Birleffi, Jennifer Thuma. Robin Segal and Ira Kruskol/Aviva Center; John Imperato/L.A. Gay and Lesbian Community Center; Jennifer Ross/Fenway Community Health Center; Linda Habalow/Youth and Family Center; Bobbie Savage and Linda Feldman/L.A. County Department of Education; Martha Pritcher/Hill House, Pittsburgh; Karen Pomer, Laurel Ollstein, Ruth Beaglehole/Business Industry School; Corky Barnes /California High School Rodeo Association; Alan Waters/FFA Enterprise, Alabama; Tammy Skubina/Benton County Extension Office; Charlie Haussman/Takini School, Cheyenne River Indian Reservation; Kathy Huse-Wika/Black Hills Special Services Cooperative; Margie Pierce/Southern California Indian Center; Su

Manuel/New Generations, Tule River Indian Reservation; Greg Janicke/Kansas City Star; Sister Pat Thalhuber; Margaret Swanson and Daniel Gabriel/COMPAS; Marc Choyt/Santa Fe Indian School; Sheena Lester/RapPages; Raymond O'Neil/Fly Paper; Ben Marcus/Surfer Publications; Mary Lou Drummy/USSF; Miles McQueen/Juice Magazine; Shirley Ito/Amateur Athletic Foundation; Karen Weisman/Amateur Softball Association; Wendy Triplett/CLAWS; Mitzi Witchger; Bob Szyman/St. Louis Wheelchair Basketball Association; Angela Perez; Mary Stevenson/Pleasant Hills High School; Tim Orr and Adriana Oliviera/BORP; Alicia Montecalvo; Stephanie Price/Home Economics Education Association; Frank LaMeira/Danfranc Productions; Dr. Gary and Vivian Ellison/Vivianna Productions; Gail Holvey/Miss North America Scholarship Pageant.

Thanks also to all the magazines, papers and other publications that were kind enough to print an article or mention when I was reaching out to girls and seeking submissions.

Aviva center for their tireless efforts in making a difference in teenage girls' lives, and to the girls there whose willingness to express themselves led me to *Girl Power*.

The newspapers and magazines who encourage teenage girls' expression and supported the book by allowing me to include pieces that they had previously published. A resource list including their addresses can be found in the back of the book.

Lastly, I would like to acknowledge all the girls who were courageous enough to pick up a pen and share their lives, their visions, their fears and their secrets. Whether their writing ended up in the book or not, they are most certainly a part of *Girl Power*.

And, as in every moment of my life, I offer my gratitude to God/Goddess.

CONTENTS

Sometimes paper is the only thing that will listen to you

—*Jennifer, Providence, Rhode Island*

INTRO

Coming of age in a time marked by social upheaval, volatile world issues, and deep personal challenges, how do young American women between the ages of thirteen and nineteen respond? How do they get a sense of who they are and where they belong? What defeats them? What gives them hope?

The voices in *Girl Power* are voices that have rarely spoken or been given a forum, but through writing are now able to be expressed and heard. They are voices of a group that shows to be significant in the shaping of society today as well as one that will grow into 51 percent of America's future: women.

For decades, the teenage years have been the most awkward time for girls, a time when they are teetering on the threshold of womanhood. Extensive studies have shown that in adolescence, girls have a tendency to go inward, shut down, lose their confidence, become self-conscious, and no longer speak freely, editing their communications.

In response to their budding sexuality, they begin to take on qualities society has equated with being "feminine": they stop expressing their opinions and trusting their own feelings. The uninhibited exuberance of childhood fades as the need for validation becomes vital. As girls start to see boys differently, and vice versa, what was once valued as a friendship is now overridden by a new sexual dynamic. Girls become either uncomfortable and guarded or, as they compete for the acceptance they so desire from boys, they judge and put down other girls. I believe this kind of behavior and these qualities are enormously magnified today due to the challenging climate of the world we live in.

While girls in the past may also have been timid about diving wholeheartedly into every aspect of teenage life, in the current generation, girls seem to have not only fear of what life will bring, but also fear for life itself.

According to the attorney general, youth between the ages of twelve and eighteen are the most likely victims of violent crimes today. Gangs are popping up everywhere—even in tiny rural communities. Living with the threat of the AIDS virus makes even the most intimate and bonding act terrifying. Children are bringing guns to school; teenage alcoholism and hard drug use have risen dramatically; the ozone layer is vanishing; the homeless population is staggering; people who see abortion as taking a life are taking the lives of those who don't. At a time when even adults and authority figures are feeling overwhelmed by the state of the world, how can a child maintain a sense of innocence and feel secure?

While working on *Girl Power*, I think what probably shocked me the most as I looked into the lives of so many teenage girls from different backgrounds and perspectives was that for every single chapter, I received writing about abuse. Girls cried out in shame, pain, and fury. It is tragic and unconscionable that so many children's lives are irreparably damaged or, at best, marred, by violations—sexual, physical, and mental.

It was, in fact, a group primarily of abused girls that led me to the idea for *Girl Power*. The concept originated when I began teaching creative writing as a volunteer at Aviva, a residential treatment center in Los Angeles for "troubled" girls. The majority of these girls, ages thirteen through eighteen, are placed at Aviva by the courts, right out of juvenile hall; the rest by the Departments of Children's Services and Mental Health. Almost all of them come from a long history of abuse, abandonment, incest, drugs, alcohol, and have committed a variety of crimes from armed robbery to prostitution. They are uncommunicative at best, and usually what does come out of their mouths is guarded and hostile.

Yet when I presented the opportunity for them to be heard, to safely put on paper what they wouldn't dare say aloud, something dramatic occurred. Without the fear of being laughed at, judged, or simply misunderstood, the girls came to life. I saw a side that not many people get to see: their depth, vulnerability, wisdom, and power. I was deeply moved and drawn into a kinship with the girls, remembering my own not-too-distant girlhood where writing and creative expression were my survival.

When I saw the effect my workshops had on the girls, and consequently on those who read their writing, this led me to explore other groups of teenage girls, to see if my notion was sound.

My sense that writing is an invaluable vehicle for growth, especially for this age group and gender, was confirmed when I found out about the Riot Grrrls, a network of angry (note the *grrr* in Grrrls) "girl revolutionaries." These young women communicate with each other through self-designed and self-written, uncensored and uninhibited photocopied publications called "zines," which they mail out, often using nicknames and aliases.

Again, paper provides a safety net against judgment, one essential for those at a supposedly self-conscious and inarticulate age.

Well before the publishing of *The Diary of Anne Frank* in the 1940s, diaries, complete with lock and key, were synonymous with teenage girls: a safe place to communicate freely no matter how outrageous, angry, or personal the entry.

The poet Jimmy Santiago Baca eloquently shares his experiences of discovering how vital writing can be in his book of prose *Working in the Dark:*

> *I wrote about it all. . . . And for the first time, the child in me who had witnessed and endured unspeakable terrors cried out not just in impotent despair, but with the power of language. Suddenly, through language, through writing, my grief and my joy could be shared with anyone who would listen. . . . I was no longer a captive of demons eating away at me, no longer a victim of other people's mockery and loathing, that had made me clench my fist white with rage and grit my teeth to silence. . . . Through language, I was free.*

And so it is with these young girls. Through writing, not only are demons freed and mockeries banished, but through self-expression, I believe, they come into their power.

I witnessed this empowerment firsthand during the many workshops I led throughout the country in the course of writing this book. I saw it in a group of teen mothers in Pittsburgh, Native

American girls on the Tule River Reservation, and lesbian and bisexual teenage girls in New York City.

My intention was that through my workshops alone—which ranged from an ongoing weekly class, to a weekend, to just an hour of exercises and assignments—I wanted the girls to feel supported and validated; to experience an increased sense of self-esteem through sharing, journaling, writing. One way of doing this was to stress my belief that there is no good or bad writing. No right way to do it, no wrong way.

I have a vivid memory of myself as a young girl, seeing a canvas with a few drops of paint splattered on it, prominently displayed at the Museum of Modern Art in New York, worth hundreds of thousands of dollars. I was shocked that a couple of drops of paint could warrant this attention. It was then I realized that "talent" is subjective, all about personal taste. Obviously many people loved and appreciated this painting. A work of art in any medium will most likely appeal to someone; a sculpture, song, or poem will touch at least one person, speak to them, move them.

Writing, as any other form of creativity, is self-expression, a sharing of feeling. How can there be a right or proper or good way to feel what you feel and express it?

If this is indeed my belief, how was I able to select which pieces to include in *Girl Power*? I wanted to show a wide range of emotions and experiences. I obviously desired to include work that moved me personally, but I also wanted to honor the "ordinary," the girls who were maybe not as adept or slick or practiced at expressing themselves on paper, but who opened up and shared their secrets and their lives.

Working on *Girl Power* gave me the extraordinary opportunity to delve into lives I would never have been aware of before, to connect with courageous, spirited young women I would not have met otherwise.

I'll never forget the incredibly exciting moment when, with only five seconds left in the game, No. 23 took a risk and shot for the basket from about fifty feet away, sinking the ball in as the clock buzzed loudly, winning the game! I felt privileged to be able to stand up and cheer, as her fellow young female teammates slapped high fives and hugged as best they could . . . all from their wheelchairs.

Or the time when I picked up the phone at 10:00 P.M. on a chilly winter night, and a young girl said she had heard about the book and wanted to write something for it, but there was a problem. She lived on the streets of Hollywood and had nothing to write with or on. Moments later, I was sitting with Mary Ann on a street corner, having brought her pens and paper, and we talked for hours.

Mary Ann was a sweet fifteen-year-old, whose sole innocence remained in her angelic face. Having fled a hideously abusive home in Alabama, she told me the only things she really missed at first, living on the streets, were her blow dryer and being able to look in the mirror in the morning. But she had gotten used to not having those things anymore. My first instincts were to take her home, give her a place to stay. But feeling that was not the appropriate thing to do, I gave her my best input on alternatives, ways off the streets, including names and numbers of several shelters. I never heard from Mary Ann again.

Attending the Riot Grrrl Convention in Washington, D.C., was remarkable and thrilling. It eerily mirrored my teenage years when my "women's consciousness raising" group held the first High School Women's Convention in the early seventies. The workshops we led back then were the *exact* same ones I attended at the Riot Grrrl Convention over twenty years later—including those dealing with fat oppression, rape, racism, and sexuality.

Having always considered myself a feminist, I was wholly prepared to confirm my beliefs that pageants are degrading and demeaning to women, fostering objectification and competition, when I was invited to be one of the judges at the Miss Teenage California Pageant. However, I must confess, I was quite surprised to find an incredibly supportive and sisterly atmosphere. I cannot be certain that all pageants are as conscious as this one was, but I knew that my preconceived notions about pageants were about to be changed when I first saw Miss Pacifica.

A large part of the judging for this particular pageant is based on the contestant's application. In it, they may include anything they'd like, to give a better idea of who they are: scholastic achievements, community work, political, social, creative endeavors. One of the things Miss Pacifica wrote of was her desire to become a heart specialist, a goal inspired by having undergone a heart transplant at age twelve. From her picture you could see that she had hearing aids peeking through her dark hair and was by no means your typical beauty by most pageants' standards. Oh, and she neglected to mention one small thing in her application. When the contestants all came out for the big opening number, Miss Pacifica was escorted out to the stage: she was also blind.

Only 257 girls were picked out of over 4,000 applicants to compete for the title of Miss Teenage California, the winner going on to the Miss Teenage America Pageant, and Miss Pacifica was one of them. She won a special "Queen of Hearts" award, and you could tell that she was transformed from that weekend on, as was everyone else who was privileged to be around her courageousness and spunk.

It was not only Miss Pacifica's presence that showed me a different way of looking at pageants, but also the fact that camaraderie was encouraged amongst all the girls. Almost everyone left with a renewed sense of self-esteem and plenty of newfound friends. I left with an altered perspective and newfound appreciation for yet another facet of teenage girls' lives.

I've been smudged with sage and cedar at a Pow Wow, grooved to open mike nights for rappers in the Inner City, listened as an entire crowd cheered on the Democrat-bashing announcer at a rodeo, baked in the sun at surfing competitions, milked a cow and plucked wool from sheep on a farm, and even "serenaded" a frat house with a group of sorority girls.

I've licked thousands of envelopes, writing in response to all the incredible letters I've received from young women, and developed relationships through writing—pen pals, if you will. I still continue to correspond on a regular basis with about twenty girls.

Speaking of "girls," in a conversation I had with a woman from a Farm Bureau about the project, she immediately became offended by my use of the word girl. For a long time, many women, myself included, have fought against derogatory words for women. But over the years, my thoughts about this have changed. I now feel that a part of claiming and reclaiming our power as girls and women is taking back those words that were once ours and have been abused and misused, and giving them a new and different connotation: *girl, chick, broad*—even words that aren't necessarily female-oriented but used as labels to alienate or ridicule, such as *outcast, jock, queer,* and others.

Jo Anne Demichele, age nineteen, writes:

> *I also believe it is powerful to take back a word that has been used against us for so long. When I own it as my own, no one can use it against me. When someone yells "queer!" at me I'm like "yeah so, that's me, I'm queer alright." I'm no longer on the defensive about being attacked. It is much more powerful to be offensive than defensive. I am taking their weapon and turning it into a positive, reaffirming word for myself. They no longer own the rights to it, it no longer hurts to hear it, I'm no longer angry and, therefore I am free from them. It is powerful to disarm your attacker. Take every word they use against you and glamorize it. . . .*

So you will notice throughout *Girl Power* that I purposely choose to use many of these words. Similarly with the section titles, where words such as *outcasts* and *insiders* are not used to perpetuate division, but, again, are intended to break stereotypes.

Also, by putting the girls and their writing into specific focuses, my intent was not to confine each girl to a particular category, but to give the book some sort of structure. I actually found that a large percentage of girls I worked with and heard from are multidimensional and fit into several chapters, not limited to just one focus: Native American teen mothers, Jocks who also live on farms, Teen Queens who surf, Homemakers who compete in rodeos.

I originally set out to include a chapter on debutantes in the "Insiders" section. My sleuthing and scheming put Nancy Drew to shame, considering that there are no offices or organizations for debs with listed numbers. I managed to obtain a list of all the current debs in Texas, as well as track down the ball chairmen for all the large debutante balls in major cities. Some people were very helpful, some skeptical. I sent out thousands of flyers, yet did not receive *one* piece of writing.

Similarly with Homemakers and sorority girls. Of the thousands I contacted, I got back very few submissions. I found it quite interesting that the only girls who were not really willing to share of themselves, all fit into the "Insider" section. Perhaps the fact that they choose not to express themselves is part of what makes them fit into the "mainstream."

Since I have been working on *Girl Power* for several years, the age I include with each girl's writing is the age they were when they wrote the piece. Many girls feel that putting their expressions and beliefs to paper may commit them to that idea forever. Keep in mind that these girls are continually growing and reexamining their lives, that the writing captures simply a moment in time. One eighteen-year-old girl, Rumeli, writes:

> *why do you have to judge me label me assume that if i said or wrote something i still feel that way? understand that i am constantly changing, redefining, relearning and that is how i want it to be.*

I have also left each piece as is, with spelling, grammar, and punctuation errors, except when I felt it interfered with understanding the content.

I have long admired the photographs of Nicola Goode. Her work combines a gritty realism with a sensitive beauty. When I first saw a series of pictures she had done of young women, I knew that I wanted Nicola to capture visually the girls whose writing appears in the book. We traveled near and far to meet and photograph these girls, and I'm so pleased to have Nicola's vision be part of *Girl Power.*

I am not a psychologist, nor an expert with a degree. I am simply a woman who, in my own trying adolescence, found writing to be my lifeline. I have been led to all the conclusions I have come to purely by the girls who were willing to share themselves and their lives. If some topics seem repetitive throughout the book, it is only because the girls, no matter how different they appear to be, have many of the same concerns and issues.

I have been overwhelmed with the depth of feeling and insight shared by each and every one of the thousands of girls I've worked with and corresponded with. Whether or not their writing was included in the book, I so appreciate the ones who felt safe enough to tell their truths in my presence, as well as the ones who felt unsafe, but did so anyway. I also acknowledge those who wanted to write and whose fears or circumstances did not allow their participation.

Every girl who takes a pen to paper and speaks her word, allowing her emotions to surface, is committing a courageous act of self-empowerment. And in the process, those who read her writing are often empowered as well.

I invite you to experience the power of girls.

Part One

Outlaws
and Outcasts

Something that makes me angry is the fact that I've wasted fifteen months of my life in placement. That when I came here I was only supposed to spent the most 6 months. It makes me angry that I went from D.C.S. and graduated to probation. It makes me angry that I felt so low of my own self that I disrespected my mother by fighting with her. It makes me angry that I cant chng change time. That I cant change my mistakes. That I cant change my mind about things. That I only can learn from past and hope memories last.

Sakinah 17

CHAPTER ONE

Homegirls

> I think I am a real nice and good girl. I
> don't do anything bad. I might make a mistake
> but I still a good girl.

Margarita might have made a few mistakes. She's shot up heroin,
been in juvenile hall several times, brought a gun to school and
threatened to kill herself, given birth to two children, and writes: "I
am a poor alcoholic." But upon meeting Margarita, one can see she
is indeed a nice and good girl. She's only fifteen.

Margarita resides at Aviva, a residential treatment center for
"troubled" girls in Los Angeles, California, one of the many
programs of this sort throughout the country. Physically, emotionally, and sexually abused, neglected, and abandoned young women
between the ages of thirteen and eighteen live at Aviva, which
boasts an on-premises school and offers family and individual therapy as part of its rehabilitation program.

The girls are in what's called "the system," placed at the center
by social workers and parole officers, some from the Department
of Children's Services, most fresh out of juvenile hall.

Out of the thirty-six girls who live there at one time, over a dozen
gangs are represented. There are also runaways, prostitutes,
junkies, thieves. Some are suicidal, others are homicidal. They're
covered with tattoos, burn marks, and scars.

And in almost every girl's room at Aviva, there on her bed sits a teddy bear.

> Yo! What's up? My name is Tonisha but they
> call me Little Smurf or Critter! I am 14
> years old and I'm a Virgo. My hobbies are
> basketball, baseball, volleyball and talking
> to my stuffed animals—(We have a lot in
> common my stuffed animals and I.)

Most of the girls I met and worked with at Aviva are defensive, defiant, aggressive and temperamental. They appear to be way beyond their years, having seen and experienced more than most people, especially those their own age. Yet beneath the surface, evidenced not only by the teddy bears and other girlish items that adorn their rooms but also by the vulnerability they occasionally allow themselves to express, they are still teenage girls. In fact, some often seem to regress and behave as if they were even younger, since most have been robbed of their childhoods by horrific events and circumstances.

Claudia, age fifteen, is a striking brunette with hazel eyes and long, wavy hair. She listens to heavy metal and enjoys writing poetry. Her writing describes her world:

> Well I have had many difficulties in my life
> with many things such as rape, molestation,
> abuse. I also have written poems that go with
> my emotions. There's only a few other topics
> I want to talk about and those are suicide,
> death, and drugs. Everything I write is about
> real life things that have or are happening
> to me. I only wish people could realize what
> is happening and that kids are doing whatev-
> er happened to them, to others...

The Homegirls' family inheritances of abuse, neglect, and disrespect often lead them to joining gangs. In a gang, not only can they act out their rage, but also gain the respect, support, love and trust they do not receive at home, creating a new family structure.

In the past several years, the number of girls in gangs, as well as girls committing violent crimes, has risen dramatically.

To join a gang, one must undergo some sort of initiation. A girl is most often "jumped in," meaning the gang members beat up on her simultaneously for a minute, sometimes longer. She can also be "diced in," "rolled in," "sexed in," or "trained in," all terms for a sexual initiation that involves rolling dice and then having sex with as many fellow male gang members as the dice indicates — usually unprotected.

Although most of the girls feel that their gangs fill an empty space in their lives, providing the care they don't receive elsewhere, they are also well aware of the consequences of belonging to one.

Yolanda is articulate and intelligent with a biting sense of humor. She describes herself as "a 16 year old African American with a 3.4 grade point average." Beside enjoying sports and going to school, she likes to "interact with my peers and other people that I don't know.... I plan to go to Howard University and get a masters in Psychology and later go on to be a lawyer or work in child development (play therapy.)"

She is also in a gang. Yolanda writes:

> There are many positive and rewarding things about being a gang member. There are people that look out for you and the rest of the little homies. We make sure that everybody always has somewhere to stay and that they are always fed. We do a lot of positive things in the community like have football, basketball and baseball games. Some of the bad things we do are kill innocent people sometimes. And we take people's lives when nobody should be taking nobody's life....
>
> I came from a single parent household and my mother was constantly working, going to school or taking care of me and my younger

brother. Me and my mom never talked so we never had a mother and daughter relationship and we really never talked about the changes that were going on in my life. So when I was 11 years old, I felt that I was grown and that I could come and go when I got ready. So I joined a local gang and started selling drugs and not going to school. I continued to do this for about 2 years come and go when I felt like it, smoke and sell drugs, and just not go to school. When I was 13 years old my brother that was 2 years old got killed by our worst enemy and that put me in a position where I did something that now I look back upon and I can't believe that I would let myself be put in a position to act in a manner like that. When I was 14 years old me and my mom decided for me to go back to school and also this was my first time that I got arrested. I got arrested for possession of a concealed weapon and for drugs but I got off with probation. Later that year after my 15th birthday, me and my homies got high and I decided to steal a car. So I went and I stole a car and there was a purse and credit cards in the trunk so I went to the mall and forged credit cards. Compton Police Department came to my house, arrested me and booked me. I went to Juvenile Hall for awhile then went to court and they placed me in Aviva. I can really say that I am happy that I made these mistakes because this has directed me to what I want to do in life. I am also happy because I can use these mistakes as stepping stones. Because just think if I would not have gotten arrested I would probably be dead or in worse places.

Eighteen-year-old Ali, who is pregnant with her second child, is rethinking her gang affiliation:

> ...I've had friends killed because of it. 2 weeks ago I had a friend killed right in front of my stepmother's house. My friends had a car wash to raise some money for his funeral. It's so hard out there. I've been just one of the lucky ones. I've been shot at and missed. I've chased. I still don't understand how I was living this life. You get involved into drugs, get put in jail for a couple of times for different things. Right now I have an uncle and also a friend doing time for attempted murder on another gang member. I just recently have a friend who just got out of L.A. after doing 10 years for attempted murder on a rival gang member.
> I don't think we should have gangs because we are fighting over stupid things, over a street or a color. What we really should do is unite together and go against those that are perpetrating us....

Serafina, age seventeen, also considers her future in the following excerpt:

> I am in a gang... I've been in it since I was young. My brothers are from it my sister isn't but I think that I stop because I'm tired of the killings and violence that's happened around my neighborhood and to my friends and family. Another reason is because I'm a female and when I have kids I don't want them to look at me as a gang banging mother I would like a lot of respect.

Like Serafina, many of the girls share their desire for respect as a mother, clearly because they never got it as a daughter. Along with the resentment many Homegirls feel toward their families, this resentment often being the impetus for them to join gangs, at the same time a common theme in the writing of these girls is the basic and simple desire for love and acceptance, especially from their mothers:

```
Dear Mommy,

    I really do miss you.  I'm surprised you
chose your husband over your little girl,
your oldest son and your mother.  Just
because he said you can't have anything to do
with them.  Well I'm not the one hurting it's
you missing your family and being totally
dependent on him.  And all I have to say now
is Bitch, I hope you suffer all through life.
Then when you want to be bothered with me you
sneak to call me, but hang up on me as soon
as you hear your husband's voice.
```

—Tanita, age 14

At the age of sixteen, a striking young brunette woman with several tattoos and shocking blue eyes consistently writes about her tormented life full of terrifying circumstances, morbidity, drugs, destruction and death. Ironically, her name is Serenity.

Reading of her past and present pain, it was no surprise that when I first met Serenity, she was hostile, raging and rebellious. In workshops, she almost always refused to participate and when she did, her writing would be scrawled heavily and almost illegibly across the page. Yet her insight and brilliance managed to peek through the furious façade.

In a poem for her deceased mother, Serenity lets us in on what happened when she was just five years old.

```
            HE TOOK HER LIFE THE WAY
            THEY'RE GOING TO TAKE MINE

     Written for my mother Maureen... Dec. 17th,
1952-Dec 30th, 1979.
```

SHE WAS MY MOTHER
NOT A DRUG USER AT ALL
A WOMAN IN THE WORLD
WHERE THE SPACE WAS TOO SMALL
THE ADDICTION GREW STRONGER
THE LOVING GREW WALLS
THAT'S WHEN HER LIFE TOOK A MASSIVE FALL
SHE WAS ALL ALONE
IN HER WORLD OF HATE
SUICIDE WAS ALL SHE SAW
THAT WAS HER FATE
SHE ATTEMPTED SUICIDE MANY TIMES BEFORE
BUT IN HER EYES, LIFE WAS ONLY A LOCKED DOOR
NO WAY TO BREAK THROUGH
NO WAY TO WALK
SHE TRIED TO FLY
BUT THE MASTER ONLY BALKED
HER LIFE WAS EMPTY
THERE WAS NO PLAN
THAT'S WHEN SHE MET DEATH
IN THE FORM OF A MAN
THE MAN WAS EVIL WITH AN INGENIOUS PLAN
TO MOLD HER OF HELL AND CUT HER LIFE SPAN
TO MAKE HER LIVE LOCKED UP IN SATAN'S CAN
HE MADE HER PREGNANT
AND CARRY HIS DEVIL'S SPAWN
AND WHEN HIS WORK WAS OVER
IT WAS TIME HE MOVED ALONG
HE DROVE HER INSANE
TO A LIFE OF DISTORTION AND PAIN
WHERE THE ONLY THING SHE LIVED FOR
WAS THE NEXT SLAM TO THE VEIN
WHEN THE MAN TURNED THE TABLES
SHE TRIED TO STOP THE PROCESS BUT
WAS UNABLE
HE KNEW THE TIMING WAS NOW
AND SHE WOULD NOT FIGHT

```
THAT IS WHEN SHE BURNED TO DEATH
ON THAT DARK AND MOURNFUL NIGHT!

    FOR MY MOTHER MAUREEN
    CAUSE OF DEATH IS SUICIDE
    MY MOTHER POURED GASOLINE ON HER BODY
    AND SET HERSELF ALITE!
         DECEMBER 30TH, 1979.
```

Claudia gives an idea about her relationship with her mother when she writes: "I would bring my mother back some bud and some tabs (acid) to make her happy."

In an excerpt from a haunting poem, she lets us further into her family life:

SADNESS

```
... Sadness is something that can make you feel sick
When a grown man has you touching his dick.
Sadness is something that cannot be stopped
Even when a grown man's taking off your top.
Sadness cannot be removed with a four-leaf clover
When a grown man touches your body all over.
Sadness is something that hurts to think about
Sadness can make you scream and shout.
There's also but one other person who's done this
  to me
This one other person made me suck his thang.
Sadness is something that you can create
Sadness is something that puts you in a depressive
  state.
This one person that did this is close to me
That's why the name I cannot tell you, can't you see.
Sadness is something that cannot be fixed
Sadness is something with lots of tricks.
You have to figure out who you can trust
This I had to tell you, it was a must.
```

Sandy is sixteen, with long blond hair that makes her pale face appear almost translucent except for, as she describes them, "nasty freckles." She dresses in velvet and flowing paisleys with lots of jewelry: part mystical, part heavy metal. She says her favorite animals are "centaurs, unicorns, pegasus and dragons." Sandy's relationship with her mother figures prominently in her ending up at Aviva:

> I am in the system of probation because when my mom got arrested, I basically had no one to go to so I went off in my own little world which was based on "drugs, music and phsy-chedelic pictures for acid trips and friends".... The police came and got them and me too. They asked me my age I said 18 so I could be put in jail with my mom because I had it planned through the hole thing so that I would be able to be with her.

* * *

The girls at Aviva all live together in a dormitorylike building, some sharing rooms. Although constantly surrounded by each other and staff members, as well as venturing out together often on activities and outings, many of the girls admit in their writing to feeling confined and alone.

PLACEMENT

Trapped
Four walls
Two windows
And one door
Alone
Scared and frightened

```
Sorry
The mistakes, the sins
Help
I'm trapped
No where to go
Nothing to do
Nothing to say
No one to talk to
No one to kiss
No one to hug
Trapped
Trapped and all alone
Because I'm in placement.
```

—Susan, age 16

One of the ways Aviva attempts to instill a sense of responsibility in the girls is to have minimum security. Although the girls are watched over, they are not behind bars and there are windows and doors throughout the building. Many have left of their own volition by AWOLing; one girl even stole the postman's truck as the mail was being delivered. Most who leave take to the only place they can with hopes of not being found and sent back to jail—the streets. Claudia AWOLed several times before she finally finished her time and found stability and love in a foster home.

```
Just go away, I'm begging you please
I have a headache that just won't ease
Now you're getting on my nerves
I sit down depressed on the corner curb
Now that I AWOLed and am on the streets,
I now realize that I'm very weak
I'm stupid, I'm bored, I'm very dumb
I'm so bored, my brain is now numb
This place is so very, very stupid
I don't know now what to do
I'm hating life right now
Life's painful like seeing a slaughtered cow
Do you know what it's like?
```

```
Do you know how to fix it?
I sure don't, I certainly wish I did.
```

* * *

Through intensive individual, group, and family therapy, the girls at Aviva are encouraged to look at problems, and are offered tools and healthy ways of dealing with them.

In her therapy, Yolanda, who turned to a gang at age eleven, has had significant insights on her displaced anger:

```
When I was younger I wasn't used to hearing
my mother or my grandma telling me no. And I
am still not used to it. I don't think I will
ever be used to it. It is very difficult for
me to be a teenager and in placement. And when
I ask my mom for something and she can't or
doesn't give it to me, it hurts a lot. I am
very angry at my mom and when I get angry at
someone, instead of placing the anger where
it belongs, I take it out on myself. I am not
used to dealing with my anger or frustrations
and sometime I get the insentive that they
hurt or made me angry because of something I
have done. I always feel that it is me—well,
if I wouldn't have said that or maybe if I
did say this they wouldn't be angry with me.
So I need to stop beating up on myself and
start placing the anger where it belongs.
```

In many situations, there is no time to consciously choose how to express anger. It erupts, and for some, it is impossible not to release it. One girl writes about pounding on walls and punching stuffed animals in her fury; another tears and rips paper to shreds as if it were a person. And one young girl's release is only found when she bites herself.

Ali finds yet another method of dealing with her feelings:

```
I get a lot of things out of writing when
I'm angry, I can't get my anger out appro-
```

```
priately.  When I'm sad I write down how I
feel.  I very much enjoy it cause I can't get
my anger out in appropriate ways and I keep
myself from getting in trouble with any anger
I do feel.  It helps me all the time.  I enjoy
writing...
```

Yet a lot of Homegirls find that the same kind of expression makes them too vulnerable, especially if their diaries and poems have been discovered by a parent or relative. Some confiscate the writing; one girl's aunt even burned her poems right in front of her face, making her shut down even further. She refused to pick up a pen again.

* * *

To focus on the healing powers of imagination, in one workshop I asked the girls to describe their ideal day, one where they could do anything they wanted, with anyone, anywhere.

Most of the days were surprisingly routine: going to movies, shopping in southern California malls, partying with homegirls, drinking Cisco. Tonisha desires to "go to Disneyland, Africa, Hawaii and Jamaica. Get budded out. Buy candy, alcohol, everything. Play Nintendo, kick back, stay black and die."

In keeping with Serenity's themes of morbidity, she writes:

```
My ideal day or experience is going to hell
to talk or meet with my mom, Jim M., Jimi H.,
Sid V., J.F.K., John L., Freddie M., Janis
J., Ghandi....
```

And Sandy lets her fantasies fly:

```
My ideal day is travelling to Paris with
George and as I and George get into our
stretch limo with pool and hot tub and wet
```

bar in it, the driver had opened up the door
and 25 to 30 naked men some with brown hair,
some with blonde, some with black, stripped
me naked and tossed me in the hot tub and were
at my every command and the bubbles were big
blue and pink splashed all over my body and
all the guys licked them off like a fruit
roll-up. And then we arrived at the Palace.
And then we all got out nude so the French
thought it was the new style and stripped off
all of their clothes. Then me and George got
out of that exotic area and got on a ship
cruise and as we looked out the port holes
and watched the sun set and the waves turn
into wild horses, so did we. I called for
room service and ordered whipped cream, cher-
ries, nuts and boy did George ever have a lot
of that. And whips and handcuffs. Then we
had a very creamy cherry-ish night.

Whether extravagant or simple, the majority of ideal days for
these girls are filled with references to what is possibly the most
universal wish: the wish for love.

If it was my day, I would go to my old man's
pad and we would go down to the park and get
money to get a hotel for the days at the
Hilton motel. We would then have a big
Lawndale party and no one else could come if
they weren't from Lawndale. Me and my old
man would have the biggest room and the
number would be 13. And we would party and
get fucked up then in the nite we would be
alone and make sweet passionate love all nite
long and try to do everything that I've
learned about sex from the girls. And then
he would get my name tattooed on him and I
would get his on me. And then we would go
out and be happy forever with each other,
getting wasted. The day would end with me
and Juan making love again all nite!!!

—Sancha, age 16

Love can also be a terrifying thing for some, like Serenity, who has experienced the damage it can cause:

```
Love is such a strange power
it envelopes you in its wicked and
  evil clutches
smashing and tearing all your emotions
trying to kill you.
```

Boyfriends play an important role in these Homegirls' lives. Whether they are really seeing someone or their fantasies have created the "perfect match," focusing on boys seems to keep the girls going. They constantly talk about them, carry their pictures, write them letters and wait for replies. Cloretta, age sixteen, ponders her relationship:

```
Right now I am very angry at my boyfriend
because he's in prison for GTA [Grand Theft
Auto] and he has about 1/2 year to do.  He
sent me  a picture but that's not going to
stop the pain that I feel for him at this
time.  I just don't know how or when to let
go of him.
  We have shared good and bad times together
and I feel like we could have more but he has
to promise that he will try to do the right
thing and not the rong.  I think that me and
him could have a great life.
```

Yet as is evident in most of the girls' writing, boyfriends, as well as family, are not always to be relied upon. Whom can these young women turn to?

```
I am what society just puts in the back of
their heads to forget about.  As if we're the
last thing in the world they need to worry or
think about.  And you know what?  It really
does suck.  We get very lonely, stressed out,
depressed and scared of how long society will
```

keep us in here. I know it's not just on
society, because a good portion goes on us,
but who is to say that we should stay in a
confined place?... It's not very reassuring
when people don't trust you. And to make it
worse, they don't get to know you. They read
a file and then again, they judge you. Not
by your personality or anything like that.
But instead by our past, or our mistakes.

—*Sandy*

Yolanda believes the antidote for the kind of alienation many
teenagers feel lies with others:

Some of the bad things that happen is they
lock innocent kids like me up. We don't only
need to be locked up we need for people to
take time up with us. It is so easy for
adults to say thumbs down but we need those
parents to also say I know he's done wrong
but I still believe in him. And if parents,
adults, and role models do this, we wouldn't
have so many young teenagers give up.

❋ ❋ ❋

Are most of these girls' futures condemned by their pasts? Is
there a way to break patterns, learned behavior, cycles of abuse,
and experience things they've never had an opportunity to experience before? Lonny, age sixteen, is getting closer to her dreams:

The thing I wish for the most in my life is
happiness. I don't feel that being in placement for thirteen years has given me much
happiness. All it has brought is more and
more sadness, loneliness, hatred and depression. Suicide has felt like the only option
at different times. But although I have

never quite succeeded, I have made quite a
few attempts.   But things are starting to
look up for me. I have a wonderful fiancee,
a best friend who's getting her mom involved
in foster parenting for me, and things are
going to get better.   I feel I finally have
a shot at a lifelong dream of happiness.

Some, like sixteen-year-old Lily, a warm and gentle Latina girl
who's been in a gang since she was eleven, have a dream for the
world:

I think that we have to stop all the racism
going around all over the world and to stop
all the rapists and the killing of innocent
people and not bomb on the peoples houses and
to lock up the people who start wars around
the world.   But we just have to go on with
our Vida Loca [crazy life]....
    Chow!!

And Serenity reaches for peace:

One day I will claim what is mine. The soul
of a child drained from her inner shell. With
no soul and to be condemned to immortal
despair has damned me to walk the land till
one day I take back my lost and crying soul.
Then I will be at peace and able to finally
let my spirit free from the abomination it
was sentenced unto. ....

Living on her own away from Aviva now, Serenity, an extraordinary young woman, attempts to do the ordinary: work at a job, do
her own laundry, pay her bills, and survive. Having used writing as
a catharsis, with suffering as her muse, she naturally hasn't been
writing much since, in her own words, she "hasn't been so
depressed."

Prevailing against her own defensive and defiant nature, Serenity allows herself to hope:

> Life may seem bleak and there is no light at the end of the tunnel. We have all passed through that dark and lonely place. We all desperately struggle to keep afloat, and sadly some of us lose sight and sink. There is no answer to the question we all ask. Why are we here. Only through trial and error and our own soul searching journeys can we begin to piece the puzzle together. Most of us growing up in my generation have gone through and overcome some pretty heavy shit.
>
> From personal experience I can say that it really does get better and no life isn't a bowl of cherries but it's not the pits either.... Never lose sight and don't ever give up. In the end we all control our own destiny....
>
> The greatest feeling of all is to prove everyone wrong and to finally succeed.

And perhaps with courage and determination, positive guidance and support, Serenity, and all the other Homegirls, will have their chance to do just that.

(All names of minors in this chapter have been changed to protect the identities of the girls. For the same reason, no photographs are included.)

so i'm told to voice my opinions...
why is it i am downgraded because
i believe our government are
hypocrites? that a choice for _anything_
should automatically be allowed?
that i do not want to be touched
when i don't want to! that sexism
is so apparant? so i say NO!,
FIGHt, and RiOt and others scorn
on me. if i stop they call me a
quitter & if i continue to be strong-
minded they   call me a bitch,
and when i   call them nothing
in return   and walk away
they call   me a wimp.
and when   i sit alone on
the circle   of grass they
wonder why i have no friends
and then laugh at me. i have no
response to you all ; just take
a look at yourselves.

Witknee Hubbs

CHAPTER TWO

Ríot Grrrls

```
i must get this out of me now.
no longer can i keep everything inside.
i am too good at keeping secrets
too good.
i am so alone that when i go out i forget how
to relate to others
this is just here.
just to share what one girl is going
  through.
maybe you know how she feels.
```

—Christina, age 17
Amherst, Massachusetts

There are a lot of girls who know exactly how she feels—alone in their bedrooms, isolated at their schools, outcasts in their own towns and cities. And they're angry about it too.

But thanks to the Riot Grrrls, they're finding out something vital: that it's okay to be mad (hence the *grrr* in grrrls), and they no longer have to do it alone.

The Riot Grrrls were born out of the "punk" scene where rebellion was expressed in attitude, appearance, style, and music. However, the philosophy of "you can do anything" and "do it yourself" seemed to apply mostly to boys, who were making the music and dictating the styles. By 1991, more and more girl bands started springing up, but ironically they often found themselves battling sexism and discrimination within a movement originally based in a consciousness about youth and oppression.

Some girls turned to each other for support and understanding and came together in a common cause: "REVOLUTION GIRL-STYLE NOW!"

In addition to weekly meetings, the Riot Grrrls network through fanzines (referred to as "zines," as in magazines), which are self-written and designed photocopied publications they hand out and mail to other girls wherever they can. In zines, they are finally free to express themselves fully, to be heard, and also to realize that they are not alone.

Since its nebulous inception (no specific person or people claim they created it), Riot Grrrl has meant many things to many people. Most girls do not attempt to define it anymore. However, it's clearly no longer just for those in the punk scene. The Riot Grrrls have reached out with open arms. From an early Washington, D.C., Riot Grrrl "manifesto":

> *RIOT GRRRL IS . . .*
> *BECAUSE we need to accept and support each other as girls; acknowledging our different approaches to life and accepting all of them as valid.*
> *BECAUSE we seek to create revolution in our own lives every single day by envisioning and creating alternatives to the status quo.*

* * *

Jasmine Kerns is an effusive nineteen-year-old beauty from Richmond, Virginia. In her "List of top 10 things," along with "real hugs and sloppy kisses, pop wheels roller skates and my younger sister Soph who rocks my world," her fave pastimes are "collecting and devouring powerful grrrl zines and Riot Grrrl meetings."

With unabashed joy, Jasmine links the momentum of her own personal growth with the RG movement:

> Everyday I get excited because I hear of the new chapters popping up all over the country —like in New York, Olympia, Richmond, New Hampshire, one in California, man . . . almost like a Benneton store or 7-11, one opening every 4 hours! Grrrl power, revolution grrrl style is REAL, is RAW, and IS NOT going to back down or go away! . . . OH, suckle to my heaving heart the sweet nectar of sister love. It smells like honeysuckles in June. It makes my toes tingle every time I think of a RG meeting where we totally supported each other through hard times, and helped each other learn how to deal with the daily subliminal/subconscious sexism we endure, and how we all grooved to ideas of putting on our own shows, and making necklaces out of shrinky-dink plastic, and building up our self-esteem and self-love . . . something I had little to none a year before. . . .

Similarly, from a Riot Grrrl in San Diego, California, who wishes to remain anonymous:

> so there's this revolution happening all across the country and all across other countries and it's the revolution girl style and as a girl revolutionary i want to say something about it . . .
>   . . . this revolution is so real and so deep for me, it is something i have been waiting for my whole life, something that i think is imperative to my survival, or at least my sanity. this revolution is in my heart and my soul, and it's in the heart and souls of a lot of other girls/women i know, and fuck you it's valid, and fuck you it's for real . . .

* * *

Over the past few years, newspapers, magazines, and news shows have begun to pay a lot of attention to the Riot Grrrls. At first, most

Riot Grrrls were open to using the media as a way to spread the word to other girls. Shortly thereafter, however, feeling that they had been misrepresented, trivialized, commercialized, and made into a new fad and trend, the Riot Grrrls changed their minds.

In her zine, *Function*, Dawn, age nineteen, from Seattle, Washington, addresses this issue:

> So much stuff has been said about what riot grrrl is, actually what some very misinformed people have said. I'm sick to death of defending riot grrrl every time I turn around, I don't even know why it should have to be defended. Riot grrrl is NOT what Seventeen, Newsweek or the LA Weekly make it out to be or any other media thing. The media attention has taken riot grrrl and twisted it and distorted the name to mean little if anything of importance. No one person can speak for all riot grrrls, they can only simply give their opinion (like I am) and it should be taken as such. . . . R.G. is meant to be empowering for grrls, having a safe comfortable space to speak openly about anything. It's about standing up for our rights and about knowing we have them. Wimmin are degraded every single day of our lifes, it's everywhere we look, t.v., magazines, streets, work, movies, speech it's everywhere. We are used as objects or holes to fuck, we are told we have to get married and depend on a man or we are nothing, old maids, hags, unwanted. We are taught to be passive, to look the other way, and boys will be boys, to cross our legs, to desire a family, to play with dolls, to open our legs, to shut our legs, to smile as we die inside (so as not to upset anyone.) We are taught to value make-up and diets and fashion models and high heel shoes, thats what grrrls grow up to feel, think, be, understand. Riot Grrrl is helping to break down all that the patriarchy has created. R.G. is standing up for your rights, my rights as a humyn. Riot Grrrl is

> showing me that I matter. I count, my opin-
> ion has worth, I don't have to sit and be
> talked over or pushed aside or just simply be
> so-and-so's "girlfriend." I'm me and can take
> a stand for my rights and not have to tip-
> toe. The ones I've been denied, you've been
> denied because we don't fit the patriarchy.
> I'm not bitter, I don't hate, I'm angry.
> Would you be? Don't tell me to "calm down,"
> "don't take things so seriously" how can I
> not when wimmin are being raped, battered and
> denied their equal rights, harassed on the
> streets. . . . I'm dying inside and I'm angry
> wimmin are dying inside and no one sees this.
> Riot grrrl is about emotions, feelings, not
> fashion, or hating boys, it's about us,
> grrrls. It's real and a threat because it
> goes against the patriarchy as anything is a
> threat that goes against the patriarchy.
> Don't make one sided judgements about riot
> grrrl because of one persons opinion, see for
> yourselves, feel for yourself. There are no
> rules. It's to break the imprisonment that
> grrrls are forced to live in.

Riot Grrrls believe that one of the most important ways of breaking the imprisonment is by speaking out.

RIOT GRRRL IS . . .
BECAUSE we need to talk to each other. Communication/inclusion is key. We will never know if we don't break the code of silence.
BECAUSE every time we pick up a pen, or an instrument, or communicate with each other, we are creating the revolution. We ARE the revolution.

In her zine *I ❤ Me*, Val Taylor, age eighteen, from Olympia, Washington, writes: "This little girl inside my heart is real. She has a voice and it will be heard."

And what better way to be heard than for hundreds of people to be reading your philosophies, desires, point of view; your secrets. In describing herself, Jennifer, age nineteen, of *Womynfolke* zine, writes: "I want to be a hearing aid, an amplifier, a transmitter, a noisemaker in my writing and in my life."

That is what creating zines provides.

Uninhibited, uncensored, and always unpredictable, zines are filled with girlish drawings and cartoons; poems and dreams; book, music, and other zine reviews; vegetarian recipes and fashion tips ("Throw that pink lacy thing away and pick up your self-esteem, dust it off, and strap a black bra on your new 'proud to be female' chest."—*Angie Tarr*) mixed in with gut-wrenching confessions and raw outpourings of emotions.

Erika Reinstein, age eighteen, from Reston, Virginia, is a vibrant girl with several tattoos, nose rings, and a lip ring; her black hair (depending on what day you catch her) full of colorful plastic children's barrettes. When Erika speaks, she commands attention, her startling blue eyes penetrating with each insightful thought expressed; when she writes, she is equally commanding:

```
     oh, girl. i want to write for you and make
you laugh and cry the way you make me. . . . i
am not sure if i am lying. when i say some-
thing i'm not sure if i made it up to get
sympathy or impress someone, or if it's the
TRUTH. i'm not sure what the truth is because
every time i try to tell it i am told to shut
up, i am told that i am lying and if i know
what's good for me i will not ever mention
that again. ever ever ever ever ever ever
ever. but i just can't seem to keep my BIG
MOUTH SHUT and i guess that's a big prob-
lem. . . .
     i think i am going to get in trouble for
real. i'm scared, 'cause i don't want to die,
but i think i might get killed. i am para-
noid. i keep seeing my blood. it is coming
out of my body and it happens over and over
again (his fist in my cunt—it bled.) i keep
thinking, what if he sees this? then i will
be in trouble and i will get the spanking of
(the end of) my life. my life. my life my life
```

```
my life. i am writing for my life, i am
running for my life.
    i am sorry this isn't nice and neat, all
spelled out in metaphors and pretty language.
this is just me and i am doing what i need to
do for survival. my life did not come to me
in a neat little package, but i need to try
and explain it to you anyway. i am writing
for you, girl, and i hope you can understand.
please try.
```

I first met Erika at the Riot Grrrl Convention in Washington, D.C., a gathering of over 100 young women from all over the country (including one who hopped freight trains from New Orleans!) who came together to empower themselves and each other. They had the opportunity to meet other girls, share zines, perform in their all-girl bands, perform spoken-word pieces, talk, scream, cry, laugh, complain, enlighten, and educate through workshops that focused on several issues, including rape, unlearning racism, exploring sexuality, and animal rights (many RGs are vegan—strict vegetarians).

Like other Riot Grrrls committed to self-expression, Erika had written on her body with a thick black marker. On one day she had running down her right arm HELLO; DADDY on the left. Emblazoned on each knuckle were the letters spelling GIRL and LOVE. Temporarily tattooed across her stomach was RAPE bookended by a heart on one side and X O X on the other. And a constant feature in her ever-changing body graffiti was on the backside of her left hand: HI, MY NAME IS ERIKA.

In an early issue of her *Fantastic Fanzine*, Erika writes about herself as someone who "has a thing about Sesame Street—not quite an obsession, but i collect toys, records, books, etc. . . . my mom gave me a train and a Big Bird puppet for x-mas. Also i own a cherry red bass guitar. it's got personality. it's got kissability."

And in the same breath:

```
    sometimes it's hard for me to do this zine
because it's so painful to write about abuse
```

and my feelings and hear other girls stories.
i get so angry and i feel like turning into
a rambo type person and going on a killing
spree. i wish i was only joking. someday this
will stop and we will all be safe. i want to
help create that someday.

* * *

Zines are an opportunity to express fully, without fear of judgment; or even if that fear still exists for some, girls can write about *that* as well, releasing it through their words. Zines are also a way to inspire.

Renee Bessette, age eighteen, from Fairport, New York, has created and contributed to many zines. From her most recent, entitled *Stumble:*

Lately, I've been getting quite a few great
zines . . . An explosion, if you will. And what
I've got to say about them is that they all
are incredible. Everyone's got something to
say, everyone is motivated to make change,
everyone is excited, ready to get involved,
make a difference. And they have. Just by
going out and doing a zine says something—it
means that this thing called "empowerment" is
in effect. Time to make a statement. And it
ain't no feeble attempt. These zines scream
"I AM MAKING A DIFFERENCE." How much more rad
can it get? I'm excited to find out. . . .
So here I am, saluting every female who does
a zine. You are kool. And for every female
who reads these zines, or somehow takes part
in making change or being creative—just
doing something that makes them feel good
about herself, I salute you too.
Go girl go.

* * *

Through zines and meetings, the Riot Grrrls have created their own support system, their own "families" who are there for each other's emotional, mental, and sometimes even physical survival and well-being—reminiscent of the Homegirls' gangs.

But what seems to set them apart from the Homegirls is that, due to class and race (although somewhat mixed, the majority of the Riot Grrrls are White and acknowledge they are "privileged"), they have opportunities many of the Homegirls have never had. Through the advantage of education, Riot Grrrls have long been aware of a vital survival tool: expression.

By getting out their frustrations, shame, hopelessness, and rage—through singing, drawing, performing "spoken word," and especially writing—they have a healthy release that the Homegirls aren't normally afforded.

In describing how she came up with the title to the zine she began writing when she was seventeen, Kelly from Endwell, New York, recounts a time when she was rummaging through some old things from her childhood and she "found a tiny shirt that said everything I need to say in capital letters and primary colors."

The shirt had a SUPERGIRL logo emblazoned on the front, which she used to name her zine:

> It reminded me of what a strong sense of SELF I had when I was little, and how that began to change as I got older. I became more hindered by doubt, and when I was completely positive about something I got really defensive and it turned into a fight between me and whoever was the smartest boy in the class (ahh, what prototypes.) This is still pretty much true, but I'm trying to trust the things that I know about me because these are things that don't have to be true by anyone else's standards.
> I am who I am by my standards.
> WE ARE ALL SUPERGIRLS.

Sharing deep emotions through writing can be a healing process. Not only does it provide a release so feelings, such as anger, do not simmer or explode inside, but it is also an alternative to lashing out at specific individuals. From *Supergirl #2:*

Okay I've had it and the keys of my type-
writer will feel the anger and rage that you
should be receiving right now. But you have
no clue. You probably never will—but that
won't stop me. I can scream on paper when you
brush me off, when you bind my tongue. . . .
   I won't shut up. I won't be intimidated. I
WILL tell you when you are hurting ME, when
you hurt ALL girls with what you say and do.
I WILL tell you NOT to use words like slut-
whorebitch. I WILL NOT shut my mouth just so
you can be nice and secure in your opinion,
an opinion which includes sexist jokes,
racist remarks, homophobic comments, gender
pride, oppressive ideology, and blind hate
blind hate blind hate.
   You know who are you because when you read
this you are thinking that this "feminist"
should SHUT UP STOP LOOKING FOR TROUBLE SHE'S
PROBABLY PREMENSTRUAL OR HATES MEN IT'S NO
BIG DEAL EVERYONE LAUGHED AT THE JOKE ABOUT
THE BLOND PROSTITUTE THIS GIRL IS MAKING A
BIG DEAL OVER NOTHING SHE DOESN'T KNOW WHAT
SHE'S TALKING ABOUT ANYWAYS.
   Yeah, you know exactly who you are.
   You aren't all of mankind, or one person
alone, but you make up a big and power-hold-
ing part of society. You are in congress, the
supreme court, the police force, the big
important bands, church, school, home. AND
IT'S TIME YOU FOUND OUT THAT THE WAY YOU ACT
SOMETIMES IS NOT RIGHT, IS NOT ACCEPTABLE TO
ME OR MY FRIENDS.
   It's about respect.
   And no I won't shut up.

Fifteen-year-old Stacy Reardon from Brockton, Massachusetts,
writes two zines called *Coddle* and *Calico*. She has an insightful
point of view abut anger:

      . . .Our rage is our power don't let it fade
don't let it die feed it to your daughters
kill all confusion but teach her don't hate

too easily because hate cancels out the power
rage supplies.

Angela, age seventeen, blond-haired and blue-eyed with an innocent and girlish smile and sparkle, writes:

> . . . Not that I don't welcome a good fight,
> but there are some things I shouldn't have to
> fight for, and humanity isn't something I
> need to earn, respect isn't something I need
> to prove myself worthy of. . . .
> I'm not going to sugar coat my anger to make
> it easier for you to swallow—from now on my
> answers will be the poison words that you
> provoke, and if you gag on them, don't expect
> me to stop you from choking.

And what do young women who have lived less than twenty years
have to be angry about? Angela wrote that she doesn't need to
prove herself worthy of respect. From the majority of the girls' writing it is clear they feel continually disrespected, especially by acts
of violation and humiliation. These acts come in many forms,
including harassment; mental, physical and verbal abuse; and rape.

Sexual harassment is a daily concern, considering that most girls
don't even feel safe walking down the street alone.

And it is not only strangers who are the perpetrators of harass-
ment. Often it is closer to home, and school, as in the case of Sara
McCool, age sixteen, from Pittsburgh, Pennsylvania. From her zine
Sourpuss #3:

> I don't understand why when boys get
> together in packs they always pull this shit
> of something like yelling, "Hey girl, my
> friend likes you." "That boy over there says
> he likes you." You have no idea how many
> times this or something like it has happened
> to me. I hate feeling like I'm part of the
> "lets-mess-with-the-ugly-girl" game. I know
> that I am not appealing to the boys who

```
usually hassle me like this, so I can't imag-
ine what they say to a girl who really turns
them on. I have never seen a pack of girls do
this. Maybe you have, but I haven't. I have
never  seen  a  pack  of  girls  get  together
around some boy and yell at him how much they
want  to  have  sex  with  him.  I  really  can't
imagine what these little boys and even grown
men expect me to respond with. I'm sure they
expect me to just continue walking and trying
to  ignore  them.  It's  like  when  boys  see  a
girl, it's like she's this walking reminder
of sex. Especially if she looks "good." It's
like if a girl wears something that makes her
look  nice,  she's  a  slut  and  thereby  is
allowed to be molested by you. She is just a
reminder  of  sex.  That's  what  she  is  and
that's all she is.
```

In addition to rage incurred by disrespectful violation, many girls write of grief, often triggered by a painful childhood memory:

```
See mommy and daddy
smile their plastic smiles:
perfect, perfect
little girl hides her face
in mommy's skirts
clinging, cringing in fear
captured in a photograph
her eyes, glassy and distant,
they tell the true story.
```

—Terry Fresina, age 17
Stoughton, Massachusetts

At Riot Grrrl meetings and in workshops, I heard a majority of girls allude to incidents of abuse. There were many who barely admitted it out loud, having taught themselves it was safer to withdraw in silence. Billie Strain, age eighteen, from Washington, D.C., is finding healing through communication, and has become vocal and expressive. An excerpt from a chilling piece by Billie entitled "I Hate You More":

listen up, daddy, and listen good. you
broke my heart, daddy. you ruined my life.
you keep us women under control and you think
your male power will keep you outta trouble.
i hate you. if i thought i could get away with
killing you, i would. not just for me, for
mom and your wife and all the other women you
abuse, all the women you mindfuck daily. you
better watch your ass, 'cause someday i'm
gonna come up from behind and boy are you
ever gonna be sorry you hurt me. don't even
try to be friends like you think i don't
remember. i remember. i wake up screaming and
i remember your eyes looking at me and your
fist beating me and your dick raping me and
my mind is reeling and wanting everything to
stop now now now now now now now.

i'm so angry when i see your face, i want
to vomit. when i can't even fuck without you
there, without crying. when i can't look in
the mirror without hearing your voice telling
me how ugly i am, telling me what kind of girl
i am. when i look at my mother and i see her
in fucking poverty while you bask in your
wealth, i feel sick. you make me sick. you
made me hate myself. you took my little girl
self and you fucked her all up. she loved
you, but i don't. i might hate myself, but i
hate you more.

Misty, age nineteen, creates many zines, including *Aqua Girl Star*, *Just Like a Girl*, and *I Can't Get Far Enough Away*. Much of her writing is an obvious response to early abuse. Even her present struggles not to re-create the cycle of abuse with her boyfriends is a running theme through most of her poems.

you're holding me down
i start to cry
you're holding me down
your hand up my blouse
that look in your eyes that tells me i'm
nothing

```
i try to pull away
              you laugh,
  "you're making it out to be something it isn't.
it's okay. hold still. it's our secret.
   no one will ever know."
  your cold uncaring hands on my body
the stench of your beer-drenched breath in my mouth
you're holding me down
  i start to cry
no one hears . . . . . . but HIM.
  you're holding me down
it doesn't take much to kill a little girl.
```

What can these girls tell us about healing? Will they ever be able to erase the memories, the intrusion, the shame? Are they ever able to trust again, to love again, to let themselves fully feel again?

From Los Angeles, eighteen-year-old Lorena Melgoza, who, along with Patricia Valdiva, does a zine entitled *U.G.L.Y.* (Unite Grrrls Love Yourself), decries:

```
I was 8, 9, 10. No, it was NOT my fault. I
didn't know what was going on. I didn't know.
I didn't understand. No one helped me. I
covered my body. I didn't want to be pretty.
I didn't want to appear attractive to any
male. Ashamed. Scared. Embarrassed. Confused.
But I tried to deny it. I tried to make-
believe that nothing had happened. I thought
I could forget about it, all the ugly details
of what he did to me, of how and where he had
touched me. That if I could just forget about
all that, I'd be alright . . .
```

As indelible as her experience was, Lorena did find some hope. Her process of reclaiming herself, and her power, began with expression, which she encourages others to find:

```
But you don't forget. You have to learn to
accept it and deal with it. You have to talk
to someone. You really do have to
tell . . . someone—Anyone. Once I began to
```

accept it and deal with it, once I told one
person, I just kept telling people. Once you
tell one person, it's not enough. I feel I've
got to tell the whole world cause I kept such
a secret locked up inside of me for so long
that I start to feel free by telling more and
more people. And see, right now there is an
11 year-old girl on tv, (on the Sally Jessy
Raphael Show) she is telling <u>her</u> story. She
too was sexually molested. She is crying. I
am crying too. I just want to hold her and
tell her how proud I am of her. And tell her
she is brave. And I wanna tell her that maybe
everything isn't alright right now, but we
can make it alright. I wish for every one of
us to come out, that could change things. We
can come out, come on strong. yell and kick
until the world finally listens and takes
action. One out of every four girls is sexually abused in this country alone by the time
she is eighteen. But also, why don't we focus
on the victim—no, the <u>SURVIVOR</u>. We need help
and support, counseling—anything and everything. People came for me, claiming to help
me. Nobody helped me. They never once showed
concern for <u>me</u>. They didn't want to know
about <u>me</u>. Or how <u>I</u> was affected. They all
just wanted <u>his</u> name, <u>his</u> whereabouts, <u>his</u>
everything. What about <u>my</u> everything? <u>My</u>
anger? <u>My</u> pain, <u>my</u> confusion, <u>my</u> life. FUCK
HIM. He's gone. I <u>AM</u> the one left standing
with it in me for the rest of <u>my</u> life. What
about <u>ME</u>?

Like the Homegirls, many of the Riot Grrrls who have been
victims of abuse still crave the love of a parent:

mommy told me
"don't go there."
she saw daddy there yesterday.
he sold an old lady with blue hair
a lottery ticket—
and a can of cat food.

```
he wished her "good luck"
and told her that the kitty
was really too fat
for its own good.
she agreed.
he was always right
about stuff like that.
i learned that,
all by myself.
he said if i told,
he'd go to jail.
he did.
he said if i told,
we wouldn't have any money.
we didn't.
he said
"if you'd just lose ten pounds,
people wouldn't say you're ugly."
people still call me ugly.
he told me
people make fun of smart girls.
he was right, as always.
the last time i saw him,
he said he was sorry.
he said he loved me.
i know i'm ugly
and i know i'm smart
i know that all the bad stuff
he said that would happen
did happen.
i just hope he wasn't wrong
about the last thing he ever said to me.
god, let him be right one more time.
```

—Terry Fresina

* * *

RIOT GRRRL IS . . .
BECAUSE we need to acknowledge that our blood is being spilt; that right now a girl is being raped or battered and it might be me or you or your mom or the girl you sat next to

*on the bus last Tuesday, and she might be dead by the time
you finish reading this. I am not making this up.*

One out of three women will be raped in her lifetime and four out
of five rape victims know their attackers. These are facts that Riot
Grrrls are painfully aware of. At the Riot Grrrl Convention in D.C.,
it was overwhelming to see the number of girls who had been date-
raped—and those were just the ones who spoke up.

Nissa Simmons, age fifteen, from Thousand Oaks, California,
writes of her experience as she seeks to release pent-up emotion by
screaming her pain on paper, calling out the name "GODDESS":

```
You asked,
I said 'NO!'
you ignored it.
Forcing my legs spread,
Your flesh pressed violently
against mine.
You stole me.
While I cry,
You laugh.
And all of this time,
all I can think about,
is how much I trusted you.
you FUCKING BASTARD!
How could you do this to me?!?!
My hatred for you,
explodes within me,
and I try to fight back,
but you only force down on me harder,
splitting me, ripping me apart.
Blood now flowing from within me, oozing
over the hard wood floor,
spilling down my legs.
You say if I tell, you will kill me, but I
feel like I'm already dead. Is this pleasure
to you? Do you think you will get away?!?!
YOU FUCKER!!!!!
I will not keep quiet!
You cannot shut me up!
NEVER!
I loved you,
but I said "NO!"
You didn't understand,
```

```
you never loved me.
(RAGE, RAGE, RAGE.)
```

                        * * *

Though the Riot Grrrls are united in speaking out against rape, abuse, and other injustices, they also struggle with teenage problems of friends, relationships, and boys. Scrawled in large print letters, surrounded by a border of colored-in hearts, HLS from New York City writes in her fanzine *Crumpy:*

```
I want to share with you but I would
  probably lose,
I want you to share with me but I would
  only take.
I want you so much because I love you
and that is why I stay away.
```

And in her zine *Kingfish #3,* Sam from San Diego, California, expresses her boy concerns:

```
i wonder if everyone feels the way i do. i
wonder if every girl at the age of 17 feels
dumb and alone. i wonder if crushes are
always crushes because i always am smashed to
emotional bits. i wonder if nothing really
matters in relationships because they always
turn out to be total shit anyways. i wonder
if i kiss lots of people because i'm hiding
my craving for real stability in my life. i
wonder if my girlfriends that have dissed me
did so because they were afraid that if they
accepted the girl revolutionary in them they
wouldn't have any more boys to kiss. i wonder
if they should care.
```

Khourey Parrish is a lanky seventeen-year-old girl from Morgantown, West Virginia, with a head of soft, short, red stubble. She describes herself: "i like girls. i am a punk. i am a riot grrrl. i am a slut. i like boys. i am a feminist. i am a girl."

Khourey had been defining herself as a lesbian until she met a boy she wanted to be with. She clearly speaks the bottom line for many Riot Grrrls in declaring, "I want the freedom to define my own sexuality":

> the spanish inquisition was held in my bedroom when information was leaked to the authorities that i slept with a boy. "people ask us what's up with you because you say you're a lesbian, but then you like boys." i was asked to be more precise in my terminology. i disagree that i have an obligation to make sure everyone understands my sexual preferences. i want the freedom to define my own sexuality. that freedom is my right. there is this idea that bi-sexuality is a transition between gay and straight—it's just a phase, it's not a serious lifestyle. i refuse to answer to gays who don't think i'm gay enough or straights that don't think i'm straight enough. . . . i will not answer to anyone.

Nor will Jasmine. From her zine *Nottababe:*

> During a protest at the U.S Capitol, my G'friend Sarah (who is a righteous womin) and I must've hugged each other at least 20 times that day, and walked arm in arm past a huge group of boys, who upon seeing us like that, their eyes nearly popped out of their heads and their jaws almost dropped in disbelief (and maybe excitement . . .) . . . but the catch is that I am not a lesbian. . . . I mean, I have never had a relationship or got together physically with another womin, but I HAVE fallen in love with their beauty, and their minds . . . why is it that I cannot fall in love with anybody? Why are there labels for everything and anything? Why is it that society teaches girls to want to fall in love with

boys only? . . . As opposed to people in general? . . . To love is human. To want human touch
is natural. It's not dirty or raunchy or
cheesy or wrong. We are weaned from our
mother's breast and from then on, weaned from
our natural instincts of human contact. So
that's why I like to freak people out. I want
to start a process of thinking . . . and even if
it is just for a minute, it is a start. I want
to start a sexual revolution . . . my sugges-
tion is that if you are with a G'friend,
anywhere, give her a BIG hug, and grab her
hand and don't let go . . . look back at people
when they stare, and smile. Because you know
what they are probably thinking, and you are
breaking the rules! And you will have the
deep sense of satisfaction that you are no
longer a member of a fucked up society that
is into constraints on love and affec-
tion . . . you are creating your own . . . your
own rules, your own agenda, your own sisterly love. Every kiss and hug is a revolution,
and a small victory. Go, Grrrl, GO!

* * *

RIOT GRRRL IS . . .
*BECAUSE I can't smile when my girlfriends are dying
inside. We **are** dying inside and we never even touch each
other; we are supposed to hate each other.*
*BECAUSE we are unwilling to let our real and valid anger
be diffused and/or turned against us via the internalized
sexism as witnessed in girl/girl jealousies. . . .*

Jealousy is a much-addressed topic in zines. Nineteen-year-old
Katherine Raymond from Quincy, Massachusetts, writes about the
subject in issue #3 of her zine *Wee Hours:*

```
              A WEE DIATRIBE:

    you know what makes me so angry? this kind
of stuff. This is from a makeup ad:
    SHE'S THE SORT OF GIRL YOU'D LOVE TO HATE.
—i.e. beautiful. What's up with trying to
foster girl jealousy? using self hatred,
which is bad enough, to foster hatred of
other girls who probably hate themselves too,
and making us all think that our only rela-
tionships can be as competitors for boys, and
making us buy stuff toward this end? so many
things lately make me realize that you don't
rise when people fall. jealousy is bullshit.
```

* * *

RIOT GRRRL IS . . .
*BECAUSE we want and need to encourage and be encour-
aged, in the face of all our own insecurities.*
*BECAUSE we are angry at a society that tells us girl =
dumb, girl = bad, girl = weak.*

Self-image is a topic every female adolescent grapples with. As
Erika sums it up: "Clinical studies show; being a teenage girl fights
self esteem better than most other leading factors." She delves
deeper into this in an excerpt from her piece entitled "It's Just
Something Inside (It Doesn't Matter)":

```
    i hate mirrors. i really do. i can't stand
my reflection, my face. i know i'm not ugly.
not that i can see it, i just know. there's
something logical somewhere inside telling me
i'm not ugly. but deep down in the pit of
everything, i don't feel it.
    i feel ugly.
    it affects my relationships. i need to be
told that i'm beautiful by my friends but
they don't tell me i'm beautiful because they
```

```
think i don't need it. . . .
    i used to have fantasies about taking a
razor and shaving off my face and when it
grew back it would be perfect. no flaws, no
points of interest whatsoever. i know i'm
stepping out of line here. this is secret,
private stuff. shame shame shame. what a
pitiful way to live, not having the ability
to see beauty in myself. i'm trying. i really
am. i want to stop with all these standards
of beauty anyway and i know i need to start
with my own reflection. it just hurts though
to never like what you see when you look at
yourself. that's all.
    that's all. . . .
```

Jasmine fights back against society and media who "play on your insecurities and try to set standards that maybe not everyone can follow" by enlightening others about several vital areas of self-worth:

```
Most "feminine" or "beauty" items are being
geared for the average, white, middle class
teenager, and that is WRONG. Fuck teen maga-
zines. Fuck TV. Fuck ANYTHING or ANYONE that
tells you that in order to be beautiful, you
must alter the way you look. . . .
    My little sister is very close to me, and
whenever I get the chance, I try to give her
a positive image about her leg hair . . . like
saying: "Oh, your leg hair is so beautiful!"
And she'll ask me—"Jasmine, why don't you
shave your legs?" And I'll usually say—
"Well, because I choose not to. It's more
comfortable, and feels cool when the wind
blows it around—kind of like kitten kisses,
and when you get older (she's 7), shave your
legs if you want to, but DON'T LET ANYONE
MAKE YOU FEEL BAD ABOUT IT, OR TELL YOU IT'S
UGLY!" I think it's beautiful. And then
she'll kiss me and hug me and I'll read her
a book about Babar. Leg hair is sexy. And so
are you.
```

In Naomi Wolf's *Beauty Myth*, she cites studies that show that 53 percent of school girls are unhappy with their bodies by age thirteen; 78 percent are unhappy with their bodies by age eighteen.

Sixteen-year-old Marcie Wyrostek shares some of the emotion that goes with low self-esteem:

```
     I cannot stop crying. Why won't the tears
stop flowing? When I was little I'd just
think of something happy and then I'd be ok,
but no happy thoughts pop into my mind at the
moment. Crying is pointless. It gives me a
headache, makes my eyes burn, makes my nose
run and causes people to ask "What's the
matter?" What do you expect me to say? Where
would I begin?
     How could I possibly explain how awful I
feel about myself; how I can't remember the
last time I was actually proud of myself; how
I can't stand any of the people I used to call
my "friends"; how I feel guilty about every-
thing I do; how I hate being fat but wish I
were thin; how I wish boys would like me even
though I'm fat so I'd be happy with myself;
how I wish I didn't depend on boys to raise
my self-esteem; how I hate boys but want them
anyway; how I know you don't really care
what's the matter with me. Nobody cares.
Maybe that's why I'm crying. Would you under-
stand this? NO, BECAUSE YOU'RE SELF-CONFI-
DENT, POPULAR, AND THIN! YOU HAVE NO IDEA
WHAT IT FEELS LIKE TO BE SO INFERIOR TO
EVERYONE AROUND YOU! SO SHUT THE FUCK UP,
WALK AWAY FROM ME, AND LET ME CRY IN PEACE!
```

Those who are trying to know and accept themselves often have the challenge of being around other girls who still don't.

Sara Smith studies art and modern dance at Hampshire College in Amherst, Massachusetts. She describes herself: "I am 4 feet 11 inches tall, and wear braces." At age nineteen, she writes:

WHAT ARE YOU SAYING TO ME?

Do you know what you are doing when you
criticize your body in front of me?
Not only R U believing what the media tells
U about how U should look and eat, but you R
pushing these negative ideas on me, your
friend. I feel sad when I see you look in the
mirror and you think your thighs R too FAT,
that your belly is too ROUND. And I feel like
shit too, because I am forced to examine MY
thighs, MY belly by YOUR (the media's) standards.
It's bad enough U impose these impossible
models on yourself, let alone making ME
uncomfortable with MY body. Watch out for the
message U send when you put yourself down,
sister.

From almost every group of girls included in *Girl Power*, I
received writing that addressed weight issues. Most of the young
women in other chapters dealt with the dissatisfaction of their
appearances by dieting, many becoming anorexic and bulimic. But
it is evident through their writing that Riot Grrrls refuse to accept
society's and the media's standards, and are fighting back, taking a
stand for themselves:

I AM XL & PROUD . . .

i am not a size 6. or 8 or 10 or 12. i am
a size 14. i am 5'11" and i weigh 178 lbs. no
matter how hard i try, i will never be super-
model skinny. (and i have tried.) nor do i
want to be. i have "big" thighs. i have
stretchmarks. i have a big belly. and i am
finally learning to like it. i am finally
trying to accept myself. after all the pain,
all the fat torment, all the "you'd be so
pretty if you just lost 15 pounds!" i finally don't care. i am beautiful. beautiful to
nobody's standards but my own. i am not 36-
24-36. i am 38-32-38. here i am. i will never

```
do ads for victoria's secret. i bet her
secret is that she can't wear her own designs
without feeling gross. call me fat, whale,  '
cow, whatever. i'll eat it up. because i
don't count calories, and your words are
zeros anyway. i'll wear hot pants, and you
can deal with it. i did."
```

—*Sam*, Kingfish #3

Nomy Lamm, age seventeen, writes: "i named my zine 'i'm so fucking beautiful' because that's what i want to hear, and it may as well start somewhere."

In describing reasons why she wrote the zine, she includes as one of her considerations: "because fat politics are not just a personal thing. It's important that we deconstruct the myths that we are fed from birth regarding fat vs. beauty, fat vs. health, etc. we need to not only accept our own bodies, we need to accept (love) other people's bodies too."

In several excerpts from her powerful zine, we get a glimpse into Nomy's process of accepting herself and her body, wholly and unconditionally:

```
    okay, in case you're having trouble figur-
ing it out—i'm fat and this zine is all about
fat oppression. in the past year i have made
a lot of progress with myself and my body
image. when i first started doing zines i was
too ashamed of my body to even say that i was
fat. although i wanted my zines to be person-
al i couldn't bring myself to talk about my
body because the only thing i could even
think to say was "why can't i lose weight?"
by the time i wrote isfb #1 i had realized
that i didn't have to hate my body, that i
could be proud of my body, that i could be
sexy, beautiful and fat (not a contradic-
tion).....................................
    i am fat. i say this not because i have low
self-esteem. but because i have high self-
esteem. i love myself. & i want to be able to
```

```
accept myself and every part of me..........
    for seventeen years i have been hating my
body. yes, my body is not like my friends',
but  neither  is  my  mind,  and  i  have  no
complaints about that......................
    i will not hate my body any longer. if i am
hating my body, i'm hating myself. my body is
not some separate entity, it is me..........
    "one size fits all" is just one more way
society has of telling me i do not exist. one
size does not, and never will, fit "all"....
    when  i  complain  of  fat  oppression,  i've
often been told "well, just lose weight. i
know it'll be hard, but you can do it." so
instead  of  changing  the  oppression,  we'll
just assimilate? imagine saying to your gay
friend who complains of homophobia, "just be
straight. i know it'll be hard, but you can
do it." just as a gay person can go against
their nature and act straight, a fat person
could perhaps go against their nature and
lose weight through starvation, bingeing and
purging, surgical mutilation, and a heavy
dose  of  psychological  abuse.  it  sounds
ridiculous, doesn't it? but this is what we
are asked to do every day.................
```

And in a list of "rules" for the reader to keep in mind, alongside "fat is not ugly," "fat people do not lack control," and "diets are 20 times more unhealthy than being fat," one stands out in all its power and glory: "if you consider me a threat, if you fear me now, then just wait. the fat grrrl revolution has begun."

* * *

Like Nomy, Val is one of many Riot Grrrls who are embracing themselves, finding the unconditional love they've always longed for—in their own hearts.

```
    The reason i named this zine 'I ♥ me' is
because i do. i love myself, and i think it
```

```
is important to love yourself. . . .
    i feel like it is important to not only
acknowledge who you are, but to accept it
also. i know that i have felt like shit at
times, we all do, but i am trying to work on
loving myself: my ups and downs, my bitter-
ness, my anxiety, my depression, my happi-
ness . . . we all have flaws and i am not here
to say that "no matter what, we are all
loving and should love each other." i am
saying that i, personally am trying to under-
stand and like myself as well as love who i
am and what actions i take every day. loving
myself is a personal revolution that is
important to me as an individual.
```

One of the many Riot Grrrl tenets is to accept parts of self that have traditionally been quashed, judged, and belittled, and to actually *glorify* them, transforming these newly formed attributes into something that's cool. This is quite evident in many of their appearances, styles, and appreciation for childhood and childlike things. From wearing cat-eye glasses and mismatched clothes to carrying *Sesame Street* lunch boxes as purses and wearing brightly colored plastic barrettes in their hair, some are starting, as Nomy and Val's zine title declares, a *Nerdy Grrrl Revolution.*

Val explains:

```
    . . . we decided to name it this because we
are nerds who want a revolution. we look like
nerds and it has been called to our attention
more than once. for example, we were in the
mall and some dumb-big-cock-jock attacked me
and tried to take my big fluffy yellow balled
hat off my head. . . .
    Another example is nomy loves seals and
wears a seal pin everywhere she goes. cute,
funny girl. So, yeah, anyways here we are and
this is our zine. enjoy and be nerdy.
```

In a zine titled *Suck My Dick*, Heather Kasunick, age nineteen, beckons girls to join the "Nerd Girl Phun Group" with the words scrawled on the top of the page (complete with a couple of letters written backwards) amidst illustrations of some of the members:

> wanna be a part of our fun group? we like
> to play, we like to boogie-woogie, we like to
> eat at taco bell, one of us is a diabetic,
> one of us wears the maxi pads with the peach
> strip, and one of us looks like punky brew-
> ster so . . . you will fit right in! come on
> over and we'll all pretend that we are in
> brownies but . . . with a . . . phunky nerd gal
> super style!

* * *

As a "nerd," a "fat" girl, an "ugly" girl, a girl walking alone down the street, a girl who says no to a boy's advances—these are all girls who are coming together in recognizing and reclaiming their personal power:

> In American society, wimmin are novelties.
> Objects. A body part. Something to use for
> convenience. Wimmin need to learn that power
> is not given, we have to take it. We need to
> realize that we don't have to stand around
> and be treated like this. Don't let anyone
> control you or dictate your life to you.
> Wimmin's bodies are sold everyday—whether we
> realize it or not. On tv, in magazines, in
> movies, on billboards—open your eyes—it's
> everywhere you look. We need to break free of
> our own stereotypes. No one can save you from
> your oppression except yourself.
> GIRLS UNITE!
> —*Misty*

And Kelly, from *Supergirl*, writes "What Girl Power Is":

> ■ feeling okay about being a girl—not left out
> or inferior
> ■ promoting girl love. It really is a good

and wonderful kind of sisterhood-friendship. Don't talk to me about school sororities; I know a different kind of sorority and we don't tolerate any kind of "pledge week," thank you, and we don't set rules for each other or leave anyone out.

■ encouraging each other. Telling each other it's good to take risks to achieve our individual goals, and congratulating each other for taking risks.

■ teaching girls and boys and older/younger people about girl issues (equality, freedom of individuality in society, safety from victimization.) These are universal issues that often affect US to a greater extent, especially for poor and minority women. When everyone understands these issues, they are almost solved.

■ learning to respect each other. How many times have you heard girls call each other a slut, or some other derogatory name? How many times have you called a girl/been called by a girl one of the many names that exist to put girls down? We can't divide ourselves into black/white rich/poor good/bad, cause we'll never really have power that way.

■ this of course comes from respecting yourself. Respect your mind and body. Respect yourself as a girl with an individual and beautiful combination of appearance, ideas, background, interests, strengths, etc etc etc.

■ being able to wear lots of lipstick or none at all, short skirts or loose jeans . . . and still be simply a girl. It's not letting anyone judge you, because it's not about limitations!

■ making noise sometimes!!!

■ GIRL POWER = GIRL LOVE = RESPECT = ENCOURAGEMENT = STRONG SELF IMAGE = DESIRE TO TEAR DOWN THE RULES = GIRL POWER = GIRL POWER = OXOXOXOX = REVOLUTION ■

❀ ❀ ❀

RIOT GRRRL IS . . .
BECAUSE I am still fucked up, I am still dealing with internalized racism, sexism, classism, homophobia, etc. . . . and I don't want to do it alone.

Riot Grrrls have overcome barriers of silence not only through their meetings and fanzines, but also through political action.

The D.C. Riot Grrrls have taken part in demonstrations such as the Pro Choice March on Washington, a "Resist the Supreme Court" rally at the Capitol, and many of them have belonged to Positive Force, a collective that organizes protests and benefits, raising money for concerns including homeless and rape-relief shelters.

Scattered throughout zines are quotes and one-line slogans: FUCK SHIT UP, START A RIOT—A RIOT OF LIFE, WAKE UP, LISTEN TO YOUR HEART, *ACT* WITH YOUR MIND, ORGANIZE A PROTEST, ACT UP!!

In Sam's *Kingfish* zine #2, scrawled in bold letters across the top of the page is: VOTE . . . **or suffer eternally in a lame paternalistic fascist society. really.**

It continues on in a smaller schoolgirl print:

> look. i'm not even fucking old enough to vote, but all i can do is implore everyone who is to vote. it is so important that we let ourselves, whoever we are, be heard. i'm sick of being ruled by rich white christian men who believe nothing i do is right, and i'm sure there are plenty of people who feel the same way, so DO SOMETHING ABOUT IT FOR FUCK'S SAKE! PLEASE!

The Riot Grrrls *are* doing something about it <u>and</u> the rest of their lives. Erika writes:

> . . .We are loving each other and ditching stupid hurtful ideas of competition. We are laughing screaming working breaking down writing singing trashing our bedrooms playing dress up

```
holding hands making our own rules and then
breaking them crying dancing playing patty cake
strapping on dildos and fucking boys with them
sticking up for each other making a spectacle of
ourselves working hard staying up all night
having sex with each other jumping on the bed
kicking the walls in . . .
   what this is is so big we can't even see it but
we can feel it, it's coming. it's here.
```

And indeed it is here. At first glance, these girls have been dissed and they're pissed. A closer, deeper look reveals a solidarity that strengthens self-concepts to combat the effects of the abusive lives that, up until now, defined many of them. Along with their shared emotions and revelations comes a commitment to change: themselves, each other, and the world, through a **"Revolution Girl-Style Now!"**

NOMY LAMM AND VAL TAYLOR

WITKNEE HUBBS AND NISSA SIMMONS ALONG WITH OTHER RIOT GRRRLS

ERICKA BABYDOLL AND MISTY

VICKY MAYORGA
FEB. 22, 1994

I never really thought about becoming a mother. The reality of it is hard. You have a lot of times of struggle but along with those struggles come a lot of precious moments that no one else but your baby can give to you. Now that I really think about it being a mother is complicated. You really have to think about what you want to show your child because everything kids see they learn. Theres a lot of mothers in the world I could

CHAPTER THREE

Teen Mothers

When the school bell rings, the girls file into the classroom dressed in baggy pants, tight scoop-neck T-shirts, tennis shoes and boots, carrying bright neon backpacks and Hello Kitty purses. They're giggling amongst themselves, arguing over boys, sharing makeup, eating candy, and drinking Cokes. They pass notes in class, whisper to their neighbors, play with their hair, and wait for recess.

At the break, these junior high and high school girls, ages thirteen, fourteen, fifteen, sixteen, cross the yard, walking over painted areas of four-square and hopscotch, avoiding balls and swings and monkey bars and jungle gyms. They continue into another building, which is filled with babies and young children playing, crying, screaming, laughing. Here, each girl goes over to one, or more, of the children, and greets her son or daughter.

Eighteen-year-old Maria Rodriguez from Inglewood, California, writes: "One thing I don't like about myself is that I get hurt fast because I am very sentimental. I like to write poems in rhymes when it's rainy and I'm sad. I like to draw when it's boring."

She continues:

    One thing I want the world to know about
    teen parenting is that it is hard to take care
    of a baby when you are still a baby yourself.

Yearly, more than a million teenage girls in the United States get pregnant. Why does this happen? What factors contribute to approximately 3,000 American teenagers a day becoming pregnant? Ofttimes, it is caused by peer pressure to be sexually active and the intense desire to fit in, be accepted.

To many girls, like Neyleda R., age seventeen, virginity equaled low self-esteem:

```
I started Jr. high at the age of 11. There
I started a new whole life. Girls wearing
make-up. Other kinds of clothes. But in
particular, they were always talking about
sex. How good it was and how grown up they
felt. They already knew I was still a virgin.
It used to feel jerky. Listening to all these
girls making fun of me. I used to think to
myself is it really, am I old fashioned? Of
course I didn't want to be called these
names. A year passed and me and my frustra-
tion grew up more. I was 12. Suddenly here I
am kissing in a car with this guy, his name
Javier. I was with him for a year going
around. Finally I ran away with him. It took
me two weeks until I was ready for it. That
night I remember when we were alone, turning
around the bed. I had wide open eyes. And I
thought this is it. This is what the girls in
Jr. high were talking about. I lost my most
precious thing in the blink of an eye. I felt
good because it was with somebody I love very
much. By the way, he is the father of my 2
year old little girl. I wish I could have
held on to my most precious thing for a longer
time.
```

While leading workshops with teen mothers throughout the country, I found, as I found with the Riot Grrrls and Homegirls, that abuse was a common component of their lives. Much of the teen mothers' writing indicates that many abuse victims have babies in reaction to their experiences. They believe that having a child will allow them to express and receive love without conditions and complications, that a baby will make them feel wanted and needed—on their own terms. Connie Pereida is one example. From Norwalk, California, Connie is seventeen years old and has a two-year-old son and a four-month-old son.

From the time I was nine years old, my life started to become a living hell. The reason for this is because that's about the time my step father started to molest me. It finally stopped at the age of 14. I went through a long term depression through the years. I kept to myself, I was both bulimic and anerexic, and I was also afraid to have a serious relationship with anyone.

Through those long years I wondered why the man I called Dad and said he loved me was doing this to me. I myself thought by not saying anything to anyone he would keep loving me. No matter what I did I thought I would be loved by him as long as I didn't open my mouth to anyone. As I grew older I knew those things I thought were wrong. I knew I would have to bring a stop to this.

When I finally did bring a stop to what was happening I believed that was it, it was all over, but silly me I was wrong. There was a lot more to come. There was the lawyers, the testifying, the hospital for the physical, and there was the waiting for the sentencing date of how long the bastard would get. When I heard how long he got, I felt like I was going to die. I learned to live with it. I learned to live with knowing he would only do a year and a half for the five years of hell he put me through.

It was hard, but I finally started a relationship with this guy. This is when I decided I wanted a baby. I wanted a baby because I wanted someone who would always love me and

be there no matter who I was or what happened
in the past. I felt as if there was still an
empty space in my life that needed to be
filled and a baby was the answer.

It is not just sexual abuse, but mistreatment in many forms
that can influence a young girl's decision to become a parent.
Nicole Williams, age eighteen, of Inglewood, California, tells of
her situation:

I want to give my daughter something I never
had which is a stable family. My mom was
never around. She's been in and out of my
life since I was born. She used drugs. So I've
been in and out of foster homes all my
life! . . . I've been in 5 placements since I
was about 10 years old. . . . I always had a
problem with being who I am, because my
family always put me down. My sister was
always the pretty one. I was always the ugly
one. She was always the smart one and I was
always the dumb one. I always got hit for
things I never did! One time I was about 12
years old and my grandmother put me in the
bathtub naked and beat me til I had whips all
over my body. It was so hard for me to even
sit down. Just because I had forgotten to
pick my clothes up when I got home from
school.

Nicole continues with the story of the time she was rushed to the
hospital after her grandmother . . .

. . .hit me upside the head with an ashtray.
. . . The reason why she do what she do is
because she is an alcoholic and drug addict.
Til this day I can't say I love you to her
because if I do, I would be lying to her. She
had already made it clear she doesn't care
about me! So you can see why I want my little
girl to have a stable home!

Another form of abuse is neglect. Although seventeen-year-old Adriana Arellano from Yuba City, California, had parents who imposed many rules, their lack of attention had far more impact on Adriana than their mandates:

> It was easy to hide because they were never there. I didn't have a relationship with either one of my parents—they were always too busy. I know why I wanted a boyfriend. I wanted someone who would pay attention to me. Someone I could talk to and someone who could tell me they loved me.

Adriana fell in love with a boy. Although not pressuring her at first, the boy did start talking a lot about sex and Adriana felt that if she didn't sleep with him, she would lose him. She writes that she had no idea that she would get pregnant. "After all, I was only 14 years old."

I also heard from many teen mothers who are not only desperately crying out for attention, but are also craving discipline, boundaries, and restrictions—evidence of being loved.

WHY DID YOU TELL ME

> Why did you tell me that I could go with Joy
>   and Cami?
> You knew that they were hanging around the
>   streets in Danville.
> I know that I asked you could I go
> but why did you say yes?
> Look at me now,
> I'm thirteen and I'm 7 1/2 months pregnant.
> Why are you screaming?
> Are you mad at me?
> Why are you telling me that I ruined every-
>   body's life?
> I don't want to move to Lexington
> Why are you making me move with you and my
>   sisters?
> I don't want to leave Daddy.

```
I'm Daddy's little girl.
Please don't make me go.
Stop yelling at me.
You are the one that told me I could go.
Oh Mama, why did you tell me?
```

—*Regina Cervantes*
Georgetown, Kentucky

Yet, other teens became mothers in the process of reacting to, and rebelling against, parents' restrictive and overprotective behavior.

When Griselda Garcia from Commerce City, Colorado, was sixteen, she just wanted to spend time with her boyfriend Hector. Her parents' reaction to her dating, however, caused her to do the very thing they were fearful of:

```
. . . I became very confused and I had mixed
feelings about going against my families'
wishes or choosing to be with Hector.
. . . When I arrived home, I found my father
standing by the door waiting for me. He was
very upset and ordered me to my room and told
me I had to stay in there everyday! . . . I was
still a virgin and I had decided that if my
father wasn't going to trust me, then I
wasn't going to try to prove that I was still
a virgin and that I was doing nothing wrong.
That day, I decided to get sexually involved
with Hector and to begin staying with him. I
also wanted to pay back my parents for their
strictness and distrust.
```

Nine months later, Griselda gave birth to her and Hector's daughter, Jessica. She is now the single parent of two children.

* * *

Like many Homegirls who, after having a child, reevaluate their gang affiliations, many teen mothers are compelled to make more responsible choices after giving birth:

> . . . I started hanging around the wrong type of people. I ended up going to jail [Sybil Brand Institute] for assault and battery. Before I went to this phasility all I wanted to do was hang out get drunk, and just kick it with my homies. Well they ended up beating up this girl one night, and she pressed charges on all of us, so we went to jail. I sat in there and thought to myself is this the type of lifestyle I want for me and my daughter, I was thinking this place is not for me.
>
> I could only see my child through a glass window, not able to hold her or kiss her, she used to see me and reach her hands out for me to hold her, and I couldn't even touch her. That hurted me more than anything in this world. I prayed to God every night. I asked Him if I get out of this, I was going to get my life back right, if not for me, for my daughter. I realize she is going to be looking up to me, and what kind of example would I be just kickin it every night, getting drunk, actin' a fool with my homies. She'll turn around and do the same thing. So I made a promise that when I got out I was going to school and to try and reach higher goals in my life.

—Natasha C., age 19

Natasha is currently enrolled at the Teen Parenting and Childcare Program at the Business Industry School in Los Angeles.

Although the majority of girls do not decide to get pregnant and feel it was a mistake that they've learned to accept and not regret, there are those who feel they have made a clear, conscious choice, like Lisette G. from Inglewood, California:

```
    I'm eighteen years old and I have a nine
month old son. A lot of people say that I am
too young to be a mother. I don't see it that
way. I want to make one thing clear. My child
came to this world because God sent him to me
and he is the one person that is going to make
a better me for tomorrow. I planned my child
and I wasn't surprised when I found out that
I was pregnant. I hate to see all those talk
show hosts that bring up topics that concern
teen mothers. Too many a time I've seen a
young woman on TV with a beautiful child say
the phrase "It was a mistake, I didn't think
it would happen to me." I feel like telling
them what did you think was going to be the
outcome of having unprotected intercourse
with someone you hardly knew or for that
reason, anyone? Don't you know about the
birds and the bees? It is likely impossible
for someone to be oblivious about sex and sex
education. Condoms are distributed all over
the place. You can even get them free! . . . I
wish we were all mature enough to discuss
family planning with our partners.
    I'm very lucky to have chosen the right
partner in my life. I may be young, but it
just feels right. My boyfriend and I while we
were dating had intercourse with protection.
We started getting serious about each other
and we discussed children. We both agreed we
wanted a child. And when I was pregnant, he
took care of me and still does.
```

* * *

Whether it is a choice to get pregnant or not, all teen mothers seem to struggle with telling their family, and the consequences that ensue. Even if there is not much of a family around, as in the case of Diana A., age seventeen, from Los Angeles:

```
Dear Dad:
    I have always wanted to tell you so many
things I didn't like about you. I will never
```

forget the day you found out that I was pregnant. I will never forget that look and everything you said to me. I always respected you
and accepted everything you did. Everybody
said I was dumb for caring for you, because you
weren't worth it. But I always defended you. I
never let anybody talk about you. That day you
found out I was pregnant, you didn't understand me. You didn't accept me the way I was.
I accepted your mistakes, all of the other
kids you had with other women. I accepted your
faults. I remember how you didn't go and see
my brothers, because you didn't want to bump
into me. I know I hurt you, but you hurt me
too just by not being on my side. You knew my
mom wasn't going to be there for me. I hoped
you were going to love me the way I was, like
I love you.
    I wish someday we can be friends like before.
                              Love, your daughter.

Teresa Walker from Lexington, Kentucky, was seventeen when
she became pregnant. She lived with her parents in, as she describes
it, "a well-to-do neighborhood with doctors and lawyers who have
the perfect children who do no wrong."

My parents were so disappointed in me, and
no one wanted my baby but me. I struggled
with whether having a baby would be the best
for my family and me. . . .
    The first few months were the toughest times
I ever experienced. I had my father tell me
I would have an abortion no matter what. But
what my mother told me hurt the most. I was
told to stand at the top of the stairs and
let her push me down them until I would
miscarry.

After giving birth to a baby girl, Teresa felt it didn't matter what
anyone else said or did—she was happy and content. Today, her
daughter is two years old and has a seven-month-old sister.

There are, however, some girls such as seventeen-year-old Erin from Valencia, California, whose pregnancies have allowed for transformations in the quality of their relationship with their parents:

> The relationship between my parents and myself has improved outrageously. Before I was pregnant, we really never talked to one another. Now we talk, go out and do things together, it is just so much nicer when you have a better relationship with your parents.

From Chicago, Zenobia Hunt is willing to work through the rough spots with her family and maintain an optimistic attitude:

> Well gals, listen up. I am 15. I have a 9-month-old daughter.
> I'm still in school and I have a great relationship with my parents (RIGHT.)
> It's not so bad (YEAH RIGHT.) Really, it's not. You just have to keep a clear head and not let anyone put a cloud over your sun. After all it's your life as well as the one you choose to bring in this world. . . . Don't get discouraged at first. If things get rough at home just sweat it out, after all, parents, like diamonds, are forever.

* * *

There are several other options for a girl to consider upon learning she is pregnant. Dina Furstenberg, age seventeen, from St. Paul, Minnesota, made a different choice:

> NOW YOU KNOW
>
> Have you ever held someone
> and loved them, and known
> you had to let them go?

Have you ever thought
of giving someone everything
you had, then realized
that would never be enough?
Have you ever struggled
to make a life for yourself,
in the hope that someone else
could have that life, too?
Have you ever seen the love
two people feel when they meet
their child for the first time,
and felt your heart break at the same time?
Have you ever seen two people
hold their child, and each other,
and felt the pain of their tears?
Have you ever felt a woman's pain
when she gives birth
then leaves the hospital alone?
Have you ever seen that one, lone child
in the hospital nursery, and not with its
 mother,
and wondered why?
Have you ever made a decision
to benefit someone else, when you knew
it would break your heart?
Have you ever felt the pain of seeing
 pictures
of your child with a beautiful family
that isn't yours?
Have you ever had to let
someone else give
your child the kind of life
it deserves, the kind of life
you can't give?
Now you know what it feels like
to place your child for adoption.

* * *

Many teen mothers wrote that they had chosen to keep their babies
out of a preconceived notion of what motherhood would be like.

From Galina McKenzie, age nineteen:

My perspective, as a child, on my life was like a fairy tale. I pictured in my mind that having a baby was going to be a easy task. It was kind of like having a cabbage patch doll, without the responsibilities. I would dress my little girl up in pretty colorful dresses. Comb her hair in pig tails. Read her a bedtime story and manage to put her to sleep without complications. I would feed her a bottle and she would drink every drop of it. Then after I got tired of playing with her, I could simply put her away and focus on another activity.

Seemingly, perception is greater than reality, because I was in for a great big surprise. . . .

Now 19 years old, I am a mother of a two year old. Yes, I still have my fun combing her hair and dressing her up, but it does not stop there. I have a great deal of responsibilities. I have a child that is totally dependent on me. It's my job to bathe her every night. It's my job to change her diapers frequently. It's my job to make sure she is getting the right nutrition and plenty of vitimins. It is my job to teach her right from wrong. It is my job to make sure her immunizations are up to date. It is my job to guide her and direct her through her childhood years. It is my job to nurture her and show her that I love her. It is my job to teach her responsibilities. Raising a child isn't always peaches and cream. Raising a child requires great effort, great input. Problems will come along, you have to know how to solve them in the right way. A mother's work is never done. This is no fairy tale.

* * *

The hardships, responsibilities, struggles, and challenges of being a teen mother don't overwhelm everyone. Orlanda Frazier, age nineteen, sees it differently. She is a student at Hill House, a teen parenting program in Pittsburgh, Pennsylvania, that offers GED training as well as classes in parenting skills, job development skills, computer training, work habits, and ethics.

```
I would like to tell the world that being a
teenage mother it isn't really hard, at least
for me it wasn't. There are a lot of opportuni-
ties out there that you can further your educa-
tion or get help with finishing your education.
There are programs that young teenagers can get
involved in. But that doesn't mean just because
it wasn't that hard for me that it's going to
be the same with you. Everyone has different
situations and in my case, her father is finan-
cially stable and I get help from both sides of
the family.
```

From all the writing I received and teen mothers I met, Orlanda is an exception. Most can't survive financially by themselves, and many are forced to rely on welfare. Families often cannot, or will not, provide for them and fathers of their children too often refuse to take on any responsibility:

```
In a few weeks, Walter is going to court and
he's going to get locked up. I'm very scared
that this might happen to me. I mean I'm
afraid that the children will not have a
father to parent them, like right now. Or I
will not have money to pay utilities or rent
or any special needs like I have now.
```

—Patty B., age 18

Eighteen-year-old Tracy W. is also faced with this problem:

```
I thought the father would always be there
to help me. Well not all the time, but at
least sometimes. The truth is he's never
around. He spends half the time in jail. The
```

other half he's running the streets, not
thinking about his son. Sometimes I get so
pissed off at him. Especially when my son is
always asking about him, wanting to be with
him, or even talk about him. It just makes me
hate him. I thought having a baby would be
half his responsibility and half my responsibility. I thought we would be a family. If I
got tired of dealing with Aaron, he could
just go to his father.

From La Mirada, California, Misty Cota, age seventeen, wistfully
yearns for the absent boyfriend/father in her poem "Butterfly."

. . . God has blessed us with this
  beautiful child
will you ever discover her gold?
So fragile, so delicate, so complete
A creation from a love we once knew.
She now entwines our lives forever
Yet you turn your cheek from our gift
Days are flying, nights are going fast
Don't think this young child is going
  to last
Her sweetness is revealed, a gleam in
  her eyes
Rosy cheeks, and a pudgy nose
on and on our baby grows
The world is a brand new place for her
Each hour there is something to learn
Don't run away and miss her first butterfly
Our little girl might not come back again.

Some fathers who do come around can prove to be more harmful
than helpful:

When I was 15 years old I had my first son.
I had my second son when I was 17 years old.
My kids don't have the same father. . . . One
day my first son's father came over to my
friend's house and put a gun to my six-month-
old's head. I was so angry and hurt! We got

up and left so now my kids fathers are at war.
I'm scared somebody is going to get hurt.

—*Demeccia C., age 18*

Despite the consequences of raising a child alone, more and more girls will no longer put up with abusive behavior from their boyfriends or husbands—especially when it involves the child.

This was the case for Jackie C., age nineteen, from Los Angeles:

So, he got mad and started telling me
things, yelling. All the time I hear the same
thing when him and I get into an argument. I
was holding my baby and he was yelling harder
and made the baby start to whimper. Then he
acted as if he was going to hit me, but he
didn't. He took my glasses off of my face and
broke them in half. Then I told him to get
out and take everything with him. Before he
did he broke my remote to my T.V. and a couple
of other things. This is not the first time
he has broke something of mine. He has broken
my glasses about four times now. Every time
I would have to pay for them.

I think I handled this situation as the best
way as I could. Before I used to let him do
whatever he wanted to me. But now I don't. I
am going to try and take steps for my child
and myself not to endure these kinds of
things anymore.

But not all teen fathers fail to live up to their responsibilities, as Lisette describes:

I'm very lucky that the father of my child
is a hard worker and a loving father. Even
though I come from a divorced family, I value
the fact that my baby's father does have
family values. Someday we plan to get
married, as for now we are simply playing the
role.

And seventeen-year-old Yesinia Mendoza believes the father of her baby shows loving sensitivity:

> When I started labor it was Sunday at night. It was very hard because I didn't have the baby until Thursday at 9:00 pm. . . . He came in and out of the room. My mom said he cried when he went downstairs to the lobby. When he went to my room I saw some tears on his eyes. . . . Now that I ask him if it hurt his feeling seeing me suffer from the contraction if it was hard on him and he said yes that it really hurt him that I was in so much pain. Because it was his fault because he wanted a baby. And then I ask him would you like another baby he says no because he doesn't want to see me suffer again.

* * *

Whether sharing the responsibility with an attentive father, an abusive father, or having no father around at all, raising a child requires making difficult choices:

> What I find the hardest is discipline, how to raise them properly. I want to be strict with them, but not too strict that they would be scared of me, but then again not easy so that they get away with things. That is so hard and important to me. Because what they come to be in life is what I have taught it's what I raised. When I get in a situation like that, sometimes I just sit and cry. I want my kids to be good in life and I want to be nice but sometimes when you're nice kids take advantage of you. And when you're mean, they don't want to be with you. I don't want my kids to be afraid of me, but I want them to respect me cause I'm their mom.

—*Elsa A., age 17*

Diana A., who wrote the pleading letter to her father after he disassociated himself from her upon learning she was pregnant, is now at home, living with her mother and her baby sister. This less than ideal situation concerns her greatly:

> In my house there are two little girls that are two years old growing up in different ways, one is my sister and one is my daughter. My mom is raising my sister in a very different way than I am raising my daughter. When it's time for them to eat, my daughter is allowed to eat as much as she wants to. If she doesn't want to eat she doesn't have to, and my sister has to eat everything. I wonder what goes through her mind when she sees my daughter being able to do more than what she's allowed to do. My sister must be confused because my mom works when I am at home and I am the one who takes care of her and I let her do what my daughter does. My sister is learning how to act when my mom is around and how to act when she's not around. I don't want my sister to think my daughter has more privileges. I worry that when they get older and if they were to be molested I'm sure my daughter will tell me and my sister would keep it a secret. My sister is very quiet and obedient sometimes I rather have someone loud and happy than someone quiet and sad.

Since Natasha has gotten out of jail and gone to school, she's made good on her word to stay out of trouble and be a responsible parent. She describes an incident where she dealt with an aspect of child-rearing in a unique way:

> Sunday I took my little girl (Bria) to the grocery store. She wanted some cookies and I told her no because she already had some at home. She fell out on the floor and started kickin and cryin, so I fell out with her and started doing the same thing, and she got up

and looked at me crazy and started walkin off.
I just laughed because I know she thought I
was crazy. But I was just letting her see that
Mommy can throw tantrums too. And to let her
see how embarrassing that can be.

Teen mothers have more than their share of pressures and problems. Some, like Jessica, age eighteen, wrote that they sometimes, regrettably, find themselves taking out their frustrations and emotions on their child:

Baby boy I want you to know how sorry I am
for what I have done to you! I need you to
know that first of all you are not the bad
one. I believe that I am because what
happened wasn't your fault. I now realize
that. Kev—I wish that you could find a way
to forgive me. Because I know that you know
I hurt you. That's why I feel so hurt for
doing what i did. I know that you are just a
little baby and that you are curious about
things. Believe me it's not your fault. It's
just that I have a lot of anger and sadness
inside and I don't know how to show it. That's
why I hope you will forgive me, because you
are the only one I have left.
                        Asking for forgiveness
                                    your Mom.

And some teen mothers have been surprised to discover that, despite their resolve to raise their child differently than they were raised, there are instincts that inherently come with being a mother:

"When I have a child I'll never do that. . . ."
Ha. What a laugh.
On that cold December day, lying on that
hospital bed,
I remembered . . .
"You can't date until high school."
"You lost your car privileges."
"You're grounded."

```
"I'm disappointed in you."
"No one said life was fair."
"I don't care if you think I'm the meanest
mom in the world."
. . . and all the rest of those things I said
I'd never say to my child.
But when I saw the nurse carrying my son away,
I no longer saw myself as a teenager,
but as a parent.
That baby was my responsibility,
and those things I thought I'd never say,
seemed like things I should say.
I had to be a parent, and I had to protect.
No one ever said life was fair,
and parents aren't always nice.
But a mother's love can always be counted on.
```

—*Dina Furstenberg*

Ali R. describes herself as: "Currently 18 years old, 5'2", medium dark skin, dark brown eyes and dark black hair. I like old cars that are fixed up such as '64 Impalas. I like going to car shows when I can. I have this character that I like 'Mickey Mouse.' I think he's a very cute character."

She describes her goals as a parent:

```
I want to teach Emily and my other child on
the way pride and joy, dignity, self respect,
and to others. How to keep their heads held
up high and not let no one bring them down.
To fight when it's needed. To think of a
future. To finish high school. I want them to
know that having a child at a young age is
difficult. I want for them to marry a good
person to wait until they get married to
think about sex. For them to come to me when
they need something or they want to talk. I
want for them to do the same—show their chil-
dren pride and joy for their nationality and
not to disrespect other people's nationality.
```

* * *

In addition to the responsibilities and challenges of caring for, providing for, and raising a child, teen mothers must also contend with society's disapproval and judgment:

> I think it's hard growing up as a teen
> mother because a lot of people treat you like
> you're scum and think that you are wrong in
> having a child at such a young age. For the
> mothers that are young like I, I wish you the
> best because it is hard but anyone can pull
> through the hard times "it gets worse before
> it gets better," remember that. It has helped
> me a lot to remember that.
>
> —*Christina, age 17*
> *Denver, Colorado*

And from Glenda Martinez, age seventeen:

> It's hard to have two kids. Sometimes I go
> on the bus some people look at you like you
> committed a crime.

Considering all the forces these girls confront on a daily basis, I was struck by the following writing from a girl in Philadelphia:

> ME, MYSELF AND I
> A VOICE ACHING TO BE HEARD
>
> My name is Sharnise Genae Carroll, and I am
> a young black woman struggling to have a voice
> in society. I am fifteen years old and I am
> six months pregnant. Being a teenager, black
> and pregnant makes it hard for me to get heard.
> It is very difficult to make it with the way
> things are today with an ongoing recession.
> And racism just makes it all the more diffi-
> cult to be very successful. Not saying that it
> is impossible, but the odds are stacked
> against me.

It was hard enough to get in a good school,
much less get a good job. I do feel very
oppressed because there are too many male
chauvinists running the show. They feel that
women never were, aren't now, and never will
be their equal on the work force.

If we had more black women having their say
in the government, then maybe there would be
all the more chance of us surviving in this
dog-eat-dog world.

Being a teen mother will not help the
circumstances at all. Getting public assistance is a big hassle, and getting a job is
unfathomable because I am under age.

I am upset because I plan on bringing a
child into a chaotic world that I have minimal say in, even though I am part of a majority. I don't want my baby growing up
believing all of the hype and stereotypes
that the media shamelessly displays each and
everyday.

I don't feel the government is doing enough
to clean up the ghettos and filth that black
families have to live in. I am so disgusted
with the system, it is made to work against us
not for us. I really hope I can make a difference in someone's life through my writing.

Sharnise has an attitude of determination, which is sometimes
necessary to be able to move forward when one feels defeated by
one's personal environment. Patty B., on the other hand, finds that
compliance is the only way for her to cope with her unfortunate
circumstances:

I wish that the community where I live
would've been like it use to be 10 years ago.
Before when I was living with my mom it used
to be safe and quiet. When my mom would give
me permission to go and play outside with my
friends, it used to be so fun. All the kids
on the block would gather up and play baseball, football or soccer. Even the ladies
from the buildings would sit outside on the

stairways and gossip. Now that place is all
fucked up. There are a lot of gang bangers,
a lot of shooting and drug dealing. Sometimes
I wish I could go outside with my kids and
play. But no! Instead I'm inside all bored
watching TV or listening to the radio. I
don't want to do that all the time. But I
guess I have to. I want my community to
change.

There is much concern about the safety of children in this country. When I asked Lisette and Nicole to write about their ideal days,
both dreamed of better, and safer, times:

Well actually I have an ideal dream. I would
live in this four bedroom two story house you
know with this big yard, beautiful rose garden
in a quiet remote area here in L.A. where there
is no crime my children can walk the streets
and play without the fear of kidnapping.

—Lisette

The first thing I would like to do is to
take me and my baby out with no one around
and to just let her wander around and do what
she wants, go where she wants without wonder-
ing if she's going to be hurt or not. To let
her think this world is hers.

— Nicole

Despite fears and concerns, or perhaps *because* of them, many
girls are taking steps to make a better life and future for their children. Eighteen-year-old Andrea A. is one of them:

Ever since I came back to school I've been
very proud of myself because now I realize
that that's the best thing for me. I really
think about me and my baby and my future. I
know that for my baby I've got to get on with
my life. I want to be someone and not depend-

ing on anyone or anything else. Sometimes I
ask myself if all of this is worth it. But I
know that in the long run I'll know that all
my struggles and sacrifices were worth it.
Sometimes I feel frustrated of life and want
to give up but I see my baby's precious little
face and it really gives me hope to go on.

There are many teen parent programs throughout the country
that offer not only a basic education, but also focus on issues related to pregnancy, parenting, and early childhood development. Yet
with all the facilities for teen mothers, only a handful have the
means to provide child care. Because of this, often girls just cannot
attend school.

Those lucky enough to be able to go are finding that programs are
becoming more scarce. Sixteen-year-old Quinndana Concepcion
from Lakewood, California, encountered this situation firsthand:

So I enrolled in the Paramount Teen Mom
Program. I liked the school. I was happy to
know that I was not the only one that was
young and pregnant. Then two months later,
the teacher told us that there was not going
to be a teen mother program in Paramount
anymore because there was not enough money
for the program.

Aware of the limited educational opportunities, and making the
most of her personal circumstances, seventeen-year-old Laticha
Allen from Chicago lashes out at those who expect her to fail:

"What are you going to do now? What about
school?" my friends and relatives ask me.
"Whatever I have to do, but I'm not dropping out of school," I reply.
I am a 17-year-old black female. I am an
honors student at Hyde Park Career Academy. I
plan to attend Columbia College in the
Fall . . . and major in journalism and broad-
cast communications and become a successful
journalist.

I am also five months pregnant.

Often—too often—friends and relatives make
snap judgements and doubt that I will become
much more than a statistic.

According to the Illinois Caucus on Teenage
Pregnancy (ICTP), in Chicago in 1991, 19.1
percent of all births were by teenagers,
which comes to a total of 11,528 births by
teenagers. ICTP also states that pregnancy is
the primary reason given for dropping out of
the Chicago schools by female dropouts.

True enough, these aren't the best statistics
for the road to success, but this doesn't give
society the right to "write off" teenage mothers and expect no social, economic, or political value from us.

With no intent to glamorize teenage pregnancy, why is there ever rarely research done
on how many teen mothers actually do finish
high school, go to college, and become func-
tional members of this society?

I have truly reached the pinnacle of my
tolerance with the idea that "it's all down-
hill from here." People envision teen mothers
as promiscuous, misguided females with low
moral standards, who ten years from now will
inevitably be on welfare, single, with tons
of kids and without an ounce of hope.

This was not my case and definitely will not
be my story. A tragedy is a disaster or
misfortune with little or no hope of being
fixed. A mistake is simply a mistake. Unless
I choose to wallow in my mistake, I can and
will succeed.

*　*　*

If their determination and desire can make it happen, indeed
these girls will have a chance to succeed. As Juana Martinez, age
eighteen, writes:

```
Women aren't objects we are women
We are dreamers we are strugglers
and we are fighters.
But the most important is that we never
  give up.
We are women.
```

Yes, they are women. They give life and nurture, set examples, discipline, work to support their children, and are responsible for them as well. But just once in a while, some, like eighteen-year-old Jahaida B. from Norwalk, California, would like to feel, and be treated, like the little girl she still is:

```
    . . . I'm sad because I think I'm ridiculous,
that everyone laughs because I too have feel-
ings because I too cry. Because I think I
shouldn't think but let time take its own
course.
    I'm sad because I need a man that will love
me, that will make me feel needed, appreci-
ated. So I could feel like a woman because
kids I already have two and I don't need
another one.
    I'm sad because I wish to have what at one
point I had
    I want to kiss and hug my mom and dad and
tell them how much I love them and have them
rock me and tell me its alright that they
will take care of me and protect me. That
everything is like it used to be. That I'm
still their little girl.
    I'm sad because I know that everything is
the way it is and that's how it's going to be
and it's never going to change because now I
am a woman and a mother and not a little girl
that too soon I left behind in the past.
    I am sad, so sad, because I know that that's
how things will always be.
```

PATTY BURGOS AND HER DAUGHTER MARLENE

DEMECCIA C. AND HER SONS, DARTEL AND ANTWOINE

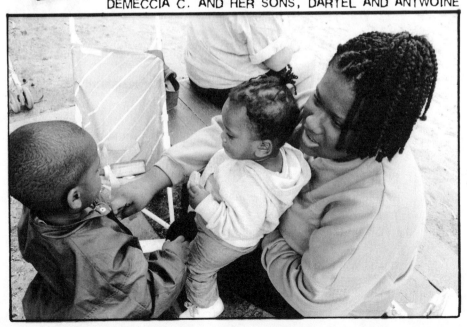

Ey, is you a guy? Is *that* a girl? What is that? Ey, excuse me, Hey you! shewt, it's a him. That's a guy. Is that a girl? It's not a girl? what is it? Ey, you dont look like a girl! Hey, excuse me is you a guy? That's a dyke that's what that is. Shewt, I wouldn't go outside with my legs lookin like that!. That's not a girl, Hey, what are you? Is you a guy, What are you? It's a dyke that's what it is, i told you its girl, it's not a girl, What is it? Shewt that's not a girl, Hey is you a girl? That's not a girl, that's not a girl, that's a dyke, that's what that is. That's not a girl.

It all comes back again and it comes back hard, it hits me in the head and knocks me over, I cannot breathe, I cannot speak, I cannot think, I will cry.

CHAPTER FOUR

Queer and Bî Gîrls

At an age when girls first experience sexual awakening, it takes a tremendous amount of courage to be true to one's feelings and adopt a lifestyle that is simply unacceptable to so many. Especially at this time when peer acceptance is so vital. The controversy over whether sexual preference is a choice or a biological fact is not at issue here. Yet every homosexual and bisexual girl who wrote makes it clear that no one would ultimately choose to be teased, belittled, judged, and ostracized.

```
"DYKE!"
From behind my back, I hear the slur for the
umpteenth time. "I'm not going to let it go
this time," I think to myself. "Let's see
who's so tough and brave now." I whip around
to face four boys who like to think of them-
selves as men.
"Who said that?" Four heads bow dumbly at
their desk. "I asked you, who said that?" Not
one of those pairs of "tough" eyes dares to
look into mine. "You're all a bunch of
cowards," I say with exasperation and walk
away.
```

Gina Ismalia Gutierez, age seventeen, is a first-generation Filipino/Portuguese American who describes herself as "a feisty, passionate, and quirky Saggitarian." In an article she wrote for her

Los Gatos, California, high school newspaper, she continues to
describe the incident:

> As soon as I walk away, frustration, disap-
> pointment and anger well up inside of me and
> I explode with unanswerable questions. I'm a
> good person and I don't try to hurt other
> people. Why can't they just leave me alone?
> Do they hate themselves so much that they
> hate me too? Do they fear me? What do they
> know about the real me? They don't even know
> who I am.
> This was not an isolated incident. I've
> experienced this harassment throughout high
> school. I have always been able to stand up
> for myself, but I've always been left with a
> vague angry feeling. . . .

Gina is comfortable enough with her sexuality to defend herself
publicly. She does not represent the majority.

Most teenage girls, such as fifteen-year-old Sara McCool, handle
harassment differently:

> Ey, is you a guy? Is THAT a girl? Ey, excuse
> me, Hey you! shewt, it's a him. That's a guy.
> Is that a girl? what is it? Ey, you don't look
> like a girl! Hey, excuse me is you a guy?
> That's a dyke. That's what it is. Shewt, I
> wouldn't go outside with my legs looking like
> that. . . . What are you? That's not a girl,
> that's not a girl, that's a dyke, that's what
> it is. . . .
> It all comes back again and it comes back
> hard, it hits me in the head and knocks me
> over, I cannot breathe, I cannot speak, I
> cannot think, I will cry.

* * *

Where do these feelings come from? For some, like nineteen-year-
old Khourey Parrish from Morgantown, West Virginia, they devel-

op quite innocently and subtly over time:

> when i was in the fourth grade, one night
> my friend demetria slept over. she told me
> all about sex. she said you be the boy and
> i'll be the girl. she said here is the hole
> where his thing goes in. she touched it. she
> said now it's time to go to sleep . . . we fell
> asleep.

> one night when i was in the fifth grade i
> was sleeping over at my friend kerry's house.
> we were lying in bed. i said have you ever
> done anything that might be considered homo-
> sexual? she said no, stupid, only boys can be
> homosexual. girls have to be lesbians. we
> fell asleep.

> one night when i was in college my friend
> erin slept over. she said she had something
> to show me. she said turn off the light. she
> said play "indian summer" again. i said what
> do we do now? she said don't talk. she kissed
> me.

For others, like Amira Antar, age sixteen, from Somerville, Massachusetts, there just comes a moment of overwhelming desire. The feelings are usually sudden, and often sparked by just a gesture or a smile:

> I never thought it could happen to me. To
> be like this. . . . I never even knew it exist-
> ed, until I discovered my feelings for her.
> She was the most beautiful woman I ever saw,
> with her straight, long blonde hair, flowing
> in the wind that first day I saw her. It was
> her face more than anything else that
> attracted me. . . .

* * *

An experience that seems to be commonly shared is the first

crush. Although not always the case, most early crushes remain secret. They are an easy way of experiencing the excitement and sensuality that comes with exploring passionate feelings—without the risk of rejection.

Several strands of her hair blew gently into her lashes. She swept them away hastily and smiled shyly at me. I was immediately charmed.

I secretly wanted for her to tilt her head back for me to feel how soft and silky her hair was as she would run it down the front of my naked body. I couldn't think of anything or anyone else who could bring such natural pleasure.

—*Shelly Bonoan, age 18*
Oahu, Hawaii

We said goodbye today. Well, actually I said goodbye to her...silently. I was afraid to say it out loud, afraid that if I did, there would be something in my voice to give it away, something that would tell her I had fallen in love with her. It was a terrible paradox: I wanted her to know, and yet desperately hoped that she might never really suspect. How would she react if she found out another woman loved her, desired her and thought of her constantly? And what if she found out it was me? Would she be embarrassed? Frightened—scared to talk to me, scared to be near me?...

Dava, I'll never forget your name. I'll never forget your face. You turn and walk away, and I know that I must let you go forever. But I will always keep a place for you where no one else can find you...not even you.

—*Baby K., age 19*
Richmond, Indiana

* * *

Those who act upon their desires are then faced with a decision. Do they "come out" and tell their family and friends, or remain isolated in their own knowingness?

Many girls wrote of this difficult and painful decision.

"The only reason I am in the closet," explains sixteen-year-old Elizabeth S., "is because of my mother. She has cancer and if I came out and told her, I know that would hurt her. Besides, if she dies, I don't want any guilty feelings thinking it was my coming out that caused her death."

And from T. J. Knight, age sixteen:

FEELINGS INSIDE

The feelings I have, I hold deep inside, for no one will ever truly understand. I'm like a time bomb unable to be diffused. I wish that someone could. Yet, I continue to hold back my feelings. For if they knew, I should surely perish in my own shame. All because of the feelings I hold inside.

Christina W. describes herself as "a white middle class queer girl from New York who believes true, honest communication, in any form, is one of the most important things to strive for." Yet she grapples with the thought of being totally honest:

i'm scared to tell my parents i am a lesbian . . . i don't know how to go about it . . . the thing that kills me is that i never talk to my parents about anything, and i feel this is way too personal to tell . . . and it's a big part of me i am hiding and i feel sucky doing so. the thing is, i think being gay fucking rules. i don't wanna be any other way. i've no problem with it. it's not fair that i'm getting worked up over their reaction. it's not fair that i need to tell them. you don't tell your parents if you're het . . .

Christina has come out to her friends and has found great support. But she's spent much time and energy dealing with the matter of telling her family:

```
    i want to bring a gay friend over, and say
"mom and dad, this is penny. she's a lesbian.
we have a lot in common!!" then i just want
to run out the door and come back hours later,
i mean i'll have to face them at one point or
another. i don't want to explain myself. i
want the burden to be on them, i want them to
think, oh, we have to understand our daugh-
ter and get over our homophobia. we have the
problem, not her. society has brainwashed us
to think loving your own sex is wrong, but if
our little christina does it, it's alright.
we must overcome our fear alone, christina
will have enough problems out in the world,
the least we can do is support her 100%. . . .
    YEAH, RIGHT, DREAM ON!!!!!!!!!!!!!!!!!!!!!
```

After some time of wrestling with the decision, Christina deter-mined that it is more important to take the risk than to continue being untrue to herself:

```
    oh, did i mention that i told my mom today?
yes, august 17th . . . christina's mom found
out the truth. what happened was she told me
about some article in the paper on homopho-
bia in the bible. while she's in general an
open-minded, liberalish gal, i was a little
curious. "she knows what's up with me," i
thought to meself. then we go for a drive cuz
i'm supposed to do my road test in four days
and maybe get my license? anyways, i tell her
how the article was interesting and say how
a lot of homophobes are not way religious,
like, for example, my dad. mom says dad
really isn't too bad that way, they've had a
lot of gay friends, who she proceeds to talk
about, and who are all male, of course. i ask
her if she's had any lesbo friends and she
```

doesn't really answer, i know she's dying to
know if i'm one. so i start on how hets think
gays of their sex are always after them which
is so lame and conceited and shit, cuz i know
she never had lesbo friends cuz they freak
her out, and she says, "are you a lesbian?"
and i just say "i guess so" all wimpy and
shit, not proud or anything, but gimme a
break, it was a tense moment. and what can i
say, she just acted as if she's asked me if
i wanted pasta for dinner and i had said yes.
like, it was no big deal. and she went on to
say how she and dad had kinda thought maybe
i was and how it was my choice and how she
respected it, but i told her it's more like
what i am, and although i think it rocks, i
didn't really choose it.

Yet Christina became frustrated later when she realized that
although her mother appeared to accept and respect her homosexuality, there were limits to her understanding. When her parents
came to a visiting weekend at school where several panels regarding sexual orientation were offered, as well as a support group
called PFLAG (Parents and Friends of Lesbians and Gays),
Christina was angry, upset, and let down when her parents left
early, without attending any of the panels:

you fucking know it you know it i told you
i told you months ago over two months ago you
block it out you ignore it you never once
have brought it up admit it you're fucking
ashamed of me you think i suck i'm not right
it isn't normal no more perfect family you
said you understood you said you could deal
ok . . . i told you it's a big deal a big deal
yeah i act like it's not important and who
cares if you know or not if you still like me
or not but i care so fucking much i want your
approval so bad i want you to accept and deal
and acknowledge but act and feel like i'm no
different than before i want you to be proud
of me but you can't you can't . . . can't tell

```
your husband keeping secrets from him of
course it's my job to tell him too my job to
break the news to everybody i bet you expect
me to apologize well no way i am me and i am
trying to like me to love me more than i do
with no help from you mommy i'm queer mommy
i'm queer . . .
```

Some, like seventeen-year-old Kendra Hillman, are lucky enough to have parents and family who are admirably supportive:

```
By May of last year, I had come out to my
sisters and my parents. My sisters were
wonderful and coming out to them has only
made us closer. At first my mother told me
that she thought I was rather young and if
I still "feel this way" when I'm "25 or
so," then she would believe I was a
lesbian. . . .
```

Since that time, Kendra and her mother have talked a lot about Kendra's sexuality and, realizing that these are feelings that Kendra has had for a long time, her mother has become more accepting:

```
My father was harder to tell than anyone
else in the family. I wasn't sure how he
would react, but he took it fairly well. I've
had a very supportive family which has made
me a lot more comfortable when I'm with my
family. I no longer feel as if I'm keeping a
secret from them. . . .
    I no longer carry the baggage that once was
the source of so much unhappiness for me. My
family has noticed that I seem much happier
and relaxed than I was before.
```

Eighteen-year-old Jody Ann McAuliffe desperately wants to tell her mother, now dead:

```
DOES ANYONE KNOW THE ADDRESS TO HEAVEN?
I NEED TO SEND THIS LETTER TO MY MOTHER.
```

Dear Mother,
   Sorry you didn't get to see your little
girl grow up to be a man. See, she went
through a lot of abuse that you didn't want
to know about. She lost her childhood,
because you refused to grow up. You married
her father, to be your father. . . .
   Although you weren't the perfect mother,
she still loved you, because she knew that
what she was going through (the abuse), was
what you went through in your childhood,
but 5 times worser than what you went
through. But unlike you, she had to grow up
to take care of you, so she wouldn't be you.
   After all the abuse, (which she had to
stop by herself), after your father's,
yours and her father's death, she opened
her eyes to discover she no longer had to
hide a secret, which she hid deep down in
her heart so that nobody, not even you,
could take it away like they took everything else away.
   Her secret was her attraction to women. . . .

Jody continues in her letter to describe meeting a wonderful
woman, one who everyone said looked and acted like her mother,
except for a "slight difference":

   . . . She didn't want to admit that Becky
was like you, because Becky gave her more
than you would have ever been capable of
giving her. Becky showed her sweet love,
nurturing, and emotional support. Plus,
Becky showed her it was O.K. to cry, which
you would never let her do, you always told
her "crying was for babies and to grow
up." . . . See Mother your little girl grew
up, for you, to be the man of the family.
Now, she only knows how to be a man, who is
strong, faithful, loving, supportive,
responsible, respectful, who gives her all
to women, and never asks for anything in
return. . . .

After her rocky relationship with Becky ends, Jody begins to see
that never asking for anything in return is part of a destructive
pattern of abuse she is willing, and ready, to let go of. She finishes
the letter to her mother:

> . . . But now things have changed emotional-
> ly. . . . I need someone who can support and
> protect me emotionally and physically from
> myself and others. Somebody who can honestly
> teach me to do things for myself, and who does-
> n't need me.
> Mother, I don't blame you for what I'm going
> through, I just wish you were here to help me
> through this, because I have so many unanswered
> questions, that only you could answer.
>
> > Help! From your little girl who grew
> > up to be a man, so you would be proud.
>
> > > Signed: Mr. Daughter.

* * *

Although Terry Fresina, age seventeen, still fights with her
mother about being out, she feels there are others who are a lot
worse off:

> Most of the people that I have come out to
> (at least young people) have been quite good
> about it. Most of them didn't make a big deal
> about it. It was just things like—if you need
> to talk. Call me—stuff like that. . . .
> However, I am very lucky compared to other
> gay people I know. I know kids who have been
> thrown out of their homes, lost support of
> their families, and been ostracized by their
> peers because they came out.

According to a 1991 report by the Department of Health and
Human Services, lesbian, gay, bi, and transgender (those in a tran-

sitional state with their gender) teenagers attempt suicide two to three times more often than heterosexual youths and account for 30 percent of all teen suicides each year.

OBSESSION

```
    I lay in bed and stare at the stars. My mind
meanders aimlessly, hoping to catch a glimpse
of reality.
    I begin to cry as thoughts of death infil-
trate my brain. My body is wracked with pain
as I begin to shake uncontrollably.
    I try to concentrate, what will my next move
be. I hold the blade close to my wrist, I
tremble. Do I want to live or will death
become my final obsession?
    I need to know as I feel the steel of the
knife draw a small stream of blood. My head
aches. I feel the familiar hammer in my eyes.
My mind and body separate.
    I see myself do it, I can't stop. I feel the
cold, thoughtless steel slice easily through
my skin. The blood is warm as my body grows
cold and the life slowly leaves my veins.
```

—T. J. Knight

Tanya Joy Knight, who has taken the name T.J. "for feminist reasons," describes herself as "currently 18, Lesbian, Christian, Honest, Caring, Loving, 8 time suicide attempt." She also adds, "They say suicide is a permanent solution to a temporary problem, but I do not view life as temporary."

Another girl who refers to herself as simply "Loner" writes from Los Angeles:

```
    On my 16th birthday, I found myself with a
gun in my mouth ready to pull the trigger,
because society didn't accept me for who I
was. I had the gun for two hours, without
moving it from my mouth. I started to think
```

of all the things that I would miss in this
world and plus, I couldn't let society win.

* * *

The teen mothers wrote of feeling judged and condemned by a
less than supportive society. Queer and Bi girls are also bombarded
with disapproval through the media, at school, from parents, teachers and religious institutions—claiming it is wrong to love one's own
sex. Homosexuality is often considered a sickness, a disease, a sin.

Anne Buster, just thirteen years old, describes herself as being
"interested in politics and am a very left wing and pro-choice open
lesbian though I try to tolerate that of others which I see as wrong
except for hatred and homophobia which have no excuses no
matter the situation."

Anne has a wisdom far beyond her years. A brilliant and ebullient
girl, she cites obscure literary passages as readily and as excitedly
as she shares a new bike route. Coming from a supportive, cultured
family (her father teaches literature, her mother is a poet, and her
brother spent years as a ballet dancer), she has been able to express
her sexuality with a clarity, and creativity, most thirteen-year-olds
aren't afforded.

Even with her keen sense of humor and joyful spirit, she wrestles
with the intense issue of condemnation:

                    I
                    Am sitting in my father's car
                    Waiting for the light to change
                    And I see the bumper sticker
                    Ahead of us
                    "God loves you!!"
                    No he doesn't,
                    I think, remembering last week's sermon
                    On the evils of homosexuality
                    And then

```
I think of Catherine
She loved me
But God condemned me
For loving her.
He shut the door
On me
Because I wasn't capable of loving a man
I tried to please
My parents, the church, society.
I tried to look for beauty
In the male body
But I couldn't find it.
And now no one can find it
In them
To forgive me
For being a lesbian.
```

Despite the condemnation many religious institutions place on homosexuality, I found many lesbians and bisexuals writing about God and their faith.

T.J., who identifies herself as a Christian, declares, "In December of '92, I decided God is just, kind, and loving. He would rather me be gay than dead."

Seventeen-year-old Lony Nelson, from Santa Maria, California, expresses frustration in the face of how others have judged her — in the name of God:

```
But as soon as I raise my voice in
protest then I'm a radical feminist. As
soon as I have an opinion on the blind
ignorance I'm a Dyke bitch who wants
special rights. As soon as I make a show-
ing, I am labeled a Liberal who has noth-
ing better to do than shoot down family
values and normal (whatever that means)
Christian morality. . . .
How dare they say I haven't known God?
They only see that I fall in love with
other women. They don't see the uncles and
aunts that were all preachers and mission-
aries of the First Southern Baptist Church
that have been prominent all my life.
```

* * *

Sweeping generalizations by society frustrate many girls who are
struggling to establish their identities. Gina continues her piece
from her high school newspaper article:

> I have no objection to the content of the
> word "dyke." But when I'm labelled by people
> who know absolutely nothing about me, I get
> angry. There is so much more to me than my
> affection orientation. . . .
>   I'm excited about moving to Massachusetts
> for college. But I'm scared of starting a
> new life far away from home. Is this
> reflected in the word "dyke?" I wish I knew
> how to cook and sort my laundry so the
> whites stay white and the brights stay
> bright. I'm afraid of getting sick 3000
> miles away from my mom. Where does "dyke"
> fit into that? I love my family and friends.
> And I feel like crying just thinking about
> it. Is this included in the definition of
> "dyke?"

Labels are destructive when they are used to separate and judge
people. They are also inappropriate, since often a person does not
know how to, or she may not care to, define herself:

> I have to ask myself "Can I really call
> myself bisexual if I've never been with
> another girl?" But then I remember that I
> called myself or felt like I was hetero-
> sexual before I was ever with a man, so
> isn't that the same? Those are the ques-
> tions that I'm confused about and these
> feelings I still can't help but feel
> strange, but it's the way I feel. I'm
> attracted to boys, but I find myself also
> attracted to girls.

—Dawn Function, age 19

For Baby K., bisexuality is not a question, it is an answer:

```
You're too queer to be straight
And too straight to be queer
You must be one or the other?
You must belong to some group,
culture, or subculture, or
you are 0 —nothing at all.
They say you can't make up your mind
They say that you can't make up your mind
They say you're confused
They say your too scared to cross the
 line . . . and stay there!
Why can't I luv a man too?
Why can't I love a woman too?
Why should I love who you think is right??
Let me tell you: I WON'T!!!
I'm not confused—I know who I am.
But 4 U I'm always: Too queer to be straight,
and too straight to be queer.
```

And Christina questions those who answer with judgment:

```
    summer has become a time for self realiza-
tions. two summers ago i stood up and yelled,
"hey, i'm bi!" last summer i stood up and
shouted "hey, i'm a dyke!" this summer i'm
standing up and screaming "hey, i'm me!"
    i'm dying to be myself, not someone who you
judge since she doesn't fit into your pre-
defined category. not a sexuality who happens
to have a personality on the side. i under-
stand the importance of labelling sexuality
to promote visibility, but when i call myself
those things all i do is put that part of me
before the rest of me, when the rest of me is
so much more important.
    i still like the word queer cuz it's so all
encompassing, but other words just serve to
build walls.
    it's about freedom from restriction, being
yourself who happens to be____ , not living
your life trying to fit into a mold that
```

wasn't made with you in mind.
    like who you please, act how you please and
judge no one.

While Gina answers herself:

    What I've finally realized is that we are
    all real people. All the labels and stereo-
    types try to keep us away from that fact, a
    fact we all know from personal experience. An
    athlete is not a dumb jock, a person of color
    is not a second-class idiot, and a gay person
    is not a sex maniac. We all have real lives,
    with real ups and downs. To say that we fit
    into a neat little package with a single-word
    label is absurd. Where is the humanity in
    that?
    Our humanity is in our eyes, the way we
    smile, the times we laugh and the times we
    cry. These things tell the real stories about
    ourselves that labels try to hide.

                        * * *

But lesbian and bisexual girls don't share only their pain and
challenges. Their "real stories" also include writings of blissful
teenage love:

    Love
    Point blank in desire
    how fast will you take me
    how fast will your hands feast on me
    Wrap, wrap your thighs
    around this warmth of nature
    remove my jeans as begged for
    tear them into shards
    I'll kiss your neck 'til morning
    With my body where you are
    suck you dry of sin
    until the morning sun
    rest inside my arms
    I'll never let you go

```
these diamonds are for you
let me in, let me in
I need you
I want you
```

—*Gloria Ever, age 17*

TO SEE YOU

```
To see your brown eyes so deep and hypnotizing
To see your beautiful face, it's a perfect example of
                heaven on earth

I long for the chance to caress your silky smooth body
The chance to kiss your tender lips, and run my tongue
              up and down your soft breast
The chance to become your companion, and walk down
              the street holding your hand
Or maybe just the chance to hold you, on the beach, at
              night, under the stars

I, have dreamt of the day in which I could wake with you
    in my arms and your breast pressed against my chest
The aroma of your perfume would still be in the air,
    the taste of your body would still be on my tongue.

There are some questions I cannot answer, why didn't God
    keep your beauty for himself, and why did he send an
        Angel to this corrupt place we call home

But the mystery that remains is how I lived without you,
        that is a mystery waiting to be solved.
```

—*Christine Soto, age 16*

FOR SONDRA I

```
I want you
To put your hand in mine
```

Together this time;
I want you
To put a smile on your lips
As I kiss each fingertip.

Your hand is all I ask for,
For now.
Your hand is not bigger than mine,
I'm glad.

Our fingers interlock
With great ease;
A perfect match.

Palm to palm, fingertips to tips,
I swear to you my love.
I swear to you my life, so
Let me kiss the inside of your wrist.

In a dark theater, I'll hold your hand
In reassurance of never disappearing;
In the pouring rain I'll kiss your palms
To show you how great my love is;
In your room I will grip your hands
In pleasure of never letting you go!

—*Shelly Bonoan*

And with love often comes heartbreak:

Every time I close my eyes you're all I see
So how am I supposed to live alone and without you? . . .
So how am I supposed to react except talking without words. Today the clouds cover the
sky with the deepest saddening gray and today
my heart's as black as the darkest velvet
kiss she gave, and the rain makes me laugh
because it washes away all my tears, and the
rain shall fall as the breath from me slips
away. . . .
The rain now seems to be a comfort as it
falls to help me close your piercing eyes, so

```
time can drip like the faces in an hour glass
and my body can breathe in an endless dream
of you. . . .
```
                                    —*Amanda Williamson, age 17*

Many hearts are broken not only from lost love, but also from the loss of friends and community. AIDS, and its destruction to the homosexual community at large, has prompted many Queer and Bi girls to become politically active and involved.

Jennie Cordova is seventeen and has a startling ancient beauty like a Goya painting. "I listen to Spanish music but I don't like dancing to it. I go out dancing to clubs and I'm starting to pass out free condoms at school and at Raves."

Jennie is very concerned about AIDS, and works for Project ABLE, where she performs plays and leads discussions educating youth about AIDS prevention at shelters, youth centers, correctional facilities, and schools.

```
                      FEAR

      When you said please
      and I said no
      Fear kept me alive
      When you said but I love you
      and I said no
      Fear kept me alive
      When you said who have you been with
      and I said no one
      Fear kept me alive
      When you said why use a condom?
      and I said AIDS
      Fear kept me alive
      When I buried you 6 feet deep
      and said good bye
      Fear kept me alive
```

                         * * *

Of the many topics these girls wrote about, alienation was perhaps the most common. Cliques and groups in school perpetuate it. The cool ones, the geeks; the in crowd, the losers; the most popular, the wallflowers; the happening girls, the last ones to get picked for the team. With the added factor of being a lesbian, Whitney Morrison, age eighteen, from Winchester, Virginia, cries out:

```
The raindrops dance on the streets.
Two children with multi-colored umbrellas
Are buying ice cream from the man in
  the truck.
I turn to watch you play the guitar.
The one light in the room allows your face
  to glow.
You smile, yet sullen, yet alone.
I feel the need to be near you,
To feel your warm embrace.
Only in time, my dear, for now we are
  unaccepted by many.
Damn this society, damn these people,
Why must we be forced to live in silence!
Slowly, but consistently the times are
  changing.
Someday we will be able to tell our secret
And not be shunned by our loved ones.
Someday we will be able to walk down the
  street hand in hand
And not be verbally assaulted.
Someday I shall be able to live freely
  with you.
But til that day . . .
We are left to sit in the shadows
And watch our life slip away.
```

Some may choose to hide in the shadows, but others, like Teresa Mendoza, age nineteen, are taking action. Teresa describes herself as "Orphaned Xicana. Mexicana. India. Lesbiana. Performance Artist. Activist. Writer. Stand-up poet."

Her take on the subject of alienation is unique and humorous:

```
            TO THE NATURAL ONES:

I am so tired.
  Oh so tired.
```

Tired of being
 Unnatural
To the natural folks
That hate so much
Oh so naturally.

I am tired,
 Oh so tired.

Tired of seeing
 Male & Female
 Man & Woman
 Adam and Eve
Everywhere I go
Showing me how it should be
How I should be
So I think maybe I should
Date a woman named Adam
And christen myself Eve.

Lony Nelson knows how continuing devaluation can move someone to anger . . .

I'm a seventeen year old lesbian and it has
been made more than plain to me that I am not
seen or heard, nor are my opinions considered. . . . I'm a seventeen year old writer,
and the words I put on paper are the purest,
most honest connection I can have with the
world around me. I want to be understood. I
want my anger, pain and frustration to make
someone who has never even met me see red.
    I can get mad, that so far is still allowed.
I'm still allowed to get angry about prejudice, homophobia, sexism and the general
laying on of stereotypes that I deal with
every day. It's O.K. that I'm hurt when a man
on the television says that queers tend to be
left for dead in military skirmishes, and by
golly that's fine with him. It's natural that
I feel affected by the swastika painted on a
school hallway or a flyer supporting the
K.K.K. It's fine that I feel threatened,

> hated, despised and ridiculed by the conser-
> vative right, because I am. . . .

. . . and the expressed anger, and search for understanding, can
move them to a place of wisdom:

> I can't speak for every seventeen year
> old, every woman or every homosexual. But on
> many of the issues that concern me most, I
> have to speak out because no one will do it
> for me. . . .
> . . .Ignorance is a disability. It takes so
> much energy to dislike someone and to keep
> those feelings fired up. Pretty soon the
> important things like compassion and human-
> ity get burned away in the effort.

Whitney Morrison is courageous enough to take a stand with no
support from others:

> I'm 18 years old and proud to say I've been
> a lesbian all my life. I live in a rural part
> of Virginia. It's hard to be an individual
> here, let alone a lesbian. This is a very
> conservative city that contains a lot of
> "right-wing" republicans and people who think
> it's a sin to be a homosexual. . . .
> I am one of two people in a high school
> populated with 800 who is openly gay. . . . I
> started a Sexual Minority Youth Group in
> Northern Shenandoah, but only two of us
> attended. I put fliers up (where allowed) and
> proceeded to get the word out. Even so, in
> order for youth to commit to a group and
> become involved they must first admit their
> sexuality to themselves. To do that, they
> have to resist society's pull toward the
> status quo and clear a path for individuali-
> ty. In filling out college applications, I
> have to write an essay about myself, etc. In
> doing so, I state that I'm an open lesbian.
> Is this going to decrease my chance of
> getting into college? Is my "lifestyle" going

to hurt my chances of working where I want,
living where I want, loving who I want?

The dominant attitude in my hometown would
answer that question, "yes." This angers and
frustrates me. I've been advocating for
myself and others out there in similar situations, and my hope is that I'm making a
difference in somebody's life. It is the
little steps that eventually lead to great
things. In whatever lies ahead I'm with my
"family," and we are armed and ready for
battle.

* * *

Fourteen-year-old Alissa Katin from Newton, Massachusetts, came out to her friends and family when she was thirteen years old: "Although they took things pretty well, people at school harassed me for most of that year." Alissa and Anne Buster not only have their youth in common, but also the fact that they are two more girls no longer willing to be kept quiet:

Two moon driven, moon ridden outcasts.
Not alone in our unique love.
Others are all around,
Being tormented and harassed as we are.
We know they are out there but we cannot
 find them.
For they are being beaten into silence
 as well.

Silence will make the death of us all.
We must stand tall and proud.
We must not give in.

Now we are protected.
We are shielded from the torment and
 harassment.
Still we are being silenced.
Still we must stand tall and proud.
Still we must not give in.

—*Alissa Katin*

I feel trapped within
My own society.
Trapped by hatred,
Morality, stupidity and prejudice
Like barbed wire around my soul
Limiting my movement.
I am living in a cage
Of homophobia
Where justice and freedom
Are dreams out of reach.
I will not live here!
Within this cage
Fit not for
The lowliest animal.
I break these bars
Of hatred.
Tearing away the barbed wire
Clinging to my soul.
I fight
To reach a goal for all
Where my dreams
Will lie in my hands
And instead of dreams
They will be considered rights
So that
The people after me
Will not have to fight the
Same wars
And my children
And my children's children
Will feel equal
To everyone
Else no matter who they love
Or who they are.

—Anne Buster

* * *

Many Queer and Bi girls have learned from their challenges and
are using their experiences and knowledge to help other girls going

through similar situations. T.J. has come a long way from her days of hopelessness and despair:

> My advice to young lesbians and bisexuals:
> #1 You are not bad and certainly will not rot in hell.
> #2 Always be proud of who and what you are. Never let anyone persuade you otherwise.
> #3 No matter who on earth leaves you and deserts you, you will always have someone/thing higher than you are to care and love you unconditionally.
> #4 You are not alone. Remember 10% that we know of, anyway.
> #5 Even if you don't believe me, I do care and I don't want to hear of any of the lesbian community disappearing due to suicide. You are valuable and special and someone does care.

There are a lot of people who care. This is evident by the number of gay and lesbian youth support services in most communities throughout the country. They provide hot lines, rap groups, activities, shelter, referrals, and information.

For all those who may judge, damn, and alienate, there are those who have compassion, acceptance, and respect for Queer and Bi girls. There are many who will always place love above hatred and intolerance.

Marcia Ventura, age fifteen, sums it up in an article she wrote for her high school newspaper in Silver Springs, Maryland:

> "Fags, homos, dykes, otherwise losers," right? . . .
> Why do people use these derogatory words? Why do people continue to hurt each other verbally, as well as physically? Why do people think that being attracted to someone of the same sex is the worst thing in the whole world, when it is really just another kind of loving?

ANNE BUSTER

JENNIE CORDOVA

Part Two

Outskirts

racking. I'll explain how it goes. You have 4 classes of haltered horses. Each class has 4 horses all simular for example aged mares. And you go and see which one is the best and grade them from best to worst.

excuse my drawings! #1 #2 #3 #4

You get 2 minuets for the side view, 2 minuets for the front 2 for the back + then you stack them and then 2 minuets to look them over again. In the class above I would probably place them 4,2,3,1. Its a competition. You compete against other judgers. Then you have 4 classes of performance. Examples: Calf roping, Western pleasure, English pleasure, Reigning, ect. The Huston Show as pretty hard 'cause you could hardly see the horses, there was so many people. They said it was the worlds biggest show. Our group took 3 of the 7 trophies. We were pretty proud.

Some of the historic + famous sights I've seen are the Alamo, Stockyards, River walk, and I know there's more

CHAPTER FIVE

Cowgirls

```
    I guess you could say that I was just an
ordinary teenage girl, but then again I am a
little different.
    I don't cheerlead, I don't come home from
school and get to call my boyfriend or all my
friends. I come home and ride all four of my
horses. . . .
```

Cobi Utterback, age fourteen, from Salinas, California, was born a Cowgirl. When she was just one month old, her mother would get on a horse and ride, holding her baby daughter until she was rocked to sleep.

Eighteen-year-old Kristie Cox, from Montague, California, shares a similar experience: "I have been riding horses since I was two weeks old, riding in front of my mother. . . ."

From the writing I received, I found that the bond many girls like Cobi and Kristie feel early on with their mothers is a closeness they experience with their entire family.

Almost all Cowgirls live on family-run ranches. Since their home is also their livelihood, unlike their "town friends," it is vital to their existence for the whole family to pitch in, sharing responsibility for the many daily tasks.

Feeding and watering animals, assisting them in birthing, moving cows, and putting up hay are only some of the numerous chores of ranching, as experienced by fourteen-year-old Teresa Dahl, from Ruby Valley, Nevada. An excerpt from her poem "My Life":

```
My horse and my saddle, my bridle and boots
My face covered with dirt moving the
   cows home
My family there with me all working
   together
That's surely the life for me

The wind in my face blowing snow all around
Just one more bunch of cows to feed
Then we'll go home
That's definitely the life for me

The struggle of pulling a calf or lamb
Then to stand and see it die
Then to pull another and save it
That's surely the life for me. . . .
```

* * *

Teachers, often teaching in one-room schoolhouses, as well as families, encourage girls to be proud of their heritage and to keep the traditions of the West alive.

One way of doing this is through "cowboy poetry," a pastime rapidly growing in popularity that gives cowboys a forum to share their folklore and stories, much as they did in olden days by campfire. As the name implies, men do most of the reciting at these readings and gatherings. But more and more women, as well as teenage girls, are beginning to participate.

Tommi Jo Casteel, age seventeen, lives with her mom, dad, and brother on 12,000 acres on the Belle Fourche River, twenty-five miles east of Sturgis, in Vale, South Dakota. "We run between 400 and 500 Black Angus mother cows, winter all our calves, raise all our own replacement heifers, and grow all our feed."

The Casteels are a very close-knit family. Tommi Jo writes: "My town friends sometimes say 'I can't believe you stayed home on Saturday night and watched TV with your parents!!', but I just smile and think 'I might do it next weekend, too!' "

Tommi Jo has been writing and reciting cowboy poetry with her mother, Jo, an accomplished writer herself, since she was nine years old. Once, after a long day of "lambing and calving" (assisting the animals in giving birth), they were running low on groceries and decided to go into town. When lambs and calves are born, iodine is put on their navels to prevent infection. Tommi Jo and her mother were in the midst of this process, their hands covered in a heavy orange tint from the iodine, when they went to the store and found themselves standing in line behind a well-put-together woman.

On the way home, they wrote "Mama's Hands" together:

```
I saw you hide your hands in line, behind
that lady fair,
    I noticed too, hers soft and white—immacu-
late from care.
    But Ma, I say, it's no disgrace, to have
workin' hands like you,
    And had she lived the life you have, she'd
have hands just like it too.
    But her hands have never hauled in wood, or
worked in God's good earth,
    They've never warmed a baby lamb, or helped
a mare at givin' birth.
    They've never felt the bitter cold, or
chopped ice for waitin' stock,
    They've never doctored sick ones, or
dressed a horse's hock.
    They've never pulled a hip-locked calf, or
packed water to the barn.
    They've probably never patched blue jeans,
or had worn ol' socks to darn.
    They've never touched a youngun, or
caressed a fevered head,
    With hands so gently folded, all night
beside his bed.
    They've never scrubbed a kitchen floor, or
```

```
done dishes every day,
    They've never guided with those hands, a
child who's lost the way.
    They've never made a Christmas gift, shaped
by a lovin' hand,
    They've never peeled apples, nor vegetables
they've canned.
    They've never wore a blister, or had
callouses to show,
    For all they've done for others, and the
kindnesses I know.
    So you see, my dearest Mama—yours are hands
of love,
    And I bet the Lord will notice, when He
greets you from above.
```

* * *

Another traditional pastime synonymous with Cowgirls and cowboys is the rodeo.

Cobi, who was rocked to sleep on a horse as a child, continued in the saddle:

```
    So the time finally came around that I was
old enough to ride by myself, I got my own
pony. I rode him everywhere. I won my first
ribbon when I was 3 years old in the barrel
racing. I just kept going to rodeo's and
trying my hardest. I'm 14 years old now and
I have won about 100 buckles and 14 saddles.
I have been the Northern California Junior
Rodeo all around champion four years in a
row. . . .
```

Kim Smith, age fifteen, from Huntsville, Missouri, has also been very successful since she began competing in rodeos at age six, winning numerous awards and titles. She believes:

```
    . . . Rodeo is one of the few sports in which
children can succeed, and experience the
```

thrill of excelling because of their own
expertise. . . . Can you think of a sport that
actually promotes family togetherness? . . . It
brings everyone closer together, traveling
weekend after weekend, grouped in a truck,
mile after dusty mile. You get to know everyone's inner self, as well as your own.

Round 'em up, head 'em out—The rodeo's in town!

Lights gleam down on costumes of silk and suede, sequins and satin, fringe, beads, bone, conch shells, snakeskin boots, Wrangler jeans, and not one cowboy or Cowgirl is without a hat. The horses whinny, calves moo, and lambs bleat as spectators fill the bleachers, eager to watch contestants race against time and each other:

RODEO

THE CROWDS IN THE STANDS THE LIGHTS
SHINING BRIGHT
THIS IS GOING TO BE ONE EXCITING NIGHT
THE GRAND ENTRY IS OVER THE RODEO
IS TO START
ALL THE CONTESTANTS SMILING WANTING TO
WIN AT HEART
THE TEAMS LOOK TO SEE HOW THEY DREW
THEIR STEER
AND THE OTHERS BEHIND THE CHUTES PREPARING
THEIR RODEO GEAR
THE RODEOS ALMOST OVER WHAT A WINNING NIGHT
NOW THE COWGIRL'S OFF TO HER NEXT RODEO SITE
THE COWGIRL'S ON THE ROAD EACH AND
EVERY NIGHT
ALWAYS HAPPY DOING WHAT IT IS SHE LIKES
THIS THE LIFE OF A COWGIRL EVERY SINGLE DAY
NEVER IN ONE PLACE ALWAYS ON THE WAY

—Erika Kauzlarich, age 17
Newhall, California

In high school rodeo, there are several events in which girls compete side-by-side with boys, including goat tying, pole bending, calf roping, breakaway roping, and ribbon roping.

But when a young woman competes on an amateur or professional level, she competes primarily in the one event for females: barrel racing.

When barrel racing, the girls and their horses try to slalom around three barrels as closely, and as fast, as they can without knocking any of them over. Speeds can reach over thirty miles per hour.

Melinda Holt, age eighteen, is the eighth in a family of fourteen children from Enterprise, Utah. In the National High School Rodeo Association, she currently ranks third in the nation, overall.

```
     "Melinda Holt, last call for Melinda Holt."
As they call my name, I feel the tension of
both my horse and I. His muscles bulging
beneath me. The next eighteen seconds all
out, exploding through the arena gate, grab-
bing the ground, feeling the horse move
beneath you. Running for the barrels and
turning full blast, not a moment to lose, one
thousandth of a second can determine the
winner. Waiting. Waiting for the announcer to
reveal our time. It seems like eternity. Did
we make it? Did we win?
```

Sixteen-year-old Penny M. Jones from Stewartsville, Missouri, also competes in barrel racing on her horse Raffles:

```
                    RACE

     My heart sounds like a drum
     as it pounds and pounds.
     My head is filled
     with rodeo sounds.

     Now I am up
     It's really my turn.
     I am so nervous,
     my stomach churns!

     I'm out of the gate!
```

```
I fly around the first turn,
I am out in the light.
My eyes seem to burn.

The barrel seems to spin
I urge the horse faster,
My breath is like fire!
This could end in disaster!

Time is adding up!
I sneak a look at the clock
Around the last barrel,
My knees begin to knock.

In the home stretch now,
speed across the line,
came in first place,
the title is mine!
```

Stacy G., age eighteen, from the tiny town of Hardtner, Kansas, describes herself: "I like country music, dancing, singing, and of course, cowboys."

Stacy feels, as many Cowgirls do, that when she is barrel racing, she is in partnership with her horse:

```
Riding barrels is very tough, fun, and is
unlike anything I've ever experienced
before....It is very competitive and frus-
trating. Training a horse to run barrels can
be very tough. Sometimes it takes a horse a
long time to pick up on how to run the
pattern....When I first started taking my
horse to rodeos, we didn't place and our runs
were always three to four seconds slow. It
was very hard to deal with. I just wanted to
do good. My horse and I were a team. It wasn't
me doing bad or him doing bad, it was both of
us doing just fine.
```

While watching these girls compete, I realized that most of them seem more comfortable, more at home, on a saddle than on the ground. With graceful movements, they become one with their horse in a precise, speedy ballet. With choreographed skill, accompanied by grunts and manure, flies and dirt, they commune in collaboration. With a tug of the reins, a lilt in the voice, they can command a beast over ten times their size and weight. On their horses, these girls are powerful.

A girl has a special love for her horse, coupled with a great deal of responsibility for its care. Cobi writes: "The animals are treated just as they are our best friends or your house pet."

Cowgirls are very protective of their sport, which has recently come under fire from animal activists who claim rodeos are nothing more than public displays of cruelty. They have even taken to protesting at events.

In response to this, Sarah Mobley, age fifteen, from Clovis, New Mexico, writes:

> There is not one thing wrong with the way I treat my horse, I also show pigs and heifers and have been confronted by these extremists at fairs and shows. I believe they have no right to say these things. There are some people who abuse their animals, but I am not one of them. I feel very strongly about this subject. . . . Animal activists are full of it.

Erika Kauzlarich, age seventeen, is a gentle yet outgoing young woman with sparkling white teeth, dark hair and eyes, and perfectly manicured nails. She exudes a warmth, making strangers feel they've known her a long time. Erika is also furious with animal activists. First, she denounces the claim that broncos' and bulls' testicles are tied to make them buck. She explains that what is used to cause bucking is called a "flank strap," made of soft sheepskin, buckled in front of the hind legs, which actually produces a sensation against the flank much like tickling. Wild animals, or animals that aren't ridden much, are used for these events and, therefore, instinctively want to get someone off their backs, especially with the added "tickling" sensation. She does not see this as abusive.

Erika further defends her sport . . . and her life:

> . . . I wish that they would just leave the
> people of the rodeo alone. I understand that
> they just want to protect the animals, but
> they should get a little more educated on our
> sport before they jump to conclusions. . . .
> They stand outside the Rodeo grounds and
> yell that we kill animals, when we don't. . . .
> In rodeo, all the animals are treated with
> respect and are very well taken care of. The
> rough stock, the calves and the cattle are
> all used for a short period of time each week-
> end, then they are put away and fed. There is
> always a veterinarian on the grounds in case
> anything should happen. I have an extreme
> love for animals. . . . Instead of investigat-
> ing us and how we harm the animals, what about
> sports like the steeple races? I've seen more
> horses break their legs and have to be put to
> sleep than I have seen any animals in Rodeo
> break a leg or get hurt to the point that they
> have to be put down. . . . In my own opinion,
> God put these animals on this earth for a
> reason, and it was not for us to kill and
> eat. . . . I just wish that these people
> wouldn't be so ignorant and would take a few
> minutes to be properly educated on the sport
> of Rodeo. If you walked by me or any person
> that was involved with Rodeo, I am sure that
> they would not mind answering a few ques-
> tions. All of us who participate in Rodeo
> have respect and I wish we would get the same
> respect back.

* * *

Erika is primarily a team roper. Her busy schedule includes
school and social activities, as well as working to pay for rodeo
entry fees.

Besides the responsibilities of constant care and feeding of a
horse, it also takes a tremendous amount of discipline, commit-

ment, and hard work to become proficient enough to compete in the rodeo.

> People get all sorts of wrong impressions about rodeo, and until they have seen one they don't realize how athletic and talented you really have to be. They don't realize the time and effort put in to practice to get better at what I do and to make myself the best person I can be.

Yet Erika, like many girls who compete in sports, is torn between her dedication and passion for rodeo and her simple teenage heart's desires. Recently, her priorities were put to the test:

> In early August we went to Reno, Nevada for 3 days. It was the best 3 days of my life. I went there to qualify so I could go to the USTRC championships in Guthrie, Oklahoma. I qualified, but chose not to go since it was the same weekend as my school's homecoming dance.

*   *   *

The saying about falling off a horse and getting right back on again is literally what those, like Stacy from Kansas, who compete in rodeos have to do:

> There is some glory to this sport when you win—but mostly it is pain. There's a lot of long hauls on the road and bruised knees, legs and arms. My legs and shins are full of scars from knocking over barrels. One time I almost got my eye poked out from the clasp on the reins hitting me in the eye!

Melinda Holt rides bravely into the arena of her fears:

> At another rodeo, everything seemed to go wrong, it had been raining all night, and the

arena was muddy. My dad and I were late
getting to the rodeo and my run was within
minutes. Could anything else go wrong? Then,
my worst nightmare came true. Coming out of
the third barrel, thoughts were going through
my head, "Oh no, I'm way off balance." As we
neared the finish line, reality struck, "I'm
not off balance, THIS HORSE IS BUCKING!!!!"
Flopping around like a rag doll, just when I
thought I was getting everything under
control, the end of the arena came. Instead
of stopping, my horse made a quick turn along
the fence, and I went tumbling down, right
into the mud. The EMT's were called in to
check for injuries, and they helped me out of
the arena. The only thing that exceeded the
embarrassment was my soreness.

Kim Smith feels that rodeo life has an edge that most "People
Don't Understand":

People just don't understand
        The dangers of it all:
                The riding,
                        The roping,
                                The racing,
    The waiting,
        The worrying,
    That the last one will
        Inch you out of
                Your check!
    People just don't understand
        About all the miles traveled,
                And the little money won—
    They think, "How neat!"
        About how many
                Different places you go
    People just don't understand
        Limping to the truck
                On bruised shins,
            Or worrying whether you can pay for gas,
    The greasy hamburgers
        And the cold fries

```
                  From last night's
                       Truck stop.
          People just don't understand
              That through it all
          Rodeo is a way of life
              Not just another boring sport!
          They
               just
                    don't
                         understand!
```

                          * * *

In most rodeos there are anywhere from twenty to eighty girls competing in each event. With these odds, many experience what Kristie Cox describes:

> I can still feel the tears trembling in my eyes and the butterflies tossing in my stomach as I positioned my powerful and stout horse Canner into the box. I can sense the panicking feeling of missing coming into my mind, but my deep concentration fought it off. I can feel Canner feeling my nervousness and the importance of the next run by the thumping of his heart bouncing off my calves.
> I can remember the early June morning like it was yesterday. . . . It was the day I learned how to overcome nervousness by deep concentration and how consistency will win every time.

Despite the mental and physical hurdles, the time, commitment, risks, and fears involved, most Cowgirls I met agree with Erika:

> In today's world of teenagers and peer pressures, going to ropings and rodeos takes me away from the everyday pressures you get from friends and school. It may seem crazy but I would rather go to a roping and have fun there

than go to a party and have people pressuring
me into doing things that don't appeal to me.

In a nation challenged by teenage drug abuse and alcoholism, some find other ways of escaping. The rodeo is also Stacy's drug of choice:

After we got done running I always had such
an adrenalin rush. Even if I was upset for us
not placing, I still felt as if I were on
cloud 9. It's like nothing I've ever experienced. After you've started competing, you
easily become hooked, it's addictive. You've
gotta have more—you can't get enough.

And another "addict" is Wendy Foster, age eighteen, from Shafter, California:

I've been competing in Rodeo's, Jackpot's
and Horse Shows since I was three years
old. . . . Rodeo has been the biggest and best
thing in my life besides my horses and
friends. . . . I love the competition of the
Rodeo life and I love the people in rodeo and
I love the fans of rodeo the people who come
and watch I get such a high of listening to
the crowd yelling and screaming for me when
I'm out in the arena competing it's such a
great rush. I know if people felt what I feel
when I'm out in that arena competing the rush
that comes over me it's like a natural high
that they wouldn't need to use drugs to get
a high or alcoholic beverages to get a buzz.

* * *

Wendy describes herself as headstrong. "Once I make up my mind," she says, "there's no stopping me." This is an important quality in being a Cowgirl. Since rodeo is very much a man's world, women and girls must work even harder to find a place for themselves. Wendy continues:

> Being a girl in rodeo has its up and downs.
> Some rodeos I have been to they put the girls
> in the other little arena. Because they feel
> the guys will bring the crowd and the girls
> events are boring so they're put in the back.
> I really feel that is discrimination towards
> the girls. The guys tend to want to take
> charge of the whole show. They don't think we
> know what we are talking about. They don't
> realize it is them who don't know what they
> are talking about. Basically they just say to
> hell with the girls. It really makes them mad
> when a girl can really show them up. I run
> barrels and team rope and I do all the other
> girls events. It really puts a smile on my
> face when you get those cocky guys who show
> up at the rodeo and start their B.S. saying
> things like girls can't rope. That's when I
> like to say do you want to put your money
> where your mouth is. They laugh and say sure
> then I can come out and stick it on my break-
> away calf or my steer, they come out and
> miss. All I can do is giggle and take their
> money. It's only a dollar bet but still it's
> their ego.

Wendy relents and adds that "not all guys are like that," and there are some who "will stick up for the girls. They're the ones who try to make the rodeo equal for everyone."

Katie McCall, age seventeen, lives with her family on a ranch in Butte Valley, which is sixty miles south of Wells in the northeastern part of Nevada. The ranch is in an extremely remote area, and the McCalls' closest neighbors are at least fourteen miles away on either side of the valley. Katie, along with her twin sister Terri, breaks through all gender barriers, setting precedents for women in the world of rodeo in an excerpt from her poem entitled "Best Friends":

> . . .We are the first girls
> In the history of the NFR
> to compete in these events
> No others have come this far.

```
I'm in Team Roping, Calf Roping,
And Steer Wrestling, too.
Terri's my partner; she rides Bareback,
And chasing cans is something she likes to do.
Our first rodeo was in Wells, Nevada
When we were only nine.
I never dreamed this glamorous life
Could hold so little shine.
This life's been hard
Right from the very beginning
We've both done much more losing
Than we ever have winning.
But now we're finally here
My dream is coming true.
We've accomplished the impossible;
Done what we promised to do. . . .
```

But we find it is only in her dreams:

```
I awoke; look around my room,
And my dream comes to an end.
But I know my vision was real
My imagination did not bend.
I fall asleep again
And come back to my story,
I'm winning the world championship,
The buckle, the fame, the glory.
And right there beside me
Is the only person who made it possible to win
My enemy, my hero,
My best friend, my Twin.
```

Perhaps, someday, Cowgirls will no longer have to dream about what they're working so hard to make a reality. Erika is setting an inspiring example:

```
Living in today's world you can say is tuff.
Women are finally being looked at as equal. I
think that there is still a majority of people
who don't realize that women can still do the
same amount of work as men. Going to team
ropings there's not very many women who
compete against the men. I never feel intim-
```

idated when I'm out in the roping arena and
there is only about 2 or 3 women out there.
My sister is one of two women who have won
their Professional Rodeo Cowboys Association
card in which she is one of two women who
compete against men in Team Roping in
California. My sister Kathy is the oldest and
I have always dreamed of being like her as far
as winning and having people accept her as a
woman in rodeo and the fact that she could
rope just as good as a man can. My sister
Tammy does the same thing and has taught me
how to be the type of person who believes in
herself and to always think positive.

Hopefully most Cowgirls will pass down to their daughters not
only pride in their heritage and traditions, but also awareness of
their strengths, their grace, their compassion and their power.

Tommi Jo sums it up in an excerpt from "My Mom and I":

My Mom she says I'm growin', and a woman
soon I'll be
She says I'm learnin' lessons 'bout someone
special—and that's me
My Mom she says that lovin' is the roughest
job of all,
And that givin' it to others makes a lady
proud and tall. . . .
My Mom and I went ridin', we checked those
babies and their Ma,
We watched new calves a buckin', was a purty
sight we saw.
My Mom and I been breakin' colts, and I've
learned her gentle touch,
My Mom says gentleness and patience, it's
that that means so much. . . .
My Mom she says a woman is the one who's
real tough,
She can ride from dark to dark, then serve
hot biscuits, sure enough.
Today she rode my saddle, and the stirrups
she didn't change,
She said to ride with dignity, out here on
God's great range. . . .

ERIKA KAUZLARICH

COWGIRLS COMPETING FOR SIERRA CIRCUIT RODEO QUEEN

Miss Mato Wakan Queen 1994-95

The big day of the pow-wow finals and The Miss Mato Wakan Queen Contest was just days away. I just completed my application and turned it in. The big day finally came. The Queen Contest was underway. We were asked Questions and we danced. Later that night I was honored and crowned the 1994-95 Miss Mato Wakan Queen. I was honored with an Honoring Song. I never experienced so much happiness in my life. I was given a crown, sash, jacket, plaque, and a peneltin blanket. My message to the youth is Be strong, never forget who you are and where you came from. Be proud of your Lakota Culture. And most of all believe in yourself.

Pila Miya
Dana j. Battese Trudell

CHAPTER SIX

Native American Girls

I have many dreams. If I could change
anything in the world, Columbus would have
never found America.

Roberta Francis Behan, age sixteen and a member of the
Northern Arapahoe Tribe of Arapahoe, Wyoming, is one of the
many Native American teenage girls who feel their lives, their
people, and their culture have been irrevocably devastated by
Western civilization.

The sacred beauty of Native American ways—experiencing a
oneness with the Great Spirit, Creator, and Mother Earth; deep
relationship to the elements; storytelling; celebration and healing
through ritual and ceremony—has been continually dishonored and
dismissed.

Broken arrowheads from long ago
Children dig them up
Bones of horses and buffalo
Whose lives have ended
Shot or run off a cliff to
land on the hard stones below
Or just trapped
All the buffalo are gone forever

yelling and screaming now they are
gone
                    —Christi Moeller, age 14
                    Vermillion, South Dakota

   While most teenage girls are just forming a concept of themselves,
finding their own identity while trying to be accepted and fit in,
Native American girls have the added challenge of living in a world
that barely recognizes their existence and frequently rejects their
culture.
   This affects the very core of their beings, as expressed in a poem
by Rachel G. Fry, age fifteen, from Omak, Washington:

                    REALIZATION

          There is a woman in the desert,
          Searching through the sand,
          Looking with a sad heart,
          For her people and her land.
          And the woman knows, and she is sad.

          And as she digs and studies,
          She finds nothing but a trace,
          Of what once walked this desert,
          Of what they call(ed) her race.
          And the woman knows, and she is sad.

          Her family is gone,
          all killed out of greed,
          no one knows what to do,
          to make the murderers take heed.
          And the woman knows, and she is sad.

          The woman cried in her heart,
          But now she is numb,
          And all she does now,
          Is wonder why they have come.
          And the woman knows, and she is sad.

          There is nothing they can do,
          To make the others halt,

```
Their number is too large,
Their ignorance is a fault.
And the woman knows, and she is sad.

The woman knows,
It is time for change,
It is death or submission,
This knowledge fills her with rage.
And the woman knows, and she is sad.
```

So many girls, like Rachel, feel helpless living in a nation that not only has historically taken from the Indian people, but also one that often perpetuates a derogatory stereotype.

The writing I received from Native American teenage girls indicates that they frequently feel that they must fight to not buy into old negative images and reject themselves. They find that self-destructive behavior is, unfortunately, all too common amongst their people, illustrated in the high rate of alcoholism, unemployment, and the fact that many do not go far from their reservations, where education and jobs are not readily available, thus remaining uneducated and impoverished.

Adrienne Thomas, a fifteen-year-old Ft. Totten Devils Lake Sioux, has some strong concerns:

```
    . . . It really bothers me when I see preju-
dice. I don't see why people watch the
Indians and look at them as if we are bad
people. I think people should treat everyone
equally, no matter what color they are.
Everyone needs to respect one another and
respect them for who they are.
    I wish there would come a day where people
don't judge others by color. I wish the white
people who are prejudice against Indians
would not look at them and think they are all
low, such as alcoholics and thieves. But I
know it is not only the Indian race that is
treated this way. This is what has been on my
mind for a very long time, and I pray one day
prejudice will end, and peace will come
throughout the world.
```

Fifteen-year-old Ralene Varela, who lives on the Tule River Reservation in California, is also determined to break through the stereotypical judgments:

> I like to be different and where I'm from I'm very different compared to everyone else but that's me. I say that because I live on a reservation and not many people venture out and dress in style they like to stick to the jeans and t-shirt kind of thing. Lately school has been becoming a challenge. I'm beginning to see who my friends are I'm beginning to realize that school is very important in our world today. For us Native Americans we are lucky to have programs and grants to go to college yet hardly anyone makes use of them. What really keeps me going and makes me strive to succeed is the fact that I can't name more than 10 people from our reservation who actually went away from it and got a good education and made something of themselves. I really want to be someone so that the younger generations know there's more than our reservation, that there's more to life than drugs and alcohol. One of the things that makes me really angry is that we as Native Americans are stereotyped and I imagine every race is but I wish some people would give us a chance to show them we are people too. We're not all the same just because some of us are violent, alcoholics or whatever doesn't mean that we're all that way. . . .

Tragically, some of the ones that are "that way" are abusive not only to themselves, but also to their familial communities, including spouses and children:

> When I was younger I was raped at the age of 2, and have had different occurrences of molestation since then. Trying to deal with

```
those at age 13, suicide was a door for me. . . .
    A lot of girls now days are having to face
problems they shouldn't have to. We need to
understand we're not the cause and we've got
to be strong. To make people understand, we
have got to understand.
```

From Menlo Park, California, Desiree Blue Arm, "16 yrs. old and still moving on," writes more about her childhood in a haunting poem:

DARKNESS

```
In a corner of the room, hides a
  little girl,
She shutters away in fear.
Who's gonna come tonight?
Crying silently to herself, for she knows
  what happens if she's heard.
No one's her friend,
they don't believe her.
Only the darkness knows what happens, after
  everyone's asleep.
Darkness is my friend, cause he sees
  and knows what happens.
He covers me with emptiness,
So I won't feel the pain.
My mind closes, as I'm lost in the numbness.
I don't want to see nothing, for my face
  is hidden.
The tears are being shed, but they're
  not being seen.
```

I received a poem that was sent to me by a concerned mother in Westminster, Colorado, who declared that the author, her fifteen-year-old daughter, was a runaway with "8 or 9 runs already this year." She wrote that the reasons were "a long story and very perplexing at the same time." She described her daughter, Alison Mouser, as a bright young woman from the Seneca-Cayuga Tribe, and stated that, as the mother of a runaway, she received a lot of comfort from the following poem by her daughter:

```
              NIGHTLY RUN


        I RUN THROUGH THE FOREST
        THE NIGHT SOUNDS BOTH
        FRIGHTEN AND EXCITE ME
   I HEAR MANY THINGS, AN OWL, A CRICKET,
        A BEAR, A COYOTE
        AND MY OWN BREATH
        FAST AND HEAVY
        FOR I AM RUNNING
        FROM WHAT?
        YOU ARE WONDERING,
   I AM RUNNING FROM NOTHING
        NOTHING AT ALL.
```

Several months after I contacted Alison's mother with interest in, and support for, her daughter's writing, I received several more poems—sent to me by Alison herself. One piece, entitled "Remember Me?", perhaps gives a glimpse into some of the feelings that might have contributed to her "long, perplexing story."

```
Remember me, the one you hurt?
Remember me, the one you lied to?
Remember me, the one you raped?
Remember me, the one you beat?
Remember me, the one you threatened?
Remember me, the one you cried to?
Remember me, the one you left?
Remember me, the one you chased?
Remember me, the one you promised?
Remember me, the one you "loved"?
Oh sorry, my mistake.
```

Dana Battese Trudell, age fifteen, is a very accomplished Santee and Oglala Lakota Indian. She sings, acts, dances, writes poetry, and is a youth advocate who speaks out on various matters. She maintains a 4.0 grade-point average, is involved with many school clubs and projects, runs cross country, and is a Junior Olympic champion. Her father is a well-known Indian activist, poet, musician, and actor, and as Dana puts it: "I guess you can say I get some of my talents from my father and the rest is up to me."

Dana has been an advocate in the fight against child abuse for six years, since she was nine years old. In her piece "A Job to Be Done," she writes about April being the month of the child on the Pine Ridge Reservation where she lives:

> . . . The Lakota people say, "Children are sacred." I think it's time we start treating them like they are instead of just saying it. The children are the future leaders of our Great Lakota Nation and they need to be respected, loved, and cared for if they are to live healthy lifestyles. I wish Child Abuse never happened to any child but it does and when we all come together and work the situation out, it can be stopped. . . .

* * *

There are, of course, also many girls I heard from who thrive in their home environment. The "ways of the family" are vital to Native Americans, the reservation being a community of extended family.

The Indian people feel it is their responsibility to perpetuate their culture and place the teachings of their ways in the hands of the family, to pass them down to each generation.

Elders are greatly respected and honored. They hold council for their tribal members and, drawing from their wisdom, they guide, support, teach, and heal. The elders of a tribe are viewed as living symbols of ancient sacred roots and are paid respect through many rituals and ceremonies.

Sonya Nicole Taylor, age sixteen, is a Chippewa Indian from Hayward, Wisconsin, who dreams of "finding a cure for AIDS and going to Korea" because she's always wanted to study Korea's government. She writes: "If I could spend a day with anyone, it would be my grandparents, so I could ask them things about our tribe from long ago."

Fifteen-year-old Charlene Holybear is from the reservation of Cheyenne River in South Dakota. She is a Lakota Sioux Indian, sharing the two branches of the Miniconjou and the Hunkpapa.

In an excerpt from her piece called "The Clown Mother," she describes the elders, one in particular, who adopted Charlene into her pueblo:

> . . . The elders in a pueblo in the northern part of New Mexico called Picuris are very traditional people. They do the sacred dances that celebrate their spirits. Their prayers are very sacred to them. . . .
>
> A visitor who comes to one of the feasts at Picuris for a Corn Dance or the Clown Day would see an old woman sitting on a lawn chair in the shadow of a building watching the dancers. One could easily tell her apart from all the other elders that are also at the dance watching their grandchildren dance. She has snow white hair, darkly tanned skin, and a slightly youthful look even though she is I think over 80 years old. . . .
>
> Once, when I was small and the pueblo had allowed me to dance their Corn Dance, we were going down the ladder of the kiva and I was laughing at this girl because her manta had fallen down to her waist. I was still laughing as I went down when I felt a tap on my shoulder. I turned around and I saw my adopted grandmother looking at me. She motioned me down the ladder, and when I got down to the ladder, she then took me to the darkest corner and started to tell me about a story. I don't remember all of it because I was too young, but what I do remember is that it was about respect for things that were special for others and to respect people as you want them to respect you. After that day, I knew that I would remember those words for the rest of my life. . . .
>
> The elders of the pueblo were people who had tried to keep the tradition alive by

> trying to teach the children about their
> culture and by teaching their language to
> their children. . . .

Tanya Wynette Jo Falls Down, age eighteen, is a Crow Indian who
lives with her grandmother in Lodge Grass, Montana.

> My Grandma was the one to raise and teach
> me how to speak my native tongue, how to
> bead, and how to cook. Grandma is a very
> respected Crow Indian. . . .
>
> The values that my grandmother taught me
> helped me through life and got me where I am
> now. I am thankful for my grandmother who
> also told me to follow my dreams and make them
> come true. She also said that you are the
> only one that can make those dreams come
> true. . . .
>
> I pray every night to the Creator to help
> me through, and I ask elders to go into the
> sweat lodge to pray for me. The sweat lodge
> is the place to go when you want to pray and
> talk to the Creator, to ask for things or to
> purify your body, and seek good vision. It is
> a traditional way of life to talk to the man
> up above and ask to go on the good path not
> the bad. He helps me to take care of myself
> and know that I do have something out there
> to reach and work for.

Olivia is an eighteen-year-old mother. She continues to live with,
and learn from, her elders as she teaches her own child:

> Olivia Poor Bear is my name. Although my
> last name is strange, it comes from a long
> generation of my family. I am part Oglala
> from Pine Ridge, South Dakota, and that is
> where my last name comes from. My other half
> is Sioux from Rosebud, South Dakota.

Olivia sews star quilts, using starbursts behind buffalo, tepees,
and other designs. She continues:

> I have learned a lot of things about my
> tribe. I hardly know how to speak Sioux, but
> I am learning that and much more. My grand-
> mother said there are many ways of our tribe
> that are forgotten. People are forgetting to
> teach their children the traditional ways. So
> therefore everything I learn from now on, my
> child will learn. I am trying my best to
> finish school because on my reservation are
> people who do not care hard enough to stop
> Indians from using alcohol and drugs.
> Therefore, I hope to get some kind of college
> degree to help with this problem to save the
> Rosebud Reservation.

Many Native American girls very much want to get educations.
Unfortunately, most schools are often far from the reservations and
require residency. A lot of girls wrote of the difficulty of having to
choose between boarding school or remaining with family, learning
the ways of their people.

Glatrina Kagenveama, from Custer, South Dakota, struggles with
this predicament:

> I was raised by my grandmother because my
> parents were lost in the busy city life
> trying to support us in spite of the miles of
> separation. I grew up learning my tradition-
> al ways and my language. I belong to the Hopi
> Anasazi Pueblo tribe from Arizona. . . .
> In our family from my mother's side we carry
> on a long passed on tradition. The family
> last name passes to the first born daughter
> of my mother, so I, thankfully, carry on our
> last name Kagenveama. Our last name has a lot
> of meaning to it. My grandmother told me it
> meant the spiritual designs of a Kachina mask
> and the great smell of rain.
> Since I grew up with my grandmother, I was
> caught between the decision of education and
> traditional ceremonies. I chose to live and
> grow with my close family, which meant to
> stay and participate in ceremonies. Several

years later I noticed I was missing out on a
lot because I didn't attend school. . . .

Glatrina eventually enrolled in the Flandreau Indian School, and
writes: "I am glad that I decided to make the right decision and
attend school."

* * *

One of the ways tribal tradition is passed down is through the
teaching of ritual and ceremony. From Adrienne Thomas, who
earlier wrote of prejudice:

> My family is strongly into our Indian ways.
> My grandfather is a medicine man, so he helps
> people who come to him for his help. I like
> being around my grandfather, because he
> teaches all his grandchildren about cere-
> monies, sweats, and the Peace Pipe. I enjoy
> this a lot. One day I want to be like
> Grandfather so I can help my people.

Sixteen-year-old Nicole Rayna Redstar Anderson, Assiniboine
Sioux and Ojibwa, writes about some of the sacred ceremonies of
her tribe:

> Some of the traditions in my family are
> really old—such as the Big Drum Ceremonies.
> At these ceremonies, people put themselves
> to the drum. These ceremonies are like pow-
> wows, but the drums that we use aren't the
> same drums we would use at a pow-wow. They
> are drums that the men have seen in dreams
> or in a vision. These ceremonies only take
> place in the spring. Big Drum Ceremonies used
> to be in a lodge or tipi, but today they have
> them in the dance halls and bingo halls. The
> Big Drum Ceremony is not supposed to be
> talked about. Things such as the drums, the
> songs, and pictures cannot be taken, or the

songs can never be recorded.
    Another ceremony we have is the Midewin
Ceremony. This ceremony is held in the fall
about the time school starts. I will just
tell you the name of this ceremony because
it is also not supposed to be talked about,
but I can tell you it is a very powerful
ceremony. This ceremony can heal, make you
have powerful visions of people, names,
medicines, and help you in life. These are
only two of our ceremonies that I can tell
you about.

Lejeune Howato also writes of ceremony, including the importance of dance:

    . . . Culture is the tradition that you have.
For example, the dances that we have and the
things that we make. It is very important for
me to learn these things because it has to be
passed down to the next generation step by
step. You must do certain things to do a ceremony. These things have to be learned over
time. If the culture dies out, then there
will be no more dances. Dances are what keep
the people together. They come together as a
community and help one another. If there are
no more dances, then what are the elderly and
the relatives supposed to enjoy? The elderly
and the relatives sit there in the sun all
day to watch their grandchildren dance. They
enjoy these dances because this is what they
did when they were little. . . .

* * *

The Pow Wow, a powerful gathering and celebration, is another
important tradition. Bringing together many tribes, it is a time of
communion in which to honor friends and elders with gratitude and
pride. A joyful event celebrating Native American culture with

music, it is also a place to compete through dance.

Both the dance and music at Pow Wows are created specifically for the event. Deeply sacred and spiritual in nature, ceremonial dances are performed with the intention of bringing about a oneness with the universe and the Great Creator.

The costumes are elaborate and festive; each bead, feather, stone, and shell bears significance. The dance competitions are broken down into several categories by age and gender. For young women the dances include Fancy Shawl, Jingle Dress, and Traditional. Each one has its own set of steps, rhythms, and costumes.

```
Some of the customs of my tribe are tradi-
tional. The Indian language our elders talk,
the pow-wows, and my younger sister's "hoop
dancing" performances have been customs for
generations. I am also a fancy shawl dancer.
I compete in most pow-wows during the summer,
and I am a former Indian princess. I have
enjoyed doing and seeing these traditional
customs carried on by my people.
```

—Sonya Nicole Taylor

At a Pow Wow, the drumming and singing, which often sounds much like chanting, give rise to a constant tribal rhythm filled with powerful emotion and spirit.

Kaci Williams, age sixteen, writes: "My culture really makes me feel proud. When I hear the drum beat, it just takes me off into some other world."

Her experience is felt by many who are similarly transported, and often healed, through the ancient beats:

```
MY TIME TO BE FREE

What it means to me, nobody knows.
I do it to relieve myself.
It's the only time I'm truly free.
I don't think about my worries,
I don't think about my insomnia,
```

```
I just listen to the beat of the
drum and try to fly like a bird.
```

—Yvonne Telles, age 16

* * *

Thirteen-year-old Graciela Avina is a Fancy Shawl and Jingle Dress dancer. On one side of her family, Graciela's ancestors are from Mexico and, on the other, of the Sisseton-Wahpeton Tribe of the Lake Traverse Reservation in South Dakota. She writes about her deep connectedness to both her cultures in her poem entitled "I Am":

```
I am a Native and a Mexican girl.
I wonder which culture I should believe.
I hear the Great Spirit call my name in
  my sleep.
I see a hawk circle around my house to
  give us protection.
I am a Native and a Mexican girl.
I pretend seeing my ancestors from Mexico.
I feel sad for the relatives I've never
  met before.
I touch my jingle dress and then I smudge
  it with sage.
I worry about my elderly relatives.
I cry when my relatives pass away.
I am a Native and a Mexican girl.
I understand why I haven't gotten my
  Indian name.
I say Indian words to my relatives when
  they do not speak English.
I dream of buffalos in clear land.
I try to be as smart as my elders.
I hope I learned something from my elders
  before they pass away.
I am a Native and a Mexican girl.
```

After Graciela wrote "I Am," she went back to South Dakota and asked her great-grandmother to hand her name down to her. During a sacred ceremony, Graciela was given her Indian name:

Mahpiyatowin/Blue Sky Woman.

The many images Graciela uses in her poem reflect the spiritual nature so indigenous to Native American culture.

Dana Battese Trudell, like many of the Native American girls I met, feels that "through all the rough phases of life, I still hang onto my spiritual beliefs. I pray every day."

In an excerpt from her piece "To Walk My Talk" she writes:

```
     . . . I believe I can achieve anything I set
my mind to. I believe in me and my people. I
believe in our language and our culture. I
believe in our land and our way of life. I
believe in the teaching of our elders. I
believe there is a plan for my life. I
believe in the power of prayer. I believe in
God, the Great Spirit. . . .
```

For Native Americans, spirituality is respect for all things, all life. Especially revered is the land from which one comes. Many, like Dana, write about their concern for not only their own land, but Mother Earth herself:

```
     I think the youth today should look at the
environment around them. Look how Mother
Earth is weeping as the land is torn apart by
all the trash you abuse her with. We are the
Seventh Generation our elders spoke of and I
think it is time for a change. Protecting
Mother Earth and Protecting the small chil-
dren from abuse means everything to me. If
you can't Protect Mother Earth, how can you
Protect your children from all the pollution,
garbage, and waste that is all over. The
Earth is your home. You can survive here. Do
not kill her. Children of Earth listen as I
tell you all I know before it's too late.
Mother Earth gives us all life.
```

Powers used in rituals and healings often come from invoking, and drawing on, properties in nature, seen and unseen. And as all living things are considered to possess a physical energy as well as a spiritual energy, flowers, plants, animals, fish, and trees are often assigned human form.

In "Charchet Waiata," seventeen-year-old Elizabeth Cofell writes about "one of my tree friends":

```
Charchet Waiata
Charchet Waiata
Looking upon your branches
I gaze into a web of
Insanity that caresses
My soul!
Charchet Waiata
Charchet Waiata
Under your boughs
I mean not to walk
On your children
It is fall
The leaves burst beneath
My feet
Charchet Waiata
Charchet Waiata
Your canopy veils me
From the rest of the
World's opinion
A vine wall that is not
Unpassable
Charchet Waiata
Charchet Waiata
Silky fingertips
Feeling the ground
Knowing it
Charchet Waiata
Charchet Waiata
Voices whispering
Blowing through the
Night
Leaves flickering
Visions
Charchet Waiata
Charchet Waiata
The forever person
Bark
```

```
Warm to touch; that's
Where the wood nymph
Hides
Smell of the
"Rough Pride"
Planted in her
Roots
Charchet Waiata
Charchet Waiata
My forever tree
My forever person
```

* * *

MY PRIDE

```
    Others try to change and
          hide, but . . .
 I'm proud of my brown skin,
  I'm proud of my big nose.
    I'm proud of my brown
      hair and brown eyes.
   I'm proud of my part in
     the middle and even
          my structure.
  Why? Because I'm Indian,
        Apache Indian!
```

—Yvonne Telles

Yvonne is an Apache Indian living in Los Angeles. She dreams of attending the Art Institute in Santa Fe, but feels she would only go if her family moved with her. "I live with my dad and my brother, my mom and stepmom died, and that among other things makes my life very difficult."

I visited Yvonne, who is also an extremely talented photographer. Black-and-white shots she has taken at various Pow Wows adorn the walls of her room, sandwiched in between posters of the Beatles and Red Hot Chili Peppers.

The sheets on her windows, acting as curtains, let in an eerie, calm light that spills over an embroidery hoop where she's hand-beading a fancy shawl to dance with at Pow Wows.

This exceptional young woman reveals herself further in an excerpt from a piece she calls "Just a Taste of Yvonne":

```
To fully describe myself,
is to tell my life story.
I'm the kind of person
who can get along with
almost anyone . . . who
can get along with me.
People usually don't know
the real me. They even
get the wrong idea.
I'm someone who is
so proud of my heritage,
there is no way anyone
will ever understand.
Who I am is where I
  come from.
Everything I do is where
I come from.
Who I hope to become
will be based on where
  I come from.
And where that is . . .
Excluding the white man's
borders and language,
I came from the land.
I don't like "Native American,"
I am not an "American,"
I am indigenous.
I am the kind of person
Who is confusing to ever
really get to know.
I even confuse myself
sometimes, because there
is no way I can put
myself into words.
I pretty much have my
own opinions on everything,
but I'm usually not heard,
```

```
I mean really heard. . . .
I know I have a lot
to learn, and as I'm
doing my part I wish
others would try the
same . . .
  with me.
```

The significance of having a voice, being acknowledged, is expressed in another compelling piece from Yvonne:

```
No!, I don't always
have to be right!
I don't always want to
be right.
I just want to be heard!
```

Eighteen-year-old Angel Arnold, from the Pomo-Wailaki-Concow Tribe, is another girl who desires to be heard and is speaking out "loud brave and clear."

An active leader in her home and school communities, she writes:

```
I feel very strong about my messages and the
main purpose of them is to reach other youth
and encourage them to bring back the culture
loud brave and clear to our future leaders of
our next generation to come. . . .
        I've done so much,
        with so little for so long,
        Now I can do almost anything—
        With nothing at all. . . .
```

In excerpts from a poem of Angel's, she affirms her hope for the future based on the power of "A Promised Prayer":

```
. . . Our pride is our honor, our power in
  our Unity
Together as one we'll share a lifetime
  of purity
Pain will be a memory we will no longer
  have to bear
```

```
Our families will sing and dance and grace
  will be shared
Mother Earth belongs to those of true heart
  and appreciation
Therefore, it's up to us to provide back her
  beauty through our care needed to save our
  Proud Nation
Visions of the day that is not far away, is
  through belief in a prayer and its blessings
  in order to eliminate the ugly past of
  yesterday. . . .
. . . A prayer in a promise shares our
  opportunity for a solid stand in
  communicating Peace, in a new world
  of triumph and Unity!
Amen.
```

Eliminating the "ugly past" is on many a Native American girl's mind. Tammy Sue Lowe, a senior at Sequoyah High School in Tahlequah, Oklahoma, is a Cherokee Indian and lives in Anderson, Missouri. She feels she has much to say and speaks to many political and community organizations. Her goal is to be President of the United States:

```
Most people, upon finding out that I am
female and minority, usually laugh when I
tell them what I want to be. If they don't
laugh, they tell me how unhonest politicians
are. I want to change all of that.
  Usually, the people who laugh or discourage
me are the ones who I always hear complain-
ing about how the government does everything
wrong. These are also the people who do noth-
ing but complain and never do anything to
change what they deem wrong.
  I cannot justify complaining about anything
I am not willing to change. Besides, I want
to be able to help my people. I grew up in a
white-dominated community, and I know first
hand the pressure applied to Native Americans
not to succeed. I've learned that unless we
can rely on ourselves and our future genera-
tions, we will never succeed.
```

```
I hope that through my work other Native
Americans will see that we can succeed.
```

While many of the Native American girls wrote of the importance of taking action, making sure history does not repeat itself, some choose to remain passive, retreating with their anger and resentment. And still others, like Tammy, may realize the necessity that for one's own soul fulfillment, for one's own inner peace, they must follow the Great Spirit's path by showing mercy and forgiveness.

```
            THE TRAIL WHERE WE DIED

Upon the trail that we walked
I saw the loss of life.
As from our home we had to leave
I witnessed only strife.
They called our trail many things,
"The trail where they cried,"
"The trail of tears," is well known
but I call it, "The trail where we died."
For on that trail, that long walk
many Cherokee spirits passed
from this land of pain and toil
to a land of beauty vast.
There the Great Spirit
rules with love and care
and protects all of His children
who have come to live with him there.
But those still on the earth
had to endure sickness and death
and feared of the moment when
they would draw a fleeting breath.
I saw before me elders fall
and women and children die.
I saw the murder of my sons,
yet I did not cry.
I witnessed the destruction of my world
as it shattered and fell apart.
Still I felt no pain
no sadness in my heart.
For in my heart there was no room
for pain to enter in.
Only room for fear and hate
of the murderous white men.
They said that we were savages
```

and threatened their white world.
But it was they who brought the death
and killed my little girl.
It was they who killed to no end
and drove us from our land,
it was they who took our lives
and buried our bodies beneath the sand.
For a very long period of time
only hate ruled my thoughts
as I could think only of sin
and the death of the whites I wrought.
In a dream I soon discovered
the error of my ways.
It was, if I ruled my life with hate
it would destroy me some day.
The scene in my dream
was of a beautiful land
where the Great Spirit
rules with a gentle hand.
Then I saw the Great Spirit,
as before him I stood.
He calmed my soul and made me smile
for He was the symbol of good.
He told me that I must change my ways
or I would never live
in the land where His children play
and no love would me, He give.
When I woke I understood
everything he had meant.
The only way to see Him
would be to share the love He had sent.
The unconditional love he showed
was not only for one race,
it was intended for everyone
who walked upon the earth's face.
To everyone He showed mercy
to everyone He showed love
to everyone He gave a second chance
as He ruled from up above.
So if I did not show mercy
if I did not show love
if I did not give a second chance
He would deny me it from above.
Now my heart is softened
as I try to forget and forgive.
The Great Spirit has directed my path
and with Him I will eternally live.

YVONNE TELLES

GIRLS AT PORTERVILLE POW WOW

You, me, the difference, and my farm

Sometimes I run outside
I scream and yell, I've got nothing to hide.
All alone, or at home
Plenty of places for me to rome.
Great Big pastures
Huge back yard, dinamite view, of the stars.
Not the ones you see on T.V.
These stars, work for free.
High hopes to make it big.
Not much offered in this small town dig.
Look someone in the eye
On the street as you pass by
Not because your scared of them,
It's someone that you know, named Jim.
In my highschool, grades 9-12,
90 students is all we've held
Knowing everyone, friend or foe —
The class of '94, 29 will go...
I believe in me.
And what I see, farmland, soil, cows & trees
My fathers, of which I have two,
Ones a farmer, the other is too.
Moms a business manager
Of "Pump-N-Stuff" stores...
need I say any more?

Tracy Hummel

CHAPTER SEVEN

Farm Chicks

Raised on the land, nurtured by the soil. Up at the crack of dawn with the crow of a rooster, serenaded by crickets at bedtime. Like their harvest, in sync with the seasons and elements, farm girls are growing and maturing.

I love being raised on a farm. I like the peace and quiet, as well as the relatively fresh air. (Of course, there is a distinct animal smell, but it's not polluted.) I like being able to go outside without being mugged. I love to go out and take a long ride on one of my horses without worrying about a ton of traffic.

Being raised on a farm is unlike anything else. You learn at a very early age to watch for snakes and other natural dangers. You learn about how babies are born, and you get to see it happen. You know where your food comes from and you understand how it got to your table.

A person raised on a farm also learns to trust others. You don't have a reason to fear people. Most farm people are good and they aren't out to get you. When you only see your family and others involved with the same things that you are, you easily get along with them. You learn to relate without fear and hostility. . . .

You enjoy lots of freedom, and you learn a
great deal of responsibility. Your parents
can let you go outside without worrying about
strangers picking you up. You can take a
horse and go exploring and be safe. You don't
just take care of your pet when you feel like
it. You have large animals that must be fed
on a regular schedule. They depend on you,
and you could lose lots of money by not doing
it. Everyone on a farm has to pitch in and
they all have their jobs.

I know that not everyone would enjoy living
on a farm, but I wouldn't trade it for
anything. Farms just seem like the only way
of life for me, and I really can't imagine
being locked in an apartment in some
city. . . .

—*Teresa Douthit, age 17*
St. Francis, Kansas

Dawn Rankin is sixteen years old and lives on a hog and cattle
farm in the South. She, too, revels in the simplicity and fulfillment
that come with country living:

Growing up on a farm is the most exciting
and useful thing that can happen to someone.
You learn to use your common sense, work
hard, be disciplined, and you get to wear
overhauls. . . .

Our farm is located on the outskirts of
Jefferson City, Tennessee. I love living in a
small town. Everybody says ma'am and sir,
much obliged and your welcome.

The average day at my house begins at 6:00
a.m. The whole family, my mom, dad and
sister, all get up and breakfast. Then we put
on our boots and go feed the hogs and cows.
We check to see that everything is running
smoothly. What we do next depends on the
season. We might work hogs and cattle or take
them to market. Then again we might be

> pulling, setting, topping, cutting, loading,
> hanging, grading tobacco. Or loading hay and
> straw, plowing fields, unloading wheat or
> corn. Or a hundred other different things.
> After a long hard day, momma, daddy, Rosy and
> me sit down to a good home cooked meal, usual-
> ly at nine o'clock p.m.

At first glance, a farm girl's life may seem similar to that of a Cowgirl. There are distinctions, however.

A farm is land cultivated primarily for agricultural production. A ranch is a large, extensive piece of land, usually in the American West, that maintains cattle (by the thousands on most ranches) and sheep.

Like Cowgirls, girls on farms must contribute many hours of the day to their families' livelihoods:

> We raise small grains such as wheat, oats
> and barley. Summer days are very long.
> Usually we are up by 7:00 a.m. and work til
> as late as 11:00 or 12:00 at night. Haying
> season is in the spring or early summer or
> whenever we have time. When asked our slow-
> est time of the year, there really isn't a
> time. My family works constantly. . . .
> We all get grouchy and nasty towards one
> another at one time or another, but it's
> usually because we lacked rest and relax-
> ation. We've tried vacations in the summer,
> but, lately there seems to be no time.

> —*Kristy Glines, age 19*
> *Lemmon, South Dakota*

Natalie Schuessler, age nineteen, is originally from the small town of Frohna, Missouri—population 250. Her father has a 320-acre farm that has been in the family for generations.

> . . . I am the only child, so I was always
> put to work. . . . Our farm is mainly used for

```
corn, beans, and hay, the main crop being
hay. Obviously, I learned to drive a tractor
before a car, doing that since I was about 8
or 9. Now that is still my main job during
summer, driving tractor or even helping load
square bales.
```

Learning to drive a tractor at such a young age, and other challenging tasks, is common on farms. After all, on a farm, every able body is put to use.

Fifteen-year-old Roseanne Rankin, the sister of Dawn who wrote of the joys of country living, writes:

```
    In describing myself, I might use the words
"redneck" or "hillbilly." I like NASCAR,
rodeos, football, baseball, drag racing,
tractor-pulls, cars, trucks, dogs, and wear-
ing hats and boots. Cornbread, biscuits,
beans, potatoes, tomatoes, hamburgers, ham
and red-eye gravy, ogra, and corn-on-the-cob
are just a few of my favorite foods. If you
are wondering how I became a redneck, here is
how. My sister and I practically grew up on
tractors and in trucks, car talk was common
at the dinner table, I was exposed to coun-
try music from the cradle, and of course farm
work. Being from the south helps, too. . . . I
got even stronger after my brothers moved
out. My sister and I had to take over all
their work. This is when I began to really
understand what all went into the job of
farming. I do everything from helping grow
our 8 or so acres of tobacco, to working hogs
(vet work), to hauling in the straw and hay.
All this hard work has taught me responsi-
bility and to be able to use the wonderful
power of common sense.
```

But farms don't just mean hard work. Country life is also full of unique play opportunities, and can often cultivate a rich imagination, as it did for seventeen-year-old Sara Schroder:

To a nine year old farm girl in southwestern Kansas, the nearest town seemed a million miles away. The thought of "THE ENTIRE WORLD" seemed so overwhelming that I was content staying around the farm and using the gift of imagination as my entertainment. . . .

My sister and I are only a year and a half apart, me being older. We always came up with something creative to do, whether it was starting our own secret club, or being pilots that soared in our plane (the top of a tree) over the land. Dad always tried to keep us happy, so he enjoyed the fact that we loved the three-wheeler he bought us to ride around the farm on, while Mom on the other hand was terrified that we would kill ourselves. That three-wheeler turned into a limousine, a semi, an airplane, a race car, and a flying dragon. . . .

One of the most memorable experiences I had involved an early morning, the blacktop in front of my house, and an airplane. It was an early morning in June and because school was out I had no desire to get up early. However on this particular morning I awoke to the sound of an airplane flying overhead. Many farmers have their crops sprayed by pilots, so I didn't think that anything was unusual. However, since I was already awake I decided to get out of bed and go downstairs. I looked out the big windows we have in the kitchen as I descended the stairs, and Dad was standing out in our yard looking up at the sky. I ran outside to join him and noticed that the sound of the plane could still be heard. The plane was circling the house, and as I watched in amazement it landed right on the blacktop! I was still standing there with my mouth hanging wide open when the plane coasted into our driveway and parked in the yard!

It turned out the pilot was a friend of Sara's father, who had decided to "pop in" for a visit.

* * *

In acknowledgment of the countless achievements and contributions they have made to their community, fifteen-year-old Jessica Hunt, her parents, and her two older sisters were named Arkansas Farm Family of the Year. Some of Jessica's many accomplishments include being president of the Builders Club, serving three years on the student council, being a member of the Spanish Honor Society, Future Farmers of America, Students Against Drunk Driving, Future Teachers of America, and also being a letterman on the Wynne High School tennis team.

The Hunts live on a 1,760-acre farm that includes 885 acres of rice and 761 acres of soybean. In an excerpt from her takeoff on Walt Whitman's "There Was a Child Went Forth," Jessica writes of moving through childhood:

```
There was a child went forth every day
And the first object she looked upon,
  that object she became.
And that object became part of her for that
  instant or for any given length of time,
Or in small bursts or throughout a
  lifetime . . .

The farm land became part of her
The comforting familiar smell of the moist
  soil as it was cultivated
The sound of the door shutting repeatedly
  before dawn
The deep growl of the diesel as it started
  every morning to transport the hardworking
  farmer
The sweet drone of the tractors as they went
  back and forth endlessly planting rows and
  rows of beans
The steady crooning of the machine pulling
  the levees for the rice
The startling zoom of the cropduster whizzing
  overhead incessantly from field to field
The loud roar of the monster combines
  stripping each plant for every bit of grain
```

```
The steady rattle of the old bob trucks
  carrying the harvest to its destiny
The sigh of the machinery being laid to rest
  at the end of a long harvest, all became part
  of the child that went forth. . . .
```

* * *

Like the Native American girls, Farm Chicks have a distinct reverence for the earth, and all other elements of nature.

From Ellis, Kansas, Ami Augustine, age eighteen, writes: "My favorite part about living on our farm is the wide-open land and sky; I love watching the summer thunderstorms roll in at night. We sit on our front porch and can see spectacular lightning shows."

The seasons are also a common theme in farm girls' writing. Since planting and harvesting are contingent upon the seasons, this is not surprising.

Sixteen-year-old Wendy Louwagie, who is one of fifty-one students in her sophomore class at Lakeview High School, writes about the seasons and her southwestern Minnesota farm:

```
My father farms about 340 acres. We plant
corn, beans, alfalfa, and oats. I like to
help him out in the field. In the spring I
dig and help pick rocks (not my favorite
job). During the summer I enjoy baling hay
and straw. I mow the lawn once a week. This
is my time to try to get rid of my farmer tan!
It usually takes a full day, with all of the
lawn we have. We don't walk or ride beans
anymore because they are sprayed by using a
field sprayer. Autumn is my favorite time of
year. There is a lot of field work to be done.
I haul loads of silage from the field back to
the yard, using a tractor and a pup (a truck
box frame pulled behind a tractor). After all
the crops are harvested, I soil save (a
conservative way of plowing), using our
newest and my favorite tractor, the 7140.
```

Cayla Rankin, age thirteen, from Satanta, Kansas, writes:

> . . . I remember going swimming in the horse
> tank during the summer. We would wait until
> an hour after lunch and put on our swim
> suits. . . .
> I loved to help water the chickens in the
> winter. There would be water that was left
> over from the day before that had turned to
> ice. I would run the water from the hose over
> it and it wouldn't thaw. So I'd get really
> mad and pick up the container and throw it on
> the ground. Then it would come out.

Fourteen-year-old Megan Dunn lives on a farm in Bourbon, Missouri. Her family raises hogs, cattle, and sheep and grows corn, wheat, soybeans, alfalfa and hay. She too describes a playful winter memory:

> Ice skating! It was the first thing that
> popped into my head when I woke up to a
> bright, but cold Saturday morning. I guess it
> was the same thing that my two sisters
> thought when they woke up, because we all
> came racing downstairs shouting, "Dad, Dad
> have you checked the ice yet?" at the same
> time. We all skidded to a stop in the kitchen.
> There was Dad sipping on some coffee and Mom
> flipping pancakes. All three of us started up
> again, "Dad, have you been at the pond?" "Dad
> is the water frozen enough to skate on?"
> "Come on, tell us." Finally, he said, "Yes,
> you can go ice skating." A shout of "hoorays"
> echoed in the kitchen. "But breakfast first"
> finished Dad. We gulped down our breakfast
> and went to put on our warmest clothes. I got
> out to the pond first. While lacing up my ice
> skates, I imagined that Dorothy Hamill just
> finished her routine at the Olympics. The
> announcer repeated the almost perfect scores
> of 5.9, 5.8, 5.9, etc. . . . It was my turn next
> to skate with the whole world watching me. I

skated out to the middle of the pond where I
looked out into the crowd, which happened to
be two black and white heifers. The pretend
music started and I began to skate.

While Megan may have had a rapt audience, Dawn, on the other
hand, has had a more frightening experience with a steer or two:

The number one physical fear of mine is
being chased by one of the bulls. I was
giving him his hay and water when all of a
sudden he started to charge at me. I had to
run about ten feet, then hurdle the fence to
get to the toolshed where there was a ladder.
I climbed up to the top of the shed and looked
down to see that he had stopped at the fence,
because it was an electric one. . . . It is
amazing how fast you can move when an eight-
hundred to fourteen-hundred pound animal gets
after you. To come over a fear, you have to
face it. That's what my dad told me. A week
later he made me face the bull and now, it
doesn't bother me to feed him or any other
animal.

* * *

In their writing, most farm girls, like Natalie Schuessler, share
that they often develop a deep bond with many different animals:

From little on, I've always had a wide variety of pets—chicks, geese, ducks, pheasants,
cats, dogs, raccoons, calves, squirrels,
flying bats. Living on a farm, we always
managed to rescue young ones, raise them on
bottles or eyedroppers, and then release them.
Two summers ago, I raised a rooster. Somehow
the chicken egg got into a duck nest and
hatched a week before the ducklings. So when
the ducks headed for the pond, I couldn't let
the chick go too. So his pen became a box in
the house, later in the garage. It took him

two years before he would associate with the
other chickens, before he would always follow
me everywhere. His name is Fred and he does
come when called.

When a girl has cared for, been responsible for, and bonded with
an animal, parting is an intensely difficult process. And sadly, it is
something they must get used to since many animals on a farm are
raised specifically to be sold.

Megan Fairbank, age fourteen, is a gentle girl with a quiet
strength and presence. She lives on a fifteen-acre farm just outside
the city limits of Corvallis, Oregon, and shares the farm with not
only her family, but also ...

> ...2 dogs, 3 cats, 2 ducks, 4 geese, 1
> gerbil, some sheep and lots of wild birds and
> small animals. Jesse [her brother] and I are
> in 4-H and take our sheep to various fairs.
> At the moment I have 3 ewes, Jesse has three
> and my parents have 1. All of which are/were
> pregnant and will/or did lamb any minute now.
> Our sheep are all well-trained, halter-
> broken, spoiled babies but we love them very
> much.

I got to meet Megan's sheep and instantly fell in love with each
one of them. I could only imagine the heartbreak of having to take
them to market, especially knowing their fate:

LAMB CHOPS

"230? 230? Megan Fairbank?"
"Right here. I'm comin', I'm comin'."
"Hurry up, and get into line. They are
already on 180."
There I was getting ready to take my lamb,
Sheepie, out of her pen. It was the last night
of Benton County Fair, and therefore the
night I hate. Not only because the fair is
almost over, but I'm tired, and it's auction
night. I had that queasy feeling in my stom-

ach that I always get. . . . I hadn't eaten
anything, knowing that I would feel funny. It
was already about 9:30 p.m. Sheep are unfortunately always last in the auction order.
After taking the blanket off, I put the
halter on Sheepie, and began to take her out
of the pen.

Sheepie was my Suffolk market lamb. I got
her in April knowing that I would have to sell
her in just a few months. I had trained, fed,
groomed, and cared for Sheepie with the
thought in mind that she would end up in someone's freezer. Of course, this did not stop
me from falling in love with her. I knew her
favorite spots to be scratched, as well as
her favorite foods: dandelions, corn and
apple-tree leaves. I knew when she preferred
to take walks, and how I could bribe her into
running down to the end of the driveway and
back. We were the best of friends. Many
people say that sheep are dumb, stupid and
have no personality (sheeponality, rather).
But that's not true, they are wonderful! Each
one has a different baa, face, and they all
act differently.

"230? 230? Come on you need to get in line."

As the moment approached, her number getting closer and closer,
Megan felt the lump in her throat:

. . . Holding Sheepie with one hand, I
brushed the tears off my cheeks with the
other. This was it, there was no turning back
now. I feebly gathered up my courage between
silent sobs and many more tears. I swabbed my
eyes once more then headed into the ring.
Bright lights and a lot of noise filled my
mind. I tried to smile as I robotically set
up Sheepie, then looked into the crowd.

Next thing I knew it was all over. Sheepie
was sold. I raced back to the pen, and as I
did I figured out how much money I made (that
is I guiltily figured out how much money I

```
made).  Let's see...Sheepie was about 130
lbs. times $1.80 per pound....That adds up
to $200+! Wow I made at least $50. Not bad,
not bad at all. But, how could I be thinking
about this! I shut Sheepie in the pen and
sobbing, went off to find my parents.
```

Her parents were proud and supportive of Megan, and after a
good cry and a hug, her hunger returned and she decided to get
some pizza with her family. She said her final good-byes to Sheepie,
and walked to the car weeping.

```
...As I fell into bed that night I had to
admit, it wasn't that bad. I had fun and even
made some money. I knew I would miss Sheepie
terribly; but I would get over it, and even
do a market lamb, or two, next year. I had
all the fun, experience, and lambs to look
forward to in the years to come.
```

* * *

Sixteen-year-old Mollie Roe's whole life is the farm. Not only does
she live and work there, in Burleson, Texas, but she's also home-
schooled. Many farm girls have firsthand experience of how life
begins and ends, and Mollie writes as she eagerly awaits the birth
of a foal from one of her favorite horses, Meg:

```
...Back in the old days (like in Spain,
during the warring years) the mares would wait
to have their foals at night to avoid getting
caught having a baby. Cause if she did she was
dead. So that's why most wait til night.
     Now when the time is about to happen, the
mare would break into a sweat, and then she'd
neigh really loud to announce its coming. Then
all the other horses will run all around cele-
```

brating the birth. That's when you have to be
careful cause the horses can go wild and cut
themselves up on the barbed wire.

One of our neighbors had a foal and that
night one of their older gueldings tried to
jump the barbed wire fence and the horse got
all cut up and our neighbor had to sew it up.
And then at another time they had another foal
and another one of their horses was caught
stomping it almost to death. So we're watching Meg very closely so that won't happen.

Weeks later, Mollie writes: ". . . Actually, Meg hasn't had her foal
yet. Can you believe it? Tomorrow she'll be two weeks late. . . . We
think she'll wait for the full moon this Saturday."

Meg did not give birth until almost one week later. Mollie and her
brother slept in the barn and got to watch the whole process:

. . . At 12:47 AM, she laid down again and
pushed the baby out. It was only a matter of
seconds—really minutes. And the baby was
already sorting out her legs and trying to
get up. She was up within a half hour. . . .

It was exciting! . . . We're sooo glad we got
a filly. . . . She's already halter and lead
broke. The baby is so frisky and likes to
kick. I have several bruises.

They named Meg's foal Crescent Moon because of the mark on
her forehead.

Fourteen-year-old Amanda Baker from Texas has had the opportunity to experience the miracle of birth often:

We live in the country near Knox City. We
are blessed with many animals; so it is a
busy place to live. We have new babies born
all the time. We have: pigs, chickens, roost-
ers, ducks, horses, rabbits, pups, dogs,
cats, rats, donkey, mule, show steers, fish
and parakeets. . . .

Amanda has been a member of the Knox City 4-H Club since its beginning. She now has her own herd of five cattle and a bull that she's raising by herself on her family's farm. Since her family has been involved in farming and ranching in the same area for almost 100 years, she feels the pressure to do her best when showing and selling her cattle, despite the closeness she feels with them:

> My steers become family pets and so gentle.
> My steers play with the dogs and cats, romp-
> ing around the trap and playing chase. I can
> get my steers to lay their heads down in my
> lap when they are tired.

* * *

From the writing I received, I discovered that one of the reasons many girls become so close to their animals is because they are not always able to have other companionship. Amanda continues:

> There has been times that I hate living out
> here. Our closest neighbor is 6 miles away and
> we are a couple a miles from town. It kinda
> gets lonesome on the prairie! When all my
> friends have to do is walk or ride their bike
> to a friend's house when their parents are
> away, busy, or at work I usually have to skip
> that opportunity because I live so far out!

Teresa, whose piece on the benefits of farm life began this chapter, struggles with similar circumstances:

> Living on a farm also presents some diffi-
> culties related to being so far away from
> what's going on in your school and communi-
> ty. You have a more limited social life. It's
> harder to be involved with things because it
> can be hard to just get to town. . . .

Many farm girls wrote of their preference to be alone, of finding comfort and insight in their solitude. Perhaps being so close to nature, and so far away from friends, forces them to enjoy being by themselves.

Candy T., age fifteen, from Oregon, Missouri, describes herself:

> I'm not like most teenagers. I don't enjoy talking on the phone or going to parties. I'd rather work on some form of a craft, or work in my flower and herb gardens, or take a long walk through the woods. I can't talk to people very well. So I express myself much better on paper.

Candy was born on the farm where she lives and finds there is little need to venture out:

> . . . We're pretty much self-sufficient. We have our own eggs, meat, vegetables and milk.
> Every year we grow a big garden of peas, beans, potatoes, tomatoes, and lots more. . . . I love working with plants and animals. In the summer evenings I either play with my animals, or work in my gardens. I do most of my thinking on the lawn mower. That's someplace where I'm totally alone.

Beckie Rowden, age nineteen, grew up on a farm three miles from town in Stark City, Missouri. With both of her older brothers gone and her friends living too far away to see them outside of school, Beckie's summers were "basically a time of solitude."

> When the loneliness of a young girl with so many thoughts and unanswered questions became too much to bear, it was then that I escaped to my personal haven, a place where the peace and serenity of nature took away my troubled thoughts.

Beckie's haven was a creek that ran through the lower section of her farm. It was surrounded by trees, and full of fish. Occasionally Beckie would happen upon a lone sandhill crane feeding on the edge of the stream:

> . . . I would stand and watch the movements
> of this beautiful bird until, sensing the
> presence of an outsider, he would spread his
> massive wings and fly away over the treetops.
> On the bank of the creek was a stump, the
> only remainder of a tree that had once stood
> over the water. It was on this stump of wood
> that I did my deepest thinking, exploring
> feelings I could not discuss with others.
> Here I felt the security I had achieved in no
> other place. I felt I was the ruler, that this
> stump was my throne upon which I would decide
> the fate of the world—or at least my own
> fate. . . .

One night, a raging summer storm came and in a matter of hours, Beckie's solace was destroyed. The water had risen over the banks and turned the fields into a "swamplike mess." Beckie had to wait several days until the water had gone down to a safe level before she could return to her beloved creek . . . or what was left of it.

> . . . Eagerly, yet with an underlying sense
> of dread, I crossed the fence and began the
> half mile trek toward the place where I had
> sought emotional refuge. I could smell the
> unmistakable scent of dead or dying fish,
> left behind as the flood waters receded.
> Brush and weeds were mangled together as a
> final mark of the water that had once before
> seemed so calm.
> I rounded the corner and came to a complete
> stop, the tears coming to my eyes at the
> sight before me. My stump of wood was gone,
> having been washed downstream. The only thing
> remaining was a large hole. The water had
> eroded away five to six feet of land. Trees
> that had once stood tall and proud lay

forlornly across the water. Nothing was the
same, nor would it ever be the same again. My
only sense of security had been washed away.
Just like the trees.

I realized then that my throne had only been
a stump, for I did not control the fate of
land, just as I had no control over my own
fate.

Now as I am an adult with adult responsibilities, I look back to those days on the
creek. I realize how sheltered I had been. I
had felt that as long as I had my stump of
wood to sit on, and nothing to do besides
watch the beauty of life around me, that
nothing could ever hurt me.

I have never returned to that spot for fear
that it has changed and eroded now to the
point that the sheer beauty I remember would
be gone forever. I prefer to conjure up memories of my simple haven, with the trees blow-
ing, the water flowing gracefully over the
rocks, and the calm serenity of a single
crane as it wades on the edge of the bank.

As solitary a farm girl's life might be, there are also many groups
for teenagers to be involved in. Future Farmers of America and
4-H are just two of the many opportunities to be with peers, make
new friends, learn valuable information, perform and hear speeches, and participate in showing and auctioning livestock and crops.

Amanda writes: "4-H has opened a whole new world up to me. I
used to be real shy to get in front of a group, but it has helped me
a lot to win District U.I.L. contest speaking."

* * *

Though most would say the farm is a place of peace, safety, and
security, it is evident that the times are changing and even country
life can't escape the influence of negative trends present in the most
densely populated cities.

From Tekoa, Washington, Suzanne J. Pollei describes herself: "I'm eighteen years old but age is not measured by years alone. I'm one of those people who never really 'fit in' anywhere. . . . Wanderlust clutches my soul, dreams always seem to know where I am. . . ."

Having recently moved to the country, Suzanne has a perspective on it that those enmeshed in it might not have. She writes about the changing times in her poem "Small Town Respectability: A Newcomers View":

```
                    YOU SMILE
          FAKE AND ABSORBED IN YOURSELF
      YOU TELL ME THERE ISN'T A DRUG PROBLEM
                    NOT HERE
        WHILE YOUR TOWN SITS BEHIND CLOSED DOOR
          INHALING THE WACKY WEED'S FUME
          YOU TELL ME THERE ISN'T RAPE
                    NOT HERE
        WHILE YOUR SON SHOVES A YOUNG GIRL
            DOWN IN THE WHEAT FIELD
          YOU TELL ME THERE ISN'T VIOLENCE
                    NOT HERE
          WHILE YOUR BABY IS BEATEN
            ACROSS THE TRACKS
                    I SMILE
        FAKE AND WONDERING IF YOU'RE REALLY
                  THAT NAIVE
        IT'S HERE AND I THINK YOU KNOW
            YOU'VE SPENT YOUR LIFE
            BUILDING A BRICK WALL
            TO HIDE THE EVIL GARDEN
          YOU CAN SAY IT DOESN'T EXIST
        BUT CAN YOU IGNORE THE GARGOYLE LOOKING
                OVER YOUR SHOULDER
```

Michelle Tharp, age fourteen, lives about ten miles outside of Bolivar, Missouri, in a tiny, close-knit community. She writes about the recent changes in her town:

```
    I know I said Bolivar is small, and it is,
    but we are starting to get gangs, drugs and
```

> violence more and more everyday it seems.
>
> Just a little while ago, a few of my friends
> and I witnessed a stabbing of a teenager by
> a teenager at the skating rink, and that's
> usually not an everyday thing in Bolivar.
>
> I guess I'm pretty glad I live in the coun-
> try. I rather be stuck here than hang out on
> the square at night and be shot! (I don't
> actually think I would be, but, hey you can
> never be too sure.)

Amanda is another girl who can never be too sure:

> A boy at school got caught with a 9 milime-
> ter, I believe that is what it was. He is in
> jail at this time. He is 16 or 17. Once again
> this is in a high school of about 100 kids.
> Imagine what it would be like in a bigger
> school!

Roseanne writes of other factors that currently affect the farming
community:

> In today's world of violence, poverty and
> fear, there's no telling if I will even be
> around tomorrow. My family could lose every-
> thing, including the farm if we are not very
> careful. I believe this is due, in part, to
> the way our government has gotten out of
> control. Not only are small, family farms in
> danger of going under because of this, but
> other small businesses too.

Farmers continually battle the uncertainties of Mother Nature—
droughts, sudden drenching rains, and floods—as well as crop-
damaging animals and pests. Today, they are also faced with
economic hardship due to unstable prices, declining land values,
and debt. In the past fifteen years, thousands of American farmers
were forced into bankruptcy. Many were forced off their land
because of economic restraints that make profitable independent
farming difficult.

Every year, 2 million acres of fertile farmland are lost to development; strip malls and condos are replacing crops of grains, vegetables, and fruits. In addition, according to American Farmland Trust, 10 million more acres are damaged by erosion and pollution from outmoded farming practices and short-sighted government policies.

Farmers are often taken for granted and treated with little respect considering the vital role they play in everyone's lives.

Seventeen-year-old Toni Gulledge resides on a farm with a foster family in Cheraw, South Carolina. She pleads for recognition of farmworkers:

DOWN ON THE FARM

I think people should appreciate the farmers of today. Most people feel that farmers are low class, stupid, tobacco chewing rednecks. People don't realize that farming deals with high tech equipment, pest controls, and stubborn animals. Some farmers go to college while others go to tech.

Another reason farmers deserve respect is because they grow the food that goes on everyone's table. If there were no farmers there would be no food.

I have heard people say it's nothing to farming. Sometimes one would say "damn the farms." Well, farming is dangerous work. My mother, brother and father have been in farm machinery accidents. It takes a lot of strength and responsibility to become and remain a farmer.

So think about it! Before you put down the farmer, stop and think about what farming is all about!

The reasons above are why it makes me so angry for someone to say "damn those farmers."

And Natalie echoes this sentiment:

Most of all I have the utmost respect for

my father. I see the long hours, from 6 a.m.
until after dark, that he puts in just to try
to make ends meet. Most days during the
summer he doesn't even have time to come home
to eat supper, so Mom and I take it out to
the fields for him. Even with modern technology and machinery it still takes so much
time and labor.
   ...America couldn't keep growing and
expanding if it weren't for farm workers—
male or female. No matter where I end up, or
what I do, I will always be a country girl at
heart....

* * *

If one lives on a farm, you can be sure one works on a farm,
regardless of gender. Yet there still exists chauvinistic ideas about
a female's place on the farm. Natalie continues:

   ...Girls raised on a farm do not get near
enough respect. Everyone thinks that just
because we're girls, we can't really <u>work</u> on
a farm. My mother and I are proof that we
work very hard. Instead of having to hire
and pay other guys to help, my mom and I are
the ones to work....
   When I came to college and told people that
I lived on a farm, I instantly got the association with cowgirls and country hicks. I
am very proud to have been raised in the country, I've learned a lot more about life than
most people. Even though I am proud of living
on a farm, I don't like these reputations
city people give us. Also, I do get tired of
the disbelieving looks I receive when I tell
people I actually do farm work. Everyone
thinks that just because we are females, we
can't do any physical work. But I love to
prove the guys wrong and watch their mouths
drop open.

And Michelle, who wrote of the violence that's come to her small town of Bolivar, also speaks out:

> Yo! Is anyone out there? Hello! Hello! Hello! Girls, we can't let the men of this world push us around and tell us how to live our lives....
>
> ...If you really stop and examine the facts, it's a male's world and always has been. Males are paid more in their careers than women are. Is it because they are stronger and have more ability to get the job done? Ha! Yeah, right!... Anyway I suppose men are paid more because they think it's their earth and they were born to rule.
>
> But ladies, this gives us no reason to shy away and make nothing of ourselves.... You can do alot with your life if you strive for what you believe in.... How can the big macho men that think they are God's gift to women stand around perfecting their muscles and running off to the drag race still criticize women when we want to make something of ourselves and help this planet? But the men say, "It's not a woman's job to be getting her hands dirty. They should be at the house preparing food for us hardworking men."
>
> Don't get me wrong guys, we still know you're wonderful at helping out in tough situations, like opening those darn jar lids and fixing the plumbing. Just kidding. We really do appreciate everything you do, but we need to be given a chance to be appreciated as well.

* * *

Farm girls, like all other teenage girls, desire to be valued and acknowledged. Especially when, unlike many other teens, they for the most part are raised with a sense of acute appreciation for their surroundings and for life itself.

Ami Augustine, capturing the feelings of many other Farm Chicks, knows she will be spending the rest of her days and nights in the only place that makes her soul flourish, much like the crops that grow on her very land:

```
          NIGHT ON A FARM

       As a child, night is fear:
   a dark trek to close the chicken coop,
        so they'll be safe and warm;
      glowing eyes reflecting from a dim
               flashlight,
      then a purr around your ankles.

      As a teen, night is adventure:
   midnight walks with coyote serenades,
     then the rustle of an unseen animal
              close at hand;
    squealing girls rushing for the light
               of the house,
      only to find our collie frolicking
               behind us.

   As a young woman, night is glory:
     raging thunderstorms rolling across
                 the sky,
    lightning flickers across a loving face,
         safe and dry on the porch;
        stars cross the heavens like dew,
    sharing secrets and trying to capture the
            moon in a telescope.

   As an old woman, what will night be:
          turning on the yard light,
   for grandchildren to play the games I no
               longer can;
      quiet evenings looking at the stars,
   remembering, wondering, waiting, hoping.
```

NICOLE DATRICE

FARM GIRLS AT A COUNTY FAIR

Part Three

Outsíders

Africa

Thats my sister over there calling me.
While staring at the ocean blue
making the waves.
She told me to listen and wait.
I hear her calling me.
She told me she'd take me in her arms.
With the sun and the rain on her dark
face
She's looked upon with sweet pleasure
and charm.
With the corn rolls and french braids.
With her head balancing the red and
green dashiki.
I hear her call to me.
The mountians and the wet lands is
where they peacefully sleep.
She's my African sister.
I admire her, dream of her, and am her.
Then I heard her scream and sing to me
the stories of her life.
She spoke of tales of Black and beauty
I hear her song in my ear forever.

Do you hear her?

by Rainen Veal

CHAPTER EIGHT

Rappers and Sístas

BLACK BEAUTY

Little Black girl, they laughed at
  you and called you black
tar black
but you smile
cause you won't give them the skin
  off your back
Little Black girl
they called your hair
kinky and nappy
but with your own hair
you're content and happy
Little Black girl they said
your nose was too wide
but you never pay any mind
to what's on the outside
Cause this little black girl
is proud of what she is
and she won't budge, sell out,
compromise, or give in
This little girl is growing into a
Black woman
concerned with nothing less
than the betterment of her race
and she has much
more on to think
about than
the features of her face.

—*Latosha Renee Guy, age 18*

There are numerous "Black Beauties" who are finding pride in themselves as girls and as a race of people that for too long have been treated like second-class citizens. They are exploring, and immersing themselves in, the beauty and strength of their heritage, as well as creating new cultural forms of expression. Rap is one such form. It is a way of telling truths, speaking out, instigating awareness, and embracing community; of fighting oppression and overthrowing traditional beliefs.

Taura Taylor, also known as T. Love, has been writing and performing raps for years. An integral part of the Los Angeles Hip-Hop community, T. Love is also a journalist, fashion stylist, and an MC, which she describes as "someone who writes their own rhymes and cares about innovating style. If you don't have style," she feels, "content doesn't even matter."

T. Love says she's a "self-proclaimed black 'rap feminist' and jill of all trades." At age nineteen, she writes of her childhood in a rap called "Pickininny":

```
Raised a black chile—some say a pickininny
Mama said, "Don't hide your pride and if'n' any
people gotta problem with the color of ya skin
defend ya kin—this is where the knowledge I
  taught you begins"
At the age of 8, life was great—and so easy
Hair nappy, I was happy with my doo bein peasy
"Your hair's got texture," moms would lecture
So never did I ever think that straight hair
  was fresher
See, I was just a pickininny
They thought I was a pickininny
Well I grew up and went to be intelligent
Did my best to transgress the hood I was
  dwellin in
Book in one hand, fist in the otha
Ready to fight—black, white, dark, light,
  any sista or any brotha
I was just a pickininny
Dark and lovely—I knew what they expected of me
My skin above me
Striven to learn but it wasn't enough to be a
```

```
bookworm
Knowledge you get from text can't teach you to earn
Respect—a threat was something I never took lightly
Ready like Freddy for anyone who wanted to fight me
Kick that ass then back to class 'cause I'll
  be doggone
If I'mma run from someone who wanted to get they
  squab on
Brain impressive, street aggressive—the urban
  innercity had me runnin wild
But bein my mom's child—
I've always been a lady
This is what she schooled her strict rules gave me
Finesse and wit and etiquette and with a kiss
She said, "Baby, you'll go beyond this
'Cause my baby ain't no pickininny."
```

In studies done by Carol Gilligan and Lyn Mikel Brown, professors at Harvard University Graduate School of Education and pioneers in the study of the development of adolescent girls, they found that African-American teenage girls had more self-confidence than girls of other races. This was partially credited to Black mothers being competent and strong role models. Gilligan and Brown found that increased self-esteem was the result of women teaching their daughters that racism is the product of other people's negative attitudes and ignorance, and not a reflection of the child as a person.

I found many daughters who claimed to have been instilled with pride by their mothers early on. T. Love is only one example.

Unfortunately, not all daughters can say this. Some had mothers who were simply too busy with their own struggles:

```
I grew up in New York City. My life has not
been an easy one. I am the oldest of five
children, born to a woman with more than her
share of troubles.
  As I grew up my mother's pain became my own.
With her life in such an uproar she called on
me, her eldest child to become the adult she
could not be. . . .
```

Stephanie Abraham, age seventeen, spent a portion of her childhood taking care of her four younger siblings, as well as being shuttled from placement to placement, separated from her brothers and sisters.

She recounts, at age eleven, being picked up from a friend's house in a huge brown station wagon by a "nicely-dressed black woman" who...

> . . . upset me trying to impress me with her
> big fancy words. She was from B.C.W. (Bureau
> of Child Welfare.) I had heard of these people
> before. They snatched innocent children from
> their parents, claiming to protect them. In
> actuality they were tearing them away from
> the security of their homes. Even if our
> homes were violent and sometimes abusive; it
> was what we, the children, knew.

During the two years her kids were in the system, Stephanie's mother turned her life around by going back to school and looking for a place for the family to live. Once she found a home, they all moved back together.

Although Stephanie had been through quite a lot of difficulties, she managed to turn the situation into a positive one, calling up a sense of determination and strength in herself.

She continues:

> . . . With such a weight upon my young shoul-
> ders I was unable to enjoy what was supposed
> to be my childhood. I have seen things no
> "child" should see. I have heard things no
> "child" should hear. Yet with all that my
> mother's lifestyle has taken from me, I am
> still able to thank her.
> Without her anger, I wouldn't know how to
> suppress my own. Without her raunchy
> language, I'd have no ideas on how to speak.
> Without her silence, I would never be able to
> enjoy my own thoughts and feelings and share
> them with those who are worthy.

More than anything, without my mother's
struggle; I wouldn't have grown on to be the
strong, intelligent, woman I am today.

* * *

The lack of a father's presence is a recurring theme in a lot of girl
rappers' lives.

When T. Love was sixteen, she used writing to expel the anger she
felt toward her father:

POPS HAD IT COMIN'

```
I have many, many, many memories
of fussin' and fightin and cursin and
 yellin—and mama askin
"Please—
not in front of the children!"
But dear ole dad was ill then
Now that he's alone, he wants his
 family back
SORRY! But I ain't havin none of that
Pops shoulda thought about THAT when he
 was illin
But daddy never cared enough to know what I
 was feelin
He never cared enough to refrain
He'd look into my eyes and refuse to see
 the pain
And at night—I was a prisoner to my bed
Thinkin that in the mornin I would find my
 mother dead
But she'd hug me and my brotha tellin us not
 to fear, wipin
away tear—she swore, "I'm gonna get us
 outta here!"
Mom's wasn't frontin—she saved a lil
 somethin
One day Pops came home to nothin
POPS HAD IT COMIN
Can somebody please—tell me who is this man?
```

Drivin a Cadillac Sedan. While I'm eatin
  cold ravioli from a can,
Pops is livin in luxury. I'm livin like a
  peasant man!
See, mama chose to pass on the upper-middle
  class
'cause it wasn't worth the caddy or my daddy
  kickin her ass
She had to prove her motherhood
She worked late nights, so me and my brotha
  could
Have a place to sleep, food to eat, clothes
  for winter
I couldda got A's but I was always in
  detention center
Hey! Wassup? Who got the doobie?
Moms on the nightshift, so I'm switchin booty
Strollin—gettin my hustle on
Been jacked, attacked and smacked and
  busted upon
Fatha won't botha 'cause he thinks I won't
  be shit
Yeah, I got the nigga's eyes but that's
  about it
POPS HAD IT COMIN...
I been through all types of pain—I been
  through all types of weather
Girl, keep it together!
Been through trials and tribulations
Pops never comprehended the shit I'd be facin
Like gettin sweated by the brothas on a
  daily basis
I've been 'round the pound, found dogs with
  friendly faces
Pops was never there for me so now I'm stuck
'Tween what's real love and what's just
  a fuck
POPS HAD IT COMIN...

Eighteen-year-old Sheron Vernese Mickie, aka Queen Dymand,
grew up fast. From a very early age, she, too, watched her father
become "distant and violent," until he left for eleven years. She
and her sister were raised by their mother in the Bronx.

As she tells her story, she asks the readers to "open your eyes and clean your ears so I can paint a picture of my life as a girl in your mind. I would appreciate if you kept it between us. Please do not reject me because I'm not the way you want me to be. I can not help it if God made me just to be me."

Sheron felt that her body was built as if it were five years ahead of her age. That, with her intelligence and proclivity to be a leader, contributed to her early precociousness. That, and a man. . . .

When Sheron was fourteen years old, she ran off with a twenty-one-year-old "fast ass drug selling boyfriend." After leaving him, she got even more heavily involved with street life—hustling and selling drugs. "I was in downtown Harlem and I was just another sister walking on a crooked line."

According to Sheron, after several run-ins with the police and eventually being "institutionalized," she finally went back to her mother, ready to take steps to change her life.

She soon discovered that significant change does not always come easily. However, Sheron's resolve to elevate her circumstances—to live a "good life"— was strong. Her first step was to return to high school. She was then elected student government president and, through accelerated study, even earned the right to graduate a year early with the ultimate testimony to a life changed: a college scholarship.

Now, as a student at State University of New York at Purchase, where she pursues her talent in writing and acting, she humbly states, "To make a long story short, I did what I had to do to make it up to myself, my God, my Family and ME."

In introducing her work, Sheron writes: "I would like to share a poem with you, it was written by myself from experience. Please keep in mind that everyone has their own struggles just like everyone has dreams."

IT'S STILL NOT LEGIT

One day I was departing from school,
watching people on the corner smoking weed to
be cool

I saw this girl named Nijja yelling and cussing
  on a rampage,
selling crazy drugs and only sixteen years
  of age.

Your life is mine, I'm gonna put your head
  to bed,
Stop sucking my style was all Nijja said.
You think it's a joke? Where the hell is
  my money?
I got caught by the cops and they took it
  all from me.

You owe me three g's and I want it with
  the swiftness,
or I'm gonna put a bullet in your head with
  the quickness.
I'll get your money as fast as I can,
but let me assure you it's hard, got damn.

What am I supposed to do I have to support
  my family,
four sisters, three brothers, a mommy and
  no daddy.
Mommy can't work cause she has to take care
  of little Jr.,
I'm the oldest so I have to bring the money
  to her.

There's too many payments,
with no help from the government.
What am I to do?
I can't let them live in torment.

Selling drugs is not all Nijja can do,
she can read, write, act, and work computers too.
But the drug money is sweet because it comes
  so quick,
let me tell you from experience, It's still
  not Legit! . . .

. . . I approached Nijja and said lend me
  your ear,
because there's a couple of things you must hear.

```
I'm surprised your conscience hasn't eaten you
  away,
from you murdering your peoples each and
  everyday.

Now your life is on the line,
you deaf, dumb and blind
Uncivilized person . . .
you need to be refined.

Negative, negative and more negativity,
working for the devil will get you money quickly?
No it will not it will only get you killed,
but if you go to school and get your education
  you will be skilled.

Can you see that's what it's all about,
lack of education makes you be without.
The knowledge which is power so you can be
  a ruler,
drugs make you go brain dead that makes
  you a loser.

Go to school and earn a good average,
so you can get a scholarship and move
  on to college.
You'll live a good life and stop being trife,
cause your intelligence will be sharper than
  a butcher knife.

Now I see your having a good time collecting
  and spending,
all that money that comes quick.
Open your eyes and acknowledge,
IT'S STILL NOT LEGIT!!
```

I heard from a number of girls like Sheron who were forced to grow up quickly. Many are needed to help care for, and even sometimes support, their struggling families as they get minimal help from social programs.

Latosha Guy, age eighteen, describes herself: "I write about connections in my mind . . . relationships, pretty people; myself and

political issues as I see them. I listen to rap, jazz, rare grooves,
gospel and funk. My favorite poets are Nikki Giovanni, Black
Panthar Assata Shukur and Langston Hughs." She addresses her
frustrations with the system in her rap "Welfare Woes":

```
beautiful girl but eyes full of despair
has no money
got four kids
goes
down
to welfare
stands in a long line, tells her whole life
story to someone she doesn't know
degrades herself and lowers her pride
when she looks at her kids
she tries to hide the guilt inside
she was trying to mend her relationship with pops
but if she is to receive welfare
seeing daddy has to stop
she thought she was supposed to be happy
but welfare is breaking up her family
she wonders what kind of well fair
is this when it doesn't wish you well
to get a helping hand
they put you through hell
she can't receive more benefits lately
and she won't
unless she has another baby
to make matters worse the foodstamps aren't last-
ing
to make sure her babies have food
she's eating less—fasting
the more she thinks
the more she gets angry with her situation
sick of worries
sick of intimidation
And so one day mommy finds a knife
and she really contemplates
taking her life
her children see her despair
and they think to themselves
there's no well, only hell in welfare.
```

Shiela Rose, aka Da Moon, appears older than her nineteen years.
An accomplished journalist for various newspapers and magazines,
she speaks of the plight of many women, lost, desperate, and abandoned in an excerpt from "Frozen Popcorn":

```
. . . South Central L.A. to the South Side of
Chicago, Harlem, where do you come from?
Is it better to be poor and righteous or rich and
  bitchy?
Starving babies—crack babies when will it end?
—Isn't all a sin?
Naked ladies with no dignity or self-respect
selling their bodies on street corners because
  she didn't receive her welfare check
She has four kids all in which she has to feed
Her man has left her to sell drugs
And satisfy his own greed
When he comes around
There is no love just screws her
Then beats her black and blue
Those are suppose to be colors of a country
  so true
for to protect but when you call
you can't get through
This can go on and on forever and
May not ever end
We've popped and stopped like frozen
Popcorn and it will happen again
and again and again. . . .
```

* * *

Racism is a fact African-American girls must live with every day.
At the age of nineteen, Keisha Wooten, from the Bronx, New York,
reminds us there is much more to be done:

```
. . . I have heard many say that "we have
come a long way." However, I have to
disagree. It is true that many have died to
get African-Americans a place in society. And
```

```
that place is noted, but we as a culture
cannot stop here. There are many ways in
which we as Blacks are not equal in society
and I feel that in 1993 it is a shame that we
are not.
```

Rainen Veal is a quiet and shy young woman with strong feelings and brave insights. Her piece on the leaders of the struggle against racial inequality is particularly inspiring because Rainen is only fourteen years old.

```
       I CAN, I AM, AND I'LL TRY TO BE . . . BLACK

I can only be free because of you
I can only be strong because you were
I can only run my fastest because you did
I can see as far as the mountains go
I can only be heard because you said I could
I can hear your voice telling me yes or no
But I can only be proud because I am black.

I am worthy of doing anything I have my mind set
I'm as smart as I want to be; only I can stop
 my world
I am perfect only by the sayings of others
I am skilled and taught well by his books
I am of the darkest skin and I'll tell you I love it
I am also charged by your great achievements
But I am proud to be African. An African Queen.

I'll try to keep everything all in your footsteps
I'll try to stand strong when they pull me down
I'll try to go far and farther to get to you
I'll try to keep faith in myself, it's hard and
 I knew
I'll try to live until I reach with final reality
I'll try to live to the day I die, only as myself
But I'll have to try my hardest to be a Princess
 in the world
whether  golden,  cinnamon,  or  sweet  chocolate
brown.
```

Following the civil unrest in Los Angeles in 1992, Rainen pleads:

```
           DEAR GOD, WHAT DO WE TELL THE CHILDREN?

It's April 29th, 1992 when the air was first nice
  and sweet
but America's people are not at peace.
A beating of a Black man has been denied.
A scene of violence is terrified.
Fires . . . , rage . . . , killings . . .
"GUILTY! GUILTY! GUILTY!"
say the people chillingly.
Once not a bad city, but now . . .
Once said "Not guilty" August 25, 1965.
April 29, 1992 it all comes to a tie.
Red, Orange, Blue, Green, seen from the sky
but we wait 'til tomorrow when the sun will rise.
We see with our own eyes, the devastation is true.
What do we tell the children?
It's very sad, the world has to wake up like this.
Racism, discrimination, a beating of a people
  all exist.
Why do we kill people? People on our own side.
On every news channel in front of our eyes.
But don't tell me—tell the children.
Don't cover their eyes.
Let them see,
let them face reality.
We need to love and respect each other
and rebuild the city, for we all need each other.
This is the world you see with your beautiful eyes.
So pay attention now, for tomorrow, help us make
this nation rise.

We all bleed the color red.
That's what we'll tell the children.
```

Shiela, Da Moon, echoes this sentiment as she attempts to define herself:

```
                    WHO AM I?

Who am I?
Am I a positive black woman?
```

```
Am I a strong black woman?
Am I a black woman with pride?
Do I love me?
If I really knew who I was
would I question who I am?
No—
I know me!
I am strong
I am positive
I am giving, caring and concerned
I love
I hate
I respect
I am a black woman in a world
that confuses nationality with race
there is only one race—the human race
I am a positive black woman
But after all of that
I still want to know
Who am I?
```

It is clear that Keisha has a strong sense of herself as "A Nubian Jewel":

```
I am WOMAN—as tall as an oak,
   as BLACK as the sand on an hawaiian beach.
invisible scars lay deep beneath my skin; I laugh
   as if nothing is wrong,
and all the while I feel the OPPRESSION of my gender
   and my culture—against my breast.
do not hate ME for my nature; but admire ME for my
   CHOCOLATE beauty.
I am this country. the soil has been toiled by the
   hands of my ANCESTORS.
you. would have starved if it wasn't for my PEOPLE
   you would have died.
I am a VOICE ringing through mt. rushmore—
   hear my plea for JUSTICE echo.
don't you dare slander ME with your gestures
even if you do, oh! yes—even if you beat
 ME with your fist,
never could you take prisoner the MIND of
   the BLACK SOUL.
my MIND will flourish in your land—MY LAND!
```

```
I am the heart beat of this plain.
I am BLACK! I am AMERICA! I am BEAUTIFUL!
```

In their raps, girls often write of themselves with pride. Zenobia, a Fort Wayne, Indiana, native who currently writes for Hip-Hop publications including *Straight from the Lip* and *One Nut Network*, wrote "Beautiful Black Woman" when she was nineteen years old:

```
Sock it to me sista girl
Wit your pretty brown skin
Go on chocolate covered baby
with your ass Black as sin
Shake that 'fro with pride,
learn to love those little fists.
Tighten that belt a little more
and show off those African hips.
Move slowly and gracefully
glide down the sand with pride,
cry in deepest sadness to the sea
for our brethren that died.
Stripped of all our titles
denied our regal thrones,
forced to disguise and camouflage
ourselves, with characteristics not our own.
Ignored, desired, neglected
and never given our proper respect
we can always find comfort in
the knowledge that our backs remain erect.
Even after we've been left as the
fatherless, motherless child
with nothing but African memories
and the warmth and favor of Allah's smile.
```

* * *

What do these girls do with their raps? How do they spread their word and make a difference with their rhyming? Few get record deals, for rap, as an industry, remains predominantly male. Instead, girls often take to the streets and clubs, the places where rap originated.

There are more and more clubs throughout the country that

provide open microphone nights, where "unknown talent" can
perform their raps in front of an audience.

```
          A CAFE CALLED THE GOOD LIFE
     never listened to rappers
     who are wack or passe
     almost every Thursday
     i'm at the Good Life Cafe
     on Exposition and
     Crenshaw
     MC's freestyle
     on thursday night
     and if their song
     is wack
     they hear
     "please pass the mic"
     never listened to rappers
     who are wack or passe
     almost every Thursday
     i'm at the Good Life Cafe
```

—Latosha Renee Guy

The Good Life is a club in Los Angeles run by Bea Hall, a woman
who has also organized a group called Youth for Positive
Alternatives. She encourages young men and women to create their
own careers and avenues of success.

When I went to the Good Life to watch an open mike night, it was
hopping with rappers. Music tracks played continually, maintaining
a steady beat. Several people at a time crammed the stage, with two
mikes being passed among them all. The sound is constant, and the
energy soars as the rappers, two at a time, battle, both furiously
spewing out rhyme. Even when an announcement needs to be
made, others keep a beat or rap behind; the groove never stops.

The scene is mostly male, but a handful of females take the stage
throughout the night.

Kimberly Hatter is a nineteen-year-old female rapper from
Houston, Texas, who goes by the name EBONY. She is presently a
first year honor student at Texas Southern University with a major

in history, and plans to attend law school. She has been rapping for almost eight years, since she was eleven:

> I grew up as a tom-boy who kept to myself, which made it inevitable that I would defy the stereotypical female role and become a rapper. There were even times in the past when I went to the extent of breakdancing with the fellows. My rap career began when I was in the fifth grade and was met by extreme disapproval from my parents. They considered rap and dancing to be specifically for MALES. They would have preferred for me to become a gospel singer as many members of my father's family. Although I received disapproval from my parents, my brothers, cousins, other family members, and friends strongly supported the idea of me becoming a female rapper. I was always the only female in a large group of boys rapping and beat boxing. . . .
>
> As I got older and entered high school, my desire to rap gradually began to fade. Fortunately, I had a boyfriend at that time who also rapped and encouraged me to continue and work on improving my skills. He not only helped me to improve my rhyme skills, but my SELF-ESTEEM as well.

EBONY went through a difficult time when her relationship with her DJ, who was also her best friend, fell apart as did a group she had formed with another female rapper. Both endings were painful for her, nearly causing her to quit rapping forever. She continues:

> I went through stages of feeling inferior to other rappers, my self-esteem fell, and I changed my rhyme style to try to compete with other people who I felt were far better than I was. Rap played such a major role in my life that I almost lost my identity at the rejection of others.
>
> To my greatest advantage, my DJ and I mended our differences to form an even stronger friend-

> ship and work relationship. Outside forces now
> have little or no effect on my rap skills or
> personal life. My confidence is at an all-time
> high and my <u>rhyme skills, technique</u>, and <u>deliv-
> ery</u> all bear witness to this positive change in
> my life. I hope to share my new-found confidence
> with the Hip-Hop community...through my
> music....

EBONY, like many of the other rappers and sistas I met and received writing from, has a clear sense of purpose and drive, and she is bound to succeed. Her goals include a desire to make a difference:

> My greatest hope is to be an inspiration to
> other females who wish to defy the limita-
> tions and stereotypes placed on their lives
> by society. I hope to provide support and
> form alliances with any females who are seek-
> ing to make any positive impacts on society.
> I would like to see more female <u>rappers,
> DJ's, promoters, producers,</u> etc.... in the
> near future.

The need for more females in the rap scene is addressed over and over again. The majority of male rap lyrics are notorious for their emphasis on crime, violence, and a reverence for a "gangsta" atti-tude. Their irreverence for women, who are commonly referred to as bitches and whores, is also infamous. Female rappers feel it is up to them to use rap to speak out for strength, pride, and power in their culture and their gender.

* * *

The Hip-Hop culture places a great deal of emphasis on image. Respect and status often come from having the right clothes, the latest sneakers, and listening to the hippest music. It is a challenge to maintain individuality, and a sense of self, within those confines.

BODY SENSES/MESSAGES FROM MYSELF

I feel a sense
A sense that you're whack and dense
immense yourself in flames
your actions are quite lame
I tame a train of thought
Your rhymes you must've bought
I caught you in the act
in the highest state of whack
your tack you should be took
please take a second look
being something that you're not
at Rap you gave a shot
I don't understand your plot
I'm hot
intense
a feeling that i sense
that you're a wimp and a big ole simp
who is it you're trying to impress
getting into this big ole' mess
I guess you do not think
or is it just a link
to your pseudo stupidity
trying hard to be like me
like me you cannot be
I do not copy what I see
original is what I am
your style you've mocked of plenty
what is your true identity?

—Shiela "Da Moon" Rose

And as these girls become stronger within themselves, most look for the same strength in boys. Zenobia attempts to dissuade a "weak" boy's attention in an excerpt from "Get off My Dick":

...Now take a look and then maybe you'd
see the way that I see how you're just clock-
ing me with all four of your eyes. I know I
hypnotize but you gotta realize that you're
in line behind a lotta other guys. I don't
try to categorize but every letter that you

bust me I file under weak! Sorry, but you
don't offer the sex appeal that I seek.

Don't mean to diss you or dog you, but
you're there even way before I call you. I
don't want somebody who can't be a man, don't
get your signals crossed again. This silly,
single, love struck shit is gettin' out of
hand, man damn!

You're coming at me like you have no heart,
like you'd just fall apart if I don't
respond—Oh how you do carry on. I'm not a
prize or a product, not a train that you can
conduct so just back up please why don't you
let me breathe? I don't mean to try and tease
just because my "everything" happens to
attract you, and this is something I gotta
do, so I'm afraid I have to ask you—GET OFF
MY DICK!

A more serious rap from T. Love warns of dangerous relationships:

WORRY FREE

I had nothin—nothin to worry about
Yeah I had doubt but my man had clout
So I got everything
A house, a common law spouse, vacations
  to the south, cars,
gold and clothes all by the time I was seventeen
I look and I see my mama, a battered wife,
  still workin at night
And I been watchin daddy beat her up all my life
Nah, unh-unh, that ain't the future I got in sight
That's why I got with him 'cause he did me right
Talkin about this man for whom I woulda died,
  I lied, defied
my motha, my brotha, my fatha, my sista, my cousin,
  my friend—
Just so I could be with him
Pops disapproved and said my move would be in sin
And then, my mama asked in a low voice,
  "How does he make his livin?"

```
But she knew, but I gotta choice and this was
  my decision
So I stepped and left behind me
All the things that remind me
Of bad times and childhood dreams. . . .
I never had to worry 'bout a thing
I never had to worry 'bout a thing
'Cause my man was gonna take me away and
  take care o' me
Buy me things I couldn't get from my parents, he
Was my man, so understand that I thought it
  was my duty
To shut the fuck up and put the dope in my cuchi
Caught—in a bust, now I'm cuffed in tryna give
  him a little hand
Now I'm spending Christmas in Sybil Brand
Thought I'd never had to worry, Worry-free
```

* * *

Religion often plays a large part in the lives of many involved with the Hip-Hop community.

Monick Monell, from Brooklyn, New York, signs her moniker in a design that looks like graffiti, spray-painted on a wall, with curved and shadowed lettering, initials and asterisks, much like gang tagging. Yet unlike a typical tag name, hers is CHURCH. She explains why in a rap of the same name:

```
Well I like to be called
            CHURCH
                  and
                  that's
                        true.
But sometimes I do
get the blues
          But I don't
turn my back
        on the
          Lord.
                  Cause I got to face
          the fact that I may go through
```

```
            some wars. The Lord is my
                       Path,
                          Light,
                              and
                          salvation
       I have no HESITATIONS
            of serving him
       Though I may go through some
   troubles the Lord is my Rock My Foundation
       He gives me Motivation
```

Whatever the source for their boldness and strength, it is clear from reading the writing of these girls that their confidence and positive perspective will take them far.

```
            AN OPEN LETTER TO THE WORLD
```

```
   Dear World,
   I am a Black child, a Black child with pride,
   dignity, strength and courage and intelli-
   gence.
   You wonder, "Is it possible for a Black
   child to possess all those qualities?" And, of
   course, the realization that I do scares you
   to death. So...as you continue in your state
   of deep, never-ending denial of my will to
   survive, you deprive me of my heritage, misin-
   form me of my accomplishments, omit my histo-
   ry from your schoolbooks, try to ban my
   musical education, tear down my community with
   drugs, disease, police brutality and more.
   I have been oppressed and enslaved for many
   years. Every time you think you've won, I, and
   all of my brothers and sisters, rise to the
   occasion, and you lose again. I'm still here,
   and I'm still Black.
   I am a Black child, here to return my
   people's dignity, to retrieve my people's
   history and, most of all, I am today's Black
   child, striving to become tomorrow's Black
   future.
```

—Shiela "Da Moon" Rose

These girls demand respect and will not tolerate being dissed by anyone—even their own brothers, who often portray women negatively through their raps. Rainen attacks the degradation of women in her piece entitled "Woman of Distinction":

```
Bitch!
Am I that dog, that you men eat?
To wear my shorts high and walk the night's street.
To wear my shorts high, my hair fake.
To disrespect a female of your own race . . .
To call her a trick, tramp, or skanch.
As for the mother that conceived you; the same.
Would you call a Queen a ho?
For I am a Nubian Princess
and my mother is a Queen.
We are educated Black women.
Yes, I am considered; for I can hold my head high.
For I can fly high. Higher than a bird in the sky.
For I have bent my back, and spread my legs too long
for a white man.
So when you say bitch, skeeza, ho, trick, or skanch
I will not turn my head.
For I am a woman of DISTINCTION.
```

* * *

These "sistas" have triumphed not just over the insecurities of teenage years, but also over the added judgments by ignorant people who do not see race as "human race," and impose their own fears and biases onto anyone unlike themselves.

In her rap "A Most Prized Possession," Latosha celebrates young black womanhood:

```
onyx, mahogany, hazelnut brown
sistas
the most beautiful creatures around
```

our beauty transcends all on earth
neither gold nor silver surpass our worth
we pray, struggle yet survive
drops of grace fall from our brow
and through the perils and frustration
we survive and manage to get ahead somehow
our strength wisdom tenacity
it all comes from within
from the melanin that makes us unique
and varies the color of our skin
onyx, mahogany, hazelnut brown
sistas
the most beautiful creatures around

LATOSHA RENEE GUY
AND
SHIELA "DA MOON" ROSE

RAINEN VEAL

T. LOVE, ZENOBIA, AND KAREN

RIDING ON WATER

IT IS AMAZING
TO THINK, TO KNOW
YOU CAN RIDE ON WATER
YOU PADDLE OUT
LOOK AROUND
THEN YOU SEE
THE PERFECT SET COMING IN
RIDING ON WATER
IT STARTS TO FORM
YOU START PADDLING
THEN YOU JUMP
SWEPT UP
RIDING ON WATER
THEN YOU'ARE SOARING
ON TOP OF WATER
YOUR HEART IS RACING
YOUR BRAIN IS SCATTERED
RIDING ON WATER
THEN IN A FLASH
IT'S OVER
YOU ARE PROUD
TO MUCH TO DESCRIBE
ONLY ONE THING TODO
YOU TURN AROUND
AND BATTLE BACK OUT
TO RIDE ON WATER.

—DANIELE DERENZI

CHAPTER NINE

Surfers and Sk8rs

With its tumultuous and sensuous power, the sea hypnotizes, then lures those under its spell, inviting them to partake in her awesome glory.

The ocean is often referred to in the feminine, symbolizing the ebb and flow of Mother Earth. With moon-regulated tides aligned with women's menstrual cycles, her vast waters represent the female depths of emotion.

> . . . I have begun to address the ocean differ-
> ently. . . . I always feel contradictory in
> trying to mimic the way some of my male friends
> go out and attempt to dominate the wave. It
> just can't be done. The ocean is too powerful.
> But I feel I can try to tap in to her power,
> respect it. But like some jealous sister or
> mother, she lashes out and is ever chang-
> ing. . . .
>
> *—Sarah Jorgensen, age 19*
> *Newport Beach, California*

Sarah describes what drew her to the ocean and the sport:

> I started surfing originally because I have
> a penchant for thrills and grew up in the

water. But looking back, I think I felt I
needed to separate myself from my Miss
Porter's existence and my mother's timid-
ness. . . . After leaving Miss Porter's, an all-
girls boarding school where I never quite fit
in, I spent a year in Santa Cruz working, lured
by the ocean and a man with salty skin and
bewitching eyes. He faded and the ocean became
clearer. . . .

* * *

I was fascinated at how almost every surfer girl expressed a very
deep soul connection from riding the ocean. An excerpt from a
poem by "Duckie" T., age fourteen, Corpus Christi, Texas:

SURFING

As the sun rises with pride
The day starts with slow waves
The crash of water sounds with our souls
Movement arises among the dunes
Blonde hair and blue eyes aren't the only ones
Anyone can do it, all it takes is soul.
Punks, preps, nerds alike
Soul, mind, and water is the life . . .
It takes more than physical ability
It takes the love of life . . .
Life is much like surfing.
Tides can come and go
And sometimes you crash
All in all remember you must have soul.

Daize Shayne, age sixteen, lives on the island of Oahu in Hawaii and
surfs at least twice a day. She describes herself as "the basic blonde
white hair and blue eyes. I'm so stoked cause I just got my braces off.
Oh yeah, and I got a tattoo on my ass. I'm kind of a tapped chick. My
style is very hippie all the way to flowers and braids in my hair. Well I
think I ought to be since my parents are still giving me their
clothes. . . ."

Daize sees surfing in her own soulful way: "It seems everything I do is art. The way I surf, the way I paint, write, draw, even the way I kiss." Sarah has a very similar take on her life:

```
    . . . I realized how writing and art and
surfing for me are one. Even if no one sees
me do any of them, they are for me, a way of
validating what I do in my life. The way I
approach the water, which color I choose to
paint with, reflect my emotions, sensibili-
ties. I wonder if this is true for everyone.
```

* * *

The ocean can be a very sensuous experience. Sight, sound, smell, and touch are all acutely awakened and can be rediscovered in the water.

Sarah continues in a poem:

```
Soft brown eyes
stare into the icy blueness
and freeze

In too deep, far too deep.

Pull me down into your saline fury
Dread my hair, make it hard for me to breathe
Make me struggle to live
Waves

Then
be velvet
Softly caress
Please keep me afloat
Give Give Give

and I will give back.
```

Eighteen-year-old Aimee Trudy Vlachos, the only girl surfer in the area of Ogunquit, Maine, asks:

DO YOU FEEL IT?

Your muscles tense up
Your breathing comes in short ecstatic breaths
as you rub your stick up and down
Do you feel it?
She's coming
You can feel her rise beneath you
oh, baby she's there
Do you feel it?
You are inside now
Your face is wet
You take a deep breath
close your eyes
Go in deeper and deeper
Do you feel it?
You feel her coming down
You ease up ready to jump off
that had to be the best one yet
but you plunge right back in
with your stick
knowing that there is more pleasure to be had
Do you feel it?

It's called surfing.

* * *

What could possibly feel more powerful than conquering something that is beyond our control? Those who face such a force as the ocean, and her sometimes violent waves, and master them can only gain a great sense of confidence and self-esteem:

. . . The sound of the pounding waves echo
through my ears like a thousand kettle drums
beating in unison with my heart. With my
surfboard becoming heavy under my arm and the
bright sun beating on my face, the waves
beckon to me. They are challenging my inner-
most determination, wanting me to give up
before I begin. But the more the waves chal-

lenge me, the braver I become.

Slowly I walk into the ocean, allowing the whiteness of the water to splash against my ankles. Wading deeper, the waves crash against my legs, pushing me back towards shore but I refuse their advice. Then onto my board I jump, and start paddling out. The crisp, cool water hits my face and I can taste the salt on my lips.

The first wave approaches me like a starving alley cat hovering over a small mouse. I begin to feel nervous, but the wave crashes over me before I have a chance to turn back. I come to the surface, gasping for air only to discover that I am alright. I turn to watch the waves flirt with the rocky shore. As my courage returns, I continue to paddle wanting to reach the outside. . . . Trying to convince myself I repeat over and over in my mind there is no quitting now! As a set of waves pass over me, I find myself almost at my desired destination. The biggest wave I had seen yet was approaching me, and as it engulfed me, I felt myself being dragged back about ten feet. Regrouping myself, I attempt to gain the ground I had lost.

After struggling past wave after wave I found myself where I wanted to be, among the surfers, on the outside.

—*Joleen Nunes, age 15*
Cayucos, California

Joleen was exhilarated by her success. But sometimes the seduction of the wave is so enticing that potential danger is ignored.

Such was the case for fifteen-year-old Andrea Olvera from Redlands, California:

. . . As we suited up and got ready, we could hear the roar of the pounding surf crashing on the beach. . . . After a long walk through blazing hot sand, we got to the beach. I

hadn't noticed that we were at "The Wedge"
until I saw six to eight foot sets pounding
the shore. No one was out and I did not recog-
nize the lifeguard's red flag, being that I
was so excited.

As I paddled out just a little behind my
brother, I couldn't help but be stoked about
the warmth my new wetsuit cuddled me in while
swimming in cool, beautiful 68 degree water.

I just came from a duck dive when I saw a
huge ten foot cleanup set coming my way. My
brother immediately jumped on the first wave,
trimming gracefully along the foamy wall of
the wave. I was busy watching my brother so
I didn't notice this massive wave coming
towards me.

I couldn't go over, I couldn't go under, I
couldn't go around, the only thing I could do
was catch and ride the monster. As quick as
lightning strikes, I was on the wave. I had
taken a late drop, so when I finally made it
down the steep face of the wave, the lip came
crashing down on me. I immediately wiped out.
When I came back up to the surface, I looked
for my board. It was about twenty yards away
and my leash had snapped.

Instantaneously, I started to swim towards
my board, when I looked over and saw another
liquid brick wall coming towards me. I knew I
couldn't make it to my board in time, so I
decided to try and body-surf to the beach and
get my board then.

So I went for it. It now has to be one of
the stupidest decisions I made in my life. As
I paddled to body-surf towards shore, I was
engulfed by a colossal amount of salt and
sand. I knew what to do during a wipeout; just
go with the flow and you'll use less breath
and energy. Silence and darkness was all I
knew of as I twisted and turned. . . .

Andrea struggled to get to the shore. Every time she got a bit
closer, she would be "eaten alive by a mass of ocean."

```
. . . Throughout all of this, thoughts were
going through my mind, weird thoughts like, I
don't want to die today I just bought a brand
new wetsuit and shoes, plus I also bought a
new surfboard a couple of days before that.
The biggest thing on my mind though was
getting air, but I couldn't because I was
being bounced, twirled and twisted by the
waves.
```

Again every time she got up, Andrea would get knocked down. Breathless, with little energy, she was finally rescued and dragged to shore by her brother. She vows she has learned many things from that day—especially about paying attention to red flags, never surfing alone, and being more cautious in a big surf.

Sarah has also battled with the forces of the sea. Once, in Mexico, she found herself being carried away by the tide and she relearned respect for the ocean; a respect, she claims, is "what we innately have as children."

```
The currents were pushing me in 3 directions
away from the shore. The surf began to rise.
I never once felt I had to resist it. It was
quite beautiful. The ocean knows when you are
scared, and will act accordingly, just as it
is able to comfort you when you cry or
rejoice with you when you're happy. It's this
weird feminine connection and I am somehow at
a loss to come to terms with it. In surfing,
you can assert yourself, using the wave as
your canvas, without the board, one can
become on the level, at its mercy, while at
the same time, exploring its depth.
A crowd gathered on the shore, so I began
to paddle in. Luckily I am a strong swimmer,
but I had to submerge myself under a break-
ing wave and let it topple me forward. When
I emerged, a Brazilian was surfing towards
me, telling me to grab the board. I don't know
what compelled me to go out in those
currents. The waves were reportedly 15 foot
(double over head). I later found out that
```

```
over 60 people last winter died right there
at that beach.
   It wasn't until I got on shore and looked
out that I realized the magnitude of the
"danger" that I had put myself in. After
surfing much smaller, familiar and more
predictable breaks, I just never felt the
need to caution myself.
```

Sarah acknowledges the ocean's power and finds value in surren-
dering to it:

```
   If it were just a sport, I don't think
people would surf for so long. Underneath all
that yuppified denial of anything illogical,
they carry an intense feeling of individual-
ity and need for self expression every time
they enter the water. We physically work
ourselves out and enter intensity so that we
can come to grips with all aspects of
life. . . . The ocean is a healer, and it taught
me a different kind of discipline. I see it
as also promoting independence and free-
dom. . . . When I face rejection in life, I can
go to the ocean and meet a challenge that
defies conquering. It comforts me as well as
making terrestrial problems look minuscule.
```

* * *

In most of the writing I received from surfer girls, they did not
examine their lives with such depth and insight as Sarah. There are
those who simply feel the feelings they get from surfing without
desiring exploration or explanation. In fact, many experience the
kind of escape and addictive joy while surfing that the Cowgirls get
from competing in rodeos.

When Kelly S., age eighteen, from Vista, California, was one of
four women surfers chosen for the U.S. Junior Surf Team in Tahiti,
nothing—not even illness and injuries—would stop her:

```
    . . . The waves broke in two feet of water
over a sharp coral reef. After repeatedly
hitting the bottom I decided to go in. When
I climbed onto the boat, my legs and feet
were dripping with blood. The sharp coral had
ripped off all my skin. The men on the boat
looked at me said a few words and laughed. I
couldn't understand what they said, but I had
a pretty good idea. One of the men grabbed a
lemon and squeezed it all over my cuts. It
hurt so bad I jumped off the boat and back
into the water! They said a few more words,
and laughed again.
    After about four hours and fifteen lemons
later, we decided to join the rest of the team
at the "right." This wave was much bigger,
much more powerful, shallower, and had twice
as many people out, but I paddled out
anyway. . . .
```

The day ended with feasts of unrecognizable, and hardly edible, foods, and the next morning Kelly woke up to a menacing thunderstorm. She also found herself incredibly ill, but it was the first day of the contest and she was determined.

```
    . . . I was so sick I hardly had the energy
to make it to the beach, plus I had to surf.
Luckily, even though the odds were against
me, I advanced on. I surfed the next two heats
and advanced, but by the fourth one I was so
sick I couldn't even paddle out. . . . I
continued to get sicker, the storm got worse,
I couldn't stand on my feet because my cuts
from the reef got infected, and I spent the
rest of my trip in bed half dead.
```

After Kelly fully recovered from her Tahitian experience, she immediately hit the waves again, as if returning to a life force:

```
    . . . I wouldn't stop surfing for anything. I
think it's like a drug. I tried it a few
times, love it and now I'm addicted. Surfing
```

```
is a good thing for me because I can express
myself by the way I surf. Surfing, next to
God, is the biggest part of my life and I
think it makes me feel worth something. I can
go out and rip perfect waves and surf how I
want to surf and no one can tell me what to
do. . . .
```

Kahli Wilson, age fifteen, lives in the small town of Gisborne in New Zealand and wrote while visiting in Honolulu:

```
Surfing in my hometown is part of the
lifestyle, just like here in Hawaii. This is
a healthy way for us teenagers to release
pressure and to enjoy ourselves. Many
teenagers back home switch to surfing for the
pure thrill they get but it also is an alter-
native to drugs and alcohol. For me, surfing
is a way of escaping from the real world where
everything is hectic and confusing. . . .
     It's always a rush going for a surf and I
believe that it is often an alternative to
many problems. A surf always clears my head
and helps keep me focused.
```

I found that surfer girls were the only group included in *Girl Power* that had such an individual focus. Although many partici-pate in surfing competitions, it is ultimately just a girl and her board, alone on the vast ocean. Unlike Pow Wows, Riot Grrrl meet-ings, and organizations like Future Farmers of America and 4-H, there is no coming together of a collective with surfing. Guinnevere Allen is trying to change that.

Sixteen-year-old Guinn, as her friends call her, describes herself as having "strawberry blonde hair, very tan skin, green eyes . . . I've been raised on the east side of Oahu in a town called Kailua. I moved to the North Shore last spring. . . . My favorite sized waves would probably be in the 4–6 ft. range, North east swell, a little offshore, but still clean and glassy with perfect pitching barrels."

Guinn is one of the founding members of the Association of Women Bodyboarders, a group dedicated to providing opportunities for women and girls to surf together and compete, without having to deal with the inequitable conditions of the men's and mixed contests.

The rapidly growing AWB promotes international contests, most recently in Japan, Portugal, and France. Members come from many countries and can find support through a quarterly newsletter.

Much like the male-dominated worlds of rap and rodeo, gender discrimination in surfing is quite evident and is clearly illustrated in professional competitions. The Association of Surfing Professionals, which determines the prize money for most of the professional surfing contests, including the Coca-Cola ASP World Tour and the U.S. Open, pays a cash prize of $105,000 to the male winner. The female winner receives $25,000, almost five times less.

Kahli is just one of the many girls who writes about discrimination out on her board:

> . . . I'm on holiday in Hawaii and I have noticed a number of female surfers out there ripping which I think is great! In Gisborne (New Zealand) where I'm from, unless they are really good, female surfers get laughed out of the water. This attitude is why so many females don't even begin to surf.

Kathy Adibi, age eighteen, has used these condescending attitudes from boys to fuel and propel her:

> . . . The most influential incident that sparked my surfing career was probably having a friend of mine named Jason tell me I could never surf because I was a girl. Being the sixth-grade tomboy that I was, something snapped in me as I heard him say that. This was the perfect opportunity to put my words into action for "a girl can do anything that a guy can" was the message I have always preached on the playground. From that point on, surfing became a major part of my

life. . . .

Besides the fact that I started surfing
because a guy told me I couldn't do it because
I was a girl, I have been given dirty looks
and/or laughed at on many occasions while
being in the water because, being a girl, I
just wasn't taken seriously as a surfer. Now,
I don't want to stereotype all guys as being
sexist because I know some guys that, though
hard to believe, aren't the least bit sexist
and completely respect and support me and my
surfing. But, I must admit, with the decent
amount of sexism I've faced, it's really hard
not to stereotype certain things. . . .

Practically every summer, Kathy goes to southern California to
surf and visit her old surf camp. There, she continually encounters
"little, spoiled, sexist boys," who "perpetuate the cycle of sexism"
and also, in her view, have no respect for the ocean:

. . . I don't think of men as objects, and I
don't give men a second-class status. And
yet, women are treated as objects and given
second-status and not a lot is being done
about it, especially in the surfing community. By the same token, I think it is ironic
that the entire surfing population exists and
depends on MOTHER NATURE and the waves SHE
brings. Finally, I think that all surfers and
all people should learn from the ancient
Hawaiians, who happened to invent surfing.
The ancient Hawaiians had no problem with
sexism in surfing for surfing was and still
should be a soulful experience having
absolutely nothing to do with a "DOMINATING
GENDER"; they cared for the oceans and the
Earth, and most importantly, they had no
societal constructs dealing with sex.

Christina Miller, age fifteen, is someone who has dealt with what
could be called reverse sexism, if not a subtle form of it:

I could not imagine that I used to wake up
in the morning and not even think about surfing. Or that I didn't surf when there was a
swell because I was "with my friends."

That's the trouble with being a girl surfer.
Most girls don't surf, so most of your
friends don't surf. My friends won't even
try.

In some ways it is good that a lot of girls
don't surf. Because you have a better chance
of getting noticed by individuals. But what
sucks is a guy will see a girl do an okay turn
and he'll tell her she rips. If that guy saw
another guy do the same thing, he wouldn't
think anything of it. Kind of ironic, huh?

I get so frustrated when I think about this.
The power of women is <u>so</u> under-rated. If more
girls surfed, trust me, more girls would rip.
If I see a girl who rips, I get so motivated. But how often is that? Once every three
months or so. . . .

The only way for women surfers to get
noticed is to get more girls to surf! Hey,
it's a great sport! Why not try it? I'm sick
of hearing that girls suck. We need to make
a difference—and if none of you can, then I
will!

Nineteen-year-old Renee Harada, a resident of Honolulu and of
Japanese ancestry, discovers that being one of the guys isn't enough:

. . . The usual morning crowd was there, and
we all gathered to talk story. We were talking about the other day when the waves were
bigger, and one of the guys asked me how it
felt being a girl, and surfing with all the
guys. Before he had asked me this question I
had never realized that most of the time it
was just me and the guys out there. I guess
I never really felt different because nobody
treated me different. I mean, sure there are
times when I get cutoff and stuff, but I never
did think it was because I was a girl.

Renee answered his question, saying she probably didn't feel any differently from anyone there, and headed to the water, not giving it a second thought. But later, sitting on the beach, she began to reflect:

> . . . As I was thinking I thought up a little analogy, it's about the sun and moon. Everyday the sun rises and shines in the sky. On some days the sun shines bright and clear, and everyone can see how great it is. But, on other days it doesn't shine so bright, so it doesn't look so great. Even on these days when the sun is hiding behind some clouds we all know it's there, it doesn't have to prove itself. Then in the evening when the sun goes down the moon comes out to shine during the night.
> This is what I thought it was like to be a girl surfing (or doing anything else). When we are surfing we are like the sun, on some days we rip and everyone notices how good we are. But, like everyone else we have our bad days and don't look so hot. The only thing is that we know how good we are, and we shouldn't have to prove it to anyone, just like the sun doesn't have to prove it's there. Then when we're not surfing we are what we are, girls. It's like the moon coming out, the girl in us comes out. Well, this is what it's like for me. I feel that when I'm surfing (or doing anything else) I'm just as good as anybody else, but I'm still a girl. . . . I want to be thought of as a good woman surfer, and not just one of the guys.

* * *

Each surfer girl I heard from made it very clear that despite the difficulties, surfing is something she would treasure forever:

The feel of the water against your freezing skin, as you duck-dive another wave, is only one of the many new experiences as you learn to surf. I remember it was a beautiful day, a tad chilly the first time I ever accomplished standing up on a surfboard. ... It was a moment which will always be imbedded in my memory, the simplicity of it all meant nothing to me, as I had achieved the first step of learning to surf.

From this moment on I was hooked, the thrill of learning a new skill made an impact on my life. I no longer saw surfing as an exclusive male activity but something that I could do. ...

The rush of adrenaline is still with me now, exactly the same as it was the first day I stood up. Simply just being out in the surf brings out a feeling of pride towards myself. I love the movement of waves as I lie on my board. The feeling of the spray against my face, being in touch with the ocean has been a part of my life since as long as I can remember. ...

Surfing has now become my way of keeping in touch with this feeling from inside, and it will, for as long as I can stand up, be a part of my life.

—Kahli Wilson

There's only one place I think about everyday, the beach. The ocean is my life, and the waves are my soul. I live to see the ocean again, I breathe to ride another wave. Out of all my times at the ocean, there's one that haunts my mind. Surrounded in water, riding a bed of foam, my longest tube ride stands out in my memory. The cool, clear water made perfect refreshment for a hot day.

I saw the wave coming in the horizon. It was a glassy four foot swell. Soon the wave came up, I paddled for it, and purposely made a

late drop. After taking the drop, I pulled a
sharp bottom turn and went straight for the
tube. A slight nose stall put me deep into
the tube. Beautiful clear blue water
surrounded me. I was lost in a tunnel so long,
so deep, that there was no return.

The moment sticks in my head like a picture.
Frozen in time, nothing can touch that
moment. It shall be embroidered till I die,
and in my last moments of life, I shall think
of it.

—Andrea Olvera

Sarah, whose writing I found to be invariably wise, sends this
challenge to other girl surfers:

. . . I know many male surfers who value the
feminine aspects of the ocean, but few who
are able to connect them with women surfers.
I respect women surfers who are competing,
but I also want to urge girls who are in the
position I was in a few years ago, to explore
the way they look at the world and to relate
what they do somehow to the rest of their
lives. I am learning that looking for meaning is okay. There isn't just one way to go
about what we are doing. It just bugs me that
there is such a singular accepted way to
approach things. Fundamentally we all get the
same beautiful rush from skating or surfing
or what not, but there is no doubt in my mind
that the forum in which we do these things,
the reasons need to be extended beyond what's
alluded to in sports magazines. . . .

* * *

Skateboarders, although quite different from surfers, are also
part of a subculture, with their own rebellious image, style, look,
and language.

> . . . Skating. I like it. You get the biggest
> rush when you do it. I guess I like the thrill
> and the risk. Cheap transportation too.
>   I really don't want to be a "skater"
> chic[k]. That would be living into some image.
> I don't consider myself a "skater," cause
> that seems so cheesey, like you have to wear
> big pants and Vans in order to be a real
> "skater." That's just a big pseudo image.
>   Alot of boy skaters laugh at you and snort
> when you say you skate. But if you show that
> you're serious and not some doofy teenybop-
> per head you'll be taken seriously. Fool boys
> can also be helpful by providing you with
> stuff (like new wheels) that you're too poor
> to buy yourself. After you scoop off them you
> have to kick their ass and show them how fresh
> you are. . . .

—Heather, age 15
Brockton, Massachusetts

The word *skating*, or as many write, *sk8ing*, refers to skate-boarding, not to be confused with ice-skating, roller-skating, or Rollerblading. Skating is more than a sport. It is a lifestyle.

From the writing I received, it appears that skating is even more male-dominated than surfing. Girls have to prove themselves continually to boys and put up with teasing, ridicule, and judgment.

Ramdasha Bikceem is an African-American self-proclaimed punk girl who, like the Riot Grrrls and their zines, does a sk8 zine called *Gunk*, and has a band by the same name. She writes:

> When I got my first skateboard I was proba-
> bly around 12 years old. It didn't really
> occur to me at the moment that what I was
> doing was considered out of the ordinary for
> alot of girls. But as I got older and start-
> ed getting more into skateboarding, I real-
> ized what role most girls played when it came
> to skateboarding. Their role was to sit on the
> sidewalk while the rest of the boys were havin

a rippin' time. At first I tried to ignore it
and I even looked down upon these girls for
not trying. I felt like nothing was stopping
me, so why couldn't they give it a try? When
I turned 14 years old, my two best girlfriends
started to skate also. We were truly an
awesome anarchic girl skate gang. But every
time we'd skate with other boys we started to
feel intimidated 'cuz we didn't know all the
latest tricks or the "cool" skate lingo. This
is when I finally started to realize why those
girls on the sidewalk didn't skate. . . . It was
because a vast majority of those boys didn't
want us there . . . we threatened their terri-
tory. I remember reading in some skate magazine how one pro skater said he was annoyed
when girls started skating because it was just
too "distracting." He went on to say that our
only function was to sit back and shut up and
watch boys skate and be their little fuckpigs
after a hard day of skating.
    Now that I'm eighteen, I don't care about
the latest skate trick or the newest lame
skate lingo. All I really care about is having
fun! I only skate with people now who are not
competitive and are interested in having fun.
Although it is still very frustrating for me
when I see girls sitting on the sidewalk
swooning over these macho shitheads. I can
only hope that they will see me there and
hopefully see themselves one day. Or at least
question what they're doing there sitting on
the sidelines. I know it's hard when the only
image girls see themselves in skate magazines
is one that is the totally typical unevolved
skate "bimbo" (I hate that word).

Eighteen-year-old Reda Rountree, from Cottondale, Florida, also
started a sk8 zine. She shares her own story of discrimination:

    The worst experience I had as a girl skater
    was when me and a guy friend of mine went to

a skate shop in Fort Walton. The guys there—
including the owner—spent the entire time
there talking to him. They acted like I
wasn't there and I couldn't possibly skate—
I'm a girl. When I asked them about a board,
they patronized me. I've had to learn how to
act around other skaters because guys don't
take girls that seriously.

Sixteen-year-old Molly Weissberg from Pittsburgh, Pennsylvania,
struggles with her own identity in the skater-boy world:

After a while, I felt like I've found the
essential skater philosophy. Get away with as
much as you can. Their goal in life is to fit
into a "boys will be boys" description, and be
as juvenile and as delinquent as long as possible. What does this description entail? Most
obviously, it does not include any kind of
respect for wimmin, nor much rational thought
for the future. It's a kind of apathy that I
just can't relate to. No, it doesn't apply to
all males who carry a skateboard, mainly to
the skater "elite." These are the ones you
meet first, the outgoing, cute ones with the
baggiest pants and the fanciest sketchbook. It
seems so easy to me, to become jaded, to agree
with them about how great they are and forget
yourself, forget that you want to be someone
and not someone's girlfriend. It seems kind of
automatic to begin to feel the need to dress
more like them (I've watched pantscuffs of
myself and other gerls grow gradually larger),
to pursue the same interests as them (why do
I feel guilty that I have never spraypainted
an 8' by 10' mural in honor of marijuana), to
forget your previous style, disregarding it as
unfashionable, immature. The whole thing
develops a false sense of importance, it's
hard to look beyond their "underground" cool-
ness to realize that the cute skater with the
highest ollies is no different than the muscu-
lar football jock with the most running yards.

* * *

Tiffany "Bridger" Graff, age sixteen, writes that her high school in Parowan, a tiny town in Utah, doesn't like her type, especially since she is the only girl there who skates and snowboards.

> I wear mascara, sometimes, besides that
> chapstick is my basic make-up. My hair is
> burgundy, and my life is skating, snowboard-
> ing, writing poetry (nobody understands),
> painting in my closet or just hanging out
> with my friends.

The street culture and style associated with skating has recently become trendy and cool—sometimes even more so than *skating* itself. There are those who dress, talk, and act like skaters without even setting foot on a board. They're called "posers." Tiffany describes how she feels about them:

> One thing I can't stand (nor will I ever be
> able to stand) is posers. The type of girls
> (or guys) who think grunge or skating is a
> fashion show! Hello! It's a way of life!
> Being who you are and being free to say or do
> whatever you want. Whenever you want. Not
> buying things to make your image better.
> Piercing your nose cuz you think people will
> think you're cool. These are the same groups
> of girls who not long ago would make fun of
> us for snowboarding or skating.

Tiffany's desire simply to be herself is often challenged. In one instance, a group of guys surrounded her at a school dance:

> ...This jerk is saying "Why aren't you
> normal?" What the hell is normal? Everybody
> is different, and you should never change for
> anybody, especially a guy. ...
> Many times I still get crap from these guys.

There are some girls, however, who have experienced camaraderie and support from boys, as friends—and more.

When Renee Tantillo, from Allston, Massachusetts, was sixteen,
she was encouraged by male friends to skate to her full potential:

> . . . By the time fall rolled around, some of
> my guy friends were much more confident of my
> abilities than I was and encouraged me to
> drop in to the four-walled ditch we hung out
> at, called "the bowl." . . . Thus, my long-
> lived passion for skating ditches was born.

And for some, like Heather, skating has taken over:

> I believe skateboarding is a substitute for
> sex. Ever since i've started skating i've
> thot less and less about the latter. My lil
> pathetic daydreams are filled w/ me doing half
> pipes and skating pool instead of making out
> in a pool. I guess this is OK maybe my ol
> libido will kik in someday. but i doubt it.
> There are the occasional moments of Longing,
> but they are swiftly chased away by visions
> of me gliding along peacefully. Maybe i'll
> find a sk8board w/ a boy attached to it. That
> would be neet. But w/ my luk the boy will be
> some asshole loser. Oh well . . . and how kum
> all the skate boys i've met are either
> conceited poop heads or completely brainless
> and/or lacking a personality? i know the
> raddest skateboy is out there, lurking. If
> you're reading this . . . Be my friend. . . .

Andria Garbiso, age seventeen, from Stockton, California, started skating at a very young age. A "little Tom Boy," she would
follow her big brother and his friends all over, trying to skate as
they did, and she'd hang out with them when they'd let her, which
was not often:

> So there I went, off by myself, practicing
> my ollies, and kick-flips. Mostly I'd just

```
try  to  jump  stuff  while  riding  really
fast. . . .
    The secret to every great skater, or athlete
of any kind, is . . . You can't be afraid to
fall. I'm not. Ask my mom. Being afraid to
fall makes you fall more. Eventually you
learn not to. (Iodine still burns.) . . .
    Eventually other extracurricular activities
came about, and skateboarding for me began to
fade, except for riding around and having my
little poodle dog pull me. We were fresh.
```

Andria seriously got back into skating several years later, "the only hang up being that I had no one to skate with. By this time my brother drove, and most girls had grown out of skating."

In her sophomore year, Andria became best friends with a girl who also wanted to skate. Together, they skated and taught each other as much as they could:

```
        . . . I even met a really great skater. One of
the best in Stockton. I liked him. My friend
tried to convince me to go out w/ him so he'd
teach us to skate better, but I couldn't let
that be the only reason.
    I liked him and he liked me, so I said yes.
Yup, now I was queen. A real Skate Betty. I
loved the attention. We'd all go skate the
banks and search for new spots w/ good long
curbs to slide. My friend was too self-
conscious to go with me and the guys, so I
tried to help her get better. We'd practice
our ollies for hours in the driveway. Trying
to get higher in one spot was not very easy.
You just have to go along and do it. The first
time I tried a waxed curb slide, I got on,
rode and dropped so hard on my butt. The board
just flew! Eventually, I laughed too. . . .
    Me and the guys always took our boards to
school. Tossed 'em in the lockers and rode
after school. I say after school, b/c we used
to skate during break at school on campus, not
near anyone, just in our own area, till the
```

faculty got nervous. Plus, I got caught riding
down the hallways by the principal after I'd
been warned twice not to. He took my board
till the end of the week. He said next time he
caught me, he'd take it till the end of the
year. So I never got caught again. But I still
skated on campus when he wasn't around.

* * *

The exhilaration and rush the girls wrote about not only comes
from skating and surfing, but also from another "board" sport:
snowboarding.

Instead of catching and gliding on a wave, or connecting with the
solid earth, girls like Tiffany are flying down the slopes:

White hills rolling before my eyes
wind whipping at my face, tugging
                my hair back
gliding across the virgin powder
forcing my body into indifferent positions.
My trail winds as a surly snake
                across his meadows
Working up my speed
forward and back my lean.
I feel as though I am one with nature,
alone on the hill, just me.

* * *

Ramdasha and the rest of the skate girls are proving themselves
to be just as skilled as boys, and at the same time enjoying themselves. To this end, they are creating new, conscious ways of thinking and living. They are understanding their power.

Even though I dislike a lot of the attitudes
that have been linked with skateboarding I
think I'll be skating as long as my body will
allow and hopefully things will change soon.

But in the meantime I'm tired of wasting my
time with these misguided young men. I see
where they've taken skateboarding and frankly
it disgusts me. I've seen what the majority
of their companies think of me and the rest
of us girls in their sexist ads. I abhor their
total dependence on the fashion industry. I
know in my heart that fashion is not the
asthetic that makes us real. I don't need or
want their validation anymore. I'm gonna do
my own thing and hopefully with the help of
other intelligent boy and girl skaters we
will redefine what used to be (and still is
most of the time) a fun sport.

Whether snowboarding, surfing, or skating, these girls are standing up for their rights—on any board they choose.

CHRISTINA MILLER

NICHOLE GREEN

Dribble, Dribble, jumpstop, pivitt, pivitt, shoot. The ball goes through the hoop. The other team has the ball, drives it down the court and shoots, its off the rim. They rebound and lay it up and it's in. Scores tied at 76. Passes the ball in, drives down the court. She stops, pivitts, she passes the ball. Times running out 9-8-7-6-5. She's at the three-point line, 4-3. she shoots its going in, 2-1-0 The crowd goes wild as the final buzzer goes off. We go home with anothe victory.
BasketBall

Mindy Stobbe

CHAPTER TEN

Jocks

Softball. Basketball. Volleyball. Football. Soccer. Track. Rowing.
Ice Hockey. Field Hockey. BMX Racing. Wrestling. Lacrosse.
Girls are doing it all.

> It took moving to a larger city, and an
> athletically competitive school, to build up
> my confidence. Since I started school, I had
> been teased by a lot of people. My ability to
> stand up to people was almost nonexistent. I
> would often come home from school and then I
> would have a comeback. An hour after each
> put-down I would imagine myself beating the
> people who beat me, just like Rocky. My quest
> has always been to come back and see those
> people and make them see how good I am. . . . I
> excelled in gym, but never enough. People
> called me a tomboy because I liked gym. . . . I
> was laughed at because I was tough, and I
> never did good enough.
> Then one day we had something called track
> and field day. . . . I won the 400 yard dash.
> From then on, things began to click. . . .

What began to click in fourteen-year-old Paula Barkman from
Pittsburgh, Pennsylvania, was an increase in self-esteem that many
girls have found through participating in sports.

My name is Laura Prinzer. I am a junior on
the Kiski Area Girls Cross-Country and Track
teams. We have finished our fourth undefeat-
ed season, and have just advanced to the
W.P.I.A.L. final meet. There, we will try to
qualify for the state meet.
    I think athletics has helped me tremendous-
ly. Being a part of a team is a great feeling, especially when it is a hardworking and
successful one. . . . I have become a much more
confident and independent person. I know that
if I work hard enough at something, I can do
it. Without sports, I don't think I would
have ever achieved this confidence.

During her first field hockey game where she "started as sweep-
er," Hannah Duffy, age fifteen, from Rindge, New Hampshire,
experienced the gamut of emotions. She writes about herself from
the point of view of her hockey stick:

    . . . She's trembling again, but this time
it's from excitement, and she's not afraid
anymore. And I can't help feeling my own
pleasure at assisting her, at helping her
improve her self-esteem. For we have it now,
a surge of power that bonds us together, that
makes me hers. Together, we are unstoppable.
And we both know it. I've felt her frustration and anger, her pride and happiness. I've
taken on her sweat and tears, her weariness
and euphoria. I complete her and she
completes me, we are one and as the game goes
on, her hands are dry and steady, and she
makes no mistakes.

Yana Shteyn, age eighteen, who qualified for the Junior Olympics
in table tennis, found strength by overcoming many obstacles on
the way:

    Originally I come from former Soviet Union,
Odessa, Ukraine. . . . Table tennis in Russia
differs greatly from the sport here in

America. For five years I trained in a sport school, in a special class for table tennis. There were twenty kids in my class, every one of us lived table tennis. . . .

Out of all those kids, I didn't stand out very much. I was a skinny, young girl. My coach didn't believe in me very much for two big reasons. I was a novice girl plus I was a daughter of a woman who worked for him.

When I turned thirteen, my life completely changed, because I came to the United States. I didn't arrive to Colorado, New York or California, instead I came to a small city of Jacksonville, Florida, where table tennis is ping-pong, a fun game. . . .

Yana and her mother found competitions and Yana started winning. She baby-sat to make money to buy tickets to the competitions, and often had to travel to other cities, sometimes spending the night in the car with her family before games.

Yana's dream finally came true. She became the number-one girl in Florida and qualified for the Junior Olympics. However, her joy was short-lived. She was banned from play on a technicality. She had come to America two months too late to be eligible for the competition.

As I look back, I have no regrets. Everything that happened to me, all I had to go through, has made me a better player, but most of all a very strong person.

Fifteen-year-old Dana J. Battese Trudell, whom we met in the Native American girl chapter, has been running since the age of six. In 1993, she was the South Dakota TAC Junior Olympic female cross-country champion:

When I run I get a lot of power. I pray and I think about things. I pray that I may do the best that I can. It's like running through time. To run the dream makes me more powerful within.

* * *

Like Cowgirls and Surfers, some Jocks, such as fifteen-year-old
Sarah Janicke from Merriam, Kansas, find a sense of escape in their
sport:

> . . . Volleyball is an important part of my
> life. It is one of the few sports that I don't
> feel embarrassed playing. When I am out there
> on the court, all my worries, shyness and
> problems dissolve from my life.
>
> The only thing I think about when I'm play-
> ing is what I need to think about: where I'm
> supposed to be on the court, my skills and my
> opponents. All my usual thoughts like "Do I
> look okay? Does he like me? Are my grades
> good enough? Am I popular?" never taunt me
> when I'm involved in a game.

Jenny Buttolph, age thirteen, who plays volleyball and basketball
in Pleasant Hill, Oregon, has a similar experience:

> One of the main reasons I play and enjoy
> sports is for me to forget about my personal
> problems and to set aside my feelings.   It
> seems that I have quite a lot of problems but
> sports lets me set them aside.

Yet Jenny also feels disturbed and troubled by "the sexism that's
involved" in sports. She continues:

> . . . For example, a men's college basketball
> game gets a lot of people to watch them where-
> as a women's basketball game gets a consider-
> able amount less. Women are just as good as
> men if not better! I don't mean to sound
> conceited but I don't think it is very fair
> to cheer on men and forget about women just
> because of their sex. I mean, where is a
> women's professional basketball team? All I
> see is women's college but men can go on to

```
the N.B.A. One main thing that I believe in
is giving everyone a fair chance.
```

This concern is evident in most of the girls' writing. Many share how daunting it is to immerse themselves fully in their sport knowing that, since there are basically no professional women's teams, they are not able to have a playing future. Most feel continually unacknowledged and dismissed.

Jessica Trybus, age sixteen, from Gibsonia, Pennsylvania, has been written up in countless local newspaper articles. Almost each week an article appears focusing on a different sport she excels in, including softball, tennis, swimming, golf, basketball, skiing, baseball, and football. With accomplishments like that, I was surprised to read about this experience:

```
When I was fourteen years old, I tried out for
one of my high school's boys ice hockey teams. I
was the first ever and only girl to try out for
this prestigious school. . . . During the clinics
before the tryouts, I was the only one of my group
to be asked to be moved up to practice with the
Junior Varsity until tryouts. . . . I made first
"cuts" and played well throughout tryouts. I
thought that I was clearly better than at least
90% of the guys. So when second tryouts came
along, I gave it all that I had. I even remember
diving along the blue line to keep the puck on
sides—and just as I did so, the whistle blew
signaling the end of tryouts. . . .
```

Jessica had to wait a week until the teams were posted. She, along with her family and friends, was confident that she would make it. On her birthday, she found out the results:

```
I didn't speak a word for two whole days.
Every time someone tried to comfort me, it
just made matters worse. After supplying
myself with ample time to think things over,
I decided that these people who cut me aren't
done with me, because I'll get them next
```

```
time. I turned right around the next week and
made the Bantam A team of a local amateur
league and really learned a lot with that
group. My ultimate high school goal is to
make the Varsity ice hockey team my senior
year at North Allegheny Senior high school.
If I feel I'm skilled and in shape enough to
try out, I expect to be judged fairly as a
player.
```

Fourteen-year-old Jenny Olson, from Pleasant Hill, Oregon, addresses the same issue:

```
Being a girl in the 90's is no easy task.
Being an athletic woman is even harder.
Almost everybody thinks that men are better
at everything, and is an image that is
imprinted unconsciously from day one. This is
unfortunate because girls can achieve so much
if they are given support instead of being
ridiculed.
```

It wasn't until 1972 that girls were even allowed a fair shot at paticipating in high school sports. With the passing of the highly controversial law referred to as Title IX, schools were forbidden to discriminate against girls in sports. The law was revolutionary.

However, according to the girls I met and heard from, being legally allowed to play on boys' teams does not protect them from mockery and disdain from their fellow teammates.

Yet many young women, like Margaret LeGates, have prevailed, earning much respect and becoming role models for other girls:

```
The smell of the mats, the roar of the
crowd, I love it all. So why does this make
me weird? Why do people stare when I enter
the gym? I guess it's because girls aren't
supposed to do certain things even if we
enjoy them.
I, Margaret LeGates, am the only girl
wrestler on the boys wrestling team at
```

> Libertyville Community High School. I was the
> first girl to participate on the high school
> level in Illinois. At 17, I've been wrestling
> for two years now at 103 pounds. This will be
> my third and final season, and I'm hoping my
> best. I would say wrestling has been one of
> the greatest experiences of my life. . . .

In eighth grade, Margaret decided to join the wrestling team. She was told she could not. She was again turned away in the ninth grade. She contacted the Women's Wrestling Federation and learned that under Title IX, she could not be blocked from participating. Once the school superintendent was informed of the law, she made the team.

After intensive training, which left her exhausted and in bed by 8:00 every night and bruised from head to toe, Margaret finally got to compete.

> . . . None of the other schools knew I was
> wrestling until the end of November when we
> had our first meet. Wrestlers and fans alike
> were surprised to see me there. That night I
> received two forfeits because the other teams
> didn't have anyone at 103 on the sophomore
> level. As the season progressed, I got more
> of the same treatment. Stares and gasps
> greeted me as I entered the room. Eventually,
> I chalked up seven more forfeits, four from
> boys who didn't want to wrestle me.
> I won one match that season. In December at
> a multiple school tournament, I was in a
> close match, and tied with a young man 7-7 at
> the end of regulation time. I pinned him in
> overtime. Everyone was cheering for me, and
> my coach, Matt Leone, was so proud. I felt
> all the obstacles had been worth it. It was
> really exciting!
> My junior season I also won one match, but
> on the varsity level. I pinned the boy in
> 4:20. This win gave me a seventh place title
> out of twelve teams. . . .

Margaret was forced to make concessions. She had to purchase a specially designed uniform and cut her hair. She also found herself faced with negative attitudes and prejudices from her male opponents and teammates.

But for Margaret it was all worth it:

> Wrestling experiences, however, have given me more gains than losses. I have gained self-respect, and respect for others' opinions. I have gained strength, and will power which will stay with me for life. I have gained respect from others, especially my peers. . . .
>
> I've been called a pioneer, and I guess in some ways I am. Since I started wrestling I know a few other girls have joined the teams at their school. . . . It makes me feel proud to know that I may have influenced other girls to follow their wishes. . . .

* * *

From Dumfries, Virginia, sixteen-year-old Nicky Croteau writes of the time when she was alone shooting baskets on a public basketball court in Pompano Beach, Florida. When other players—all men—showed up, every one of them avoided Nicky:

> . . . More and more pour in; they begin to crowd up the courts. I still have my basket to myself. The baskets are now over-crowded. They've started up a couple of games on half-courts with groups sitting near waiting to play, and I STILL have my hoop to myself. This is ridiculous! The ones in line could play a game at my basket . . . if I play, too. So I decide to show them my stuff. Maybe if they see I can play, they'll join me. So I do some fancy dribbling that I've been working on for awhile and pop a few shots. Still—no reaction. Maybe this is a step

ahead for women. Maybe it's good they're not
assuming they can just take the basket from
me. Maybe I'm getting really annoyed, too.
The game next to me ends. I grab my ball,
walk over to the nearest guy and say, "May I
play?", realizing I sound really stupid; no
one else asks like that. The guy says sure,
and I followed him onto the court. I felt
pretty damn uncomfortable I'd like to add.
There were nine black guys standing there
looking at me. (By the way, I'm a not so tall
white girl).
    "Hi." I said.
    Another great comment. A couple of them
smiled. (Possibly laughing at me to themselves). But no one responded. They just
began shooting around. I joined them. . . .

But, to no surprise, Nicky was the last person picked for a team.
The game began and Nicky made a basket quickly. It was apparent, however, that the men had let her score with little or no
defense. She confronted them and asked them to play seriously.
Then they went all out, "stuffing" her three times in a row, with no
middle ground.

    I got used to it though. Eventually, as the
game went on, I got better. I made a couple
of shots, and I even made the winning point
for my team. After the game, a few of the guys
asked me where I was from, where I played,
etc. . . . I answered them, talked for awhile,
grabbed my ball and walked away. I did manage
to hear some comments on the way to the car.
    "Damn. She was pretty good. I've never
played against a girl before," said one of
the players. "These are the 90's, better get
used to it," responded one of my teammates.
That really made my day.
    I've been back to the courts a few times
since then, and you'd be surprised how much
respect I've earned. I'm never the last one
picked anymore.

* * *

Some girls, like Shona Williams, age thirteen, find that playing on coed teams, with all the teasing and the "smart comments," makes for a more competitive game:

> I played tackle football last season. All
> boys were on my team and I think I was the
> only girl in our league. . . . My first game I
> played I could hear boys making smart
> comments and stuff. And to tell you the truth
> I kinda liked it because they were making fun
> of me, but when the game started I gave them
> the beating of their life. Most of my games
> I heard smart comments, but they really
> didn't realize that they were just making me
> stronger by saying that rude stuff. I liked
> playing with guys though because they know
> more about football.

Fourteen-year-old Jacylyn De Board's frustration in an all-girl softball league forced her to choose the only option she felt she could:

> I made the all-star team every year I
> played. After my second year of league I
> stopped playing because I had become the best
> pitcher in league and I didn't have any kind
> of competition.

* * *

In addition to social pressures and physical pain, girl Jocks, with their rigorous and time-consuming practices, tryouts, and competitions, must sacrifice the social life other teens seem to crave. What keeps them going?

> It's the feeling you get after you've run
> your ten billionth lap, after you've shot

your 100,000 free throws, after you practiced
your spike approach approximately 4,800
times. If you could describe the feeling in
a word it would be euphoria or pain. But that
feeling that every muscle in your body is
aware of, makes everything worthwhile. I can
do anything. I know it because I <u>have</u> run ten
billion laps and shot 100,000 free throws.
Because I've heard the laughs and the "girls
can't play sports" jokes. Well guys, you
better check your bucks because the next time
you're streaking down the court for a lay-in,
the hand that stuffs the ball down your
throat might just belong to a girl. And you
can bet that she'll be feeling that euphoria.

—Chelsea McAlister, age 14

Nineteen-year-old rower Jessica Smith competes in the Foot of
Charles regatta in Boston, the novice equivalent of the Head of
Charles—the biggest regatta in the United States, held annually in
Boston on the Charles River.

She's a coxswain, the "captain" of her boat. It is up to her to
manage eight rowers—steering, giving directions, and motivating
each girl to race her best race.

. . . "Okay, taking it up. Full pressure,
full steam ahead crossing the starting line.
Let's go! We've worked hard for this day,
let's show them how it's done! Pushing off,
remembering your body angles . . . make every
stroke your best stroke. Keep it going, keep
it going! Let's show some power! We're a
powerhouse, we're looking great and working
hard! Power ten on this one!" And so we rowed
our hardest and our best ever. The steering
came as naturally to me as breathing. I
hardly thought about my next words to the
rowers. It all came from within, from somewhere deep in my subconscious. All my hard
work, reading articles and manuals, taking
comments from the rowers and advice from the

coach, listening to the varsity coxswains and
pumping them for information, stressing,
worrying, sleepless nights and morning rows—
it was all paying off.
  We sailed under the Weeks Bridge and around
the sharp corner as if we had wings.
Suddenly, the finish line was on us. So soon?
I was almost disappointed. I called a power
ten—ten of the hardest, best possible
strokes—for the finish line and we flew
across. We didn't come in first, but no one
had passed us either. We paddled for about
fifty yards beyond the finish line, and
weigh-'nuffed. We had done it! We were
incredible! The adrenalin in that boat could
have rowed the whole race over again, backwards, eight arms tied behind eight backs of
the eight rowers who had pulled us through
the water like a hot knife slicing through
butter. (I, of course, would need both hands
to steer.) . . .

Of African-Italian descent, seventeen-year-old runner Danielle
Purfey lives in Allison Park, Pennsylvania. Among other numerous
achievements, Danielle is a seven-time National Junior Olympian,
and was named Athlete of the Year in 1990 and 1988 by the USA
Track and Field Southern Region.

                      I KNOW THE ANSWER

We trot to the starting position like
  thoroughbreds
The Others pawing and prancing.
There's one last moment of hesitation,
One last forced breath and, in the split
  second I wonder . . .
Why am I here?
The terror
The smoke
The gun

                      BANG!
I'm in my own world now, with just enough

```
room for me.
A pack of 15 girls is what reality pushes,
While solidarity is what I imagined,
Instead I'm all alone on this icy blue
 colored track.
I see no one else.
I hear no one else.
I run this race for me and only me . . .
While giving much thanks to all who have
helped me climb this steep mountain of success.
I have completed my second lap in moments . . .
                        Right on schedule.
The third lap begins to wrestle with me but
I stay strong and claim the victory.
I cry tears of pain,
                      . . . yet shed tears of joy.
I'm down to the last 100 meters.
Every step represents everything I've worked for
And the uncountable hours of sacrifice.
Every step seems like another day—a lifetime . . .
just waiting to pass.
I can see the bright white line now
I'm so anxious to cross.
I raise my arms in ecstasy
And no longer ask
Why am I here?
I know the answer.
```

Danielle writes of "giving much thanks" to all who have helped her "climb this steep mountain of success."

Many girls have received much support and valuable insight from those around them. Heather K. Ehrman, nineteen years old, is from Merrimack, New Hampshire:

```
My parents, teachers, coaches and friends
encouraged me to believe that I can achieve
whatever I choose to accomplish due to my
ambition, hard work, and desire for happi-
ness. This is an important discovery between
leaving a childhood and becoming an adult. A
little girl would be frightened to think of
the uncertainty that lay in her future. As a
```

young woman, her fear remains but it has
evolved into the excitement of unknown possi-
bilities. . . .

Other times, what is intended as support can actually feel like
pressure, and instill self-doubt:

I am fifteen years old and I am a fast pitch
softball player. I have had a glove on my
hand since I was a little girl. My father got
me started because of his love for the game.

Because my father was a pitcher, I am a
pitcher. I started this position two years
ago. My father says I have great potential
but I just have to develop and go through the
transition every pitcher goes through. He
also tells me to practice just a little bit
harder. Believe me, I do practice. I play
from March to August and practice and condi-
tion from September to February.

My problem is, my father was a great pitcher. He expects it all to come naturally to
me, but sometimes I have a hard time with it.
In the last season I have come very close to
the strike zone, but not right on.

It is very frustrating for me. I love pitching, I could do it for hours, I just wish I
could be as good as I want to be. I do expect
a lot from myself. I just realized that this
season. I expected it to all come together.
I told myself that this would be my season.
Well, it turned out to be a horrible season.
Except for a few games which I pulled through
that made me proud of myself, I felt like my
father felt differently.

It seems like whenever I do something good
he's not there to see it, but when I do something bad he is and I don't hear the end of
it. I always feel like he's disappointed or
let down. That's what I get though for having
a softball dad.

My plan for the future is to practice a lot
harder. I am very ambitious. Soon I am going

```
to have what it takes. I did make a promise
to my father though, some day I will strike
him out!
```

—Sarah Fritz
Zimmerman, Minnesota

There are many demands on teenage girls in sports as they struggle to fulfill their own personal goals amidst the expectations of others.

Jami Strinz is a fifteen-year-old all-around jock from Pleasant Hill, Oregon. She's played volleyball, soccer, and basketball. In softball, her underhand fast pitch puts many boys to shame. Three years ago, at twelve years old, her pitch clocked in at fifty-five miles per hour. She hasn't been timed since, but is certain it's only gotten faster. She writes:

```
It really doesn't matter how old you are,
you'll always have pressure on you, due to
sports. I've learned that you have to take
control, and if you think you can't, you
better find another line of work.
```

Fifteen-year-old Tara Koenig from Elk River, Minnesota, experienced just too much pressure:

```
Since I was young, I've never been one to
sit around. I've always been busy, busy,
busy. I became extremely active after I
entered junior high with maintaining a
straight A average and also competing in
sports. But, somehow, I always ended up being
able to handle all the stress . . . until this
year. . . .
My schedule was filled with swimming and
weightlifting in the mornings, which meant
getting up at 5:00 A.M. After practice, I
went directly to school. Following school, I
headed back to the pool for a practice usual-
ly lasting until 5:15. I worked as a life-
guard until around 7:00. When I finally
```

        arrived home, I always seemed to be loaded
        down with homework. Unable to put it off, I'd
        stay up until 1:00 or 2:00 A.M. just to wake
        up and do it over again. With swim meets on
        Thursdays and Saturdays, my week was filled.
        Loss of sleep, exhaustion, and stress took
        its toll.

Indeed, Tara became sick and was diagnosed with mononucleo-
sis. Her life immediately had to change as she could no longer swim
and could only attend school for three hours a day while she recu-
perated. The days were full of emotion and upset, impatience and
frustration. She continues:

        . . . Sometimes I wish that I could go back
        to when I was a child and my biggest worry
        was if I'd have to clean up the dishes after
        supper. Life was so carefree back then. The
        most magical thing was to wake up with a
        bright new morning to greet you. But I know
        there is no way to go back. So, with me, the
        stress keeps building up more and more until
        something gives. This Fall, it was my health.

                        * * *

Many Jocks feel, as the Teen Queens will tell us, that there is a
fine line between encouragement from well-meaning parents and
teachers, and persuading a girl to persist after her desire fades:

        As a teenage girl, I have had a lot of
        pressure in sports. Not only from my friends
        around me at school, but from my family, and
        especially my coach. I started playing
        soccer as a little first grader, not know-
        ing how I would like it. As years past, it
        became my favorite sport. I was an average
        soccer player, until one coach came into the

picture. He started teaching me skill. A few years later, I was what you called naturally talented in soccer. At age twelve, I had already been on two varsity soccer teams, and made an advanced out-of-school team.

When I finally became a teenager, I started having a social life, with a boyfriend. I was playing an instrument, and trying to keep straight A's. With all this, and soccer, it was too much. My soccer coach wanted me to drop everything else, and just concentrate on soccer. I didn't drop everything but soccer was at the top of my list, along with good grades. I wasn't happy with this decision because it didn't feel like my own. Pressure from my parents and coaches was what made up my mind.

It seemed like everybody was happy about me playing soccer because I was good at it. My love for this sport wasn't, or didn't seem like it was there anymore. I wasn't going to quit soccer because I had a talent for it. I wasn't going to give a talent up that could excel me in life.

My coach always calls me before a tryout to make sure I don't have doubts about going. If I do, he'll put in the right words to make me go. He doesn't make the decision for me, but the pressure is so strong that I feel I have to tryout, or else I won't get a scholarship, and go on with soccer. I don't know if I like it or not. I'm at a point in my life where I feel I have to go along with it, and if I don't, I won't have an alternative for the rest of my life.

People around me think that I love soccer, and I do, but the pressure draws me away from the love for it, and makes me feel as though I'm playing for everybody else, not me. For me to love a sport, I have to be playing for myself, not everybody else.

—Karli Holob, age 13

Coaches can make an indelible impression on a young girl's life, both positively and negatively. Morgan Holbrook, age thirteen, was greatly affected by the behavior of her coach:

> A few years ago I was on a softball team and the coach only picked 3 or 4 girls to pitch and no one else and I even practiced a lot at pitching and showed him, but he didn't care. He just had the girls that he picked pitch no matter what. My friend thought the same way, she and I both thought they weren't very good so I don't think it was very fair. Also, when he was throwing us grounders just because I didn't catch it he started yelling at me and literally told me I sucked and made me feel so bad. That's why I didn't play softball for a year.

Jenny Olson, age fourteen, understands the profound effects a coach can have on a girl's experience in athletics and in life:

> I really enjoy sports, yet at the same time, I find that it pushes my stress level to the max. I think that the area where most of the stress is produced is from the coaches. I personally do like to win, but the most important part of the game is to enjoy it. Some coaches are the win-no-matter-what-it-takes type of coaches. This is very unfortunate because it teaches the players low self-esteem.

Fortunately, there are also those coaches whose encouragement, insight, and support have greatly inspired those on their teams. Seventeen-year-old Shannon Elliot from Pittsburgh, Pennsylvania, has been swimming competitively for thirteen years. The past two years she has been state champion in the 200-yard Freestyle. Last year, she placed second in the 500 Freestyle. Shannon writes of her relationship with her coach:

> Even if he does have insatiable expectations of his swimmers and strenuously trains

them like no other, I would not trade him for
anyone. He helps me learn to make decisions,
handle peer pressure and cope with my personal problems. He handles my uncompromising
moods, my opinionated disposition and my
unwavering stubbornness. Not only does he
tolerate me, but he is making me a better
person. We have our fair share of disagree-
ments and fights, but we also experience
victory and success together. I spend more
time with this person, during the swim
season, than I do with my parents. As I look
at my state medals, framed and hanging on the
wall, they represent Corky Semler, my swim
coach, role model and second father. . . .
  He is able to motivate teenagers through
reason, not fear. He is also able to instill
discipline while having fun. . . . Corky also
teaches me to be fair and not to judge others
too quickly. . . . He has also made me realize
I need to balance work and fun.

* * *

Another pressure that is inherent in sports is the intensity of
competition. It is expected between teams—after all, that's what
makes a game. But Lisa Hope Barclay, age sixteen, from
Brownsville, Oregon, found herself face-to-face with an unusual
circumstance, another sort of competition she was not prepared for:

  . . . I participate in a sport called BMX
(Bicycle Motorcross.) I started BMX at the
early age of 7 in 1985. My nickname at the
track was "Sleeper." I was called this
because I would wait until the last half of
the track to make my move.
  In my early years of racing BMX, I struggled to beat my twin sister, Lori. . . . I had
a hard time racing against my sister all of
the time because she usually won. She is
younger than me but started racing 4 months

earlier than me. The weird thing about this
is at Nationals I would usually beat Lori.
When it came to the pressure, I could handle
it better.

One Saturday my sister and I were racing in
Corvallis Indoor. We both raced for the same
team at this time, so we were more competitive than ever. Going into the main event, I
had first sewn up. To get second, I had to
finish third. The girl in third was very
slow. There was no way I could finish third!
When we were staging up to the gate my
sister, Lori, said that she wished she would
win because she is one of the four on the team
sheet. For our team to get first over all,
she needed to get first. I felt bad (in my
mind I wanted our team to finish first, first
to me was no big deal) . . . and gave up the
race.

Our team got first that night, but got
accused of cheating to get our team to win.
I lied and said that my ankle hurt because of
a crash earlier in the week. One other team
tried to fight us, and I turned on the tears
so they would think that it really hurt. To
this very day you are the only person I have
told this to. It was one of the greatest pressures of my life.

Joan J. Ryoo, an eighteen-year-old Korean-American, is now on
the varsity water polo team at Harvard University. For many years,
she swam competitively, and won, by focusing only on herself:

. . . By the fourth meet of the season, I had
learned the art of seclusion in a crowd, of
separating myself from the clamor and excitement of swim competitions by building walls
so thick and soundproof, only the gun of the
referee could penetrate the woven silence of
my universe. Inside, it was only me and the
race ahead. . . .

However, little did I realize that with all
I gained in erecting psychological parti-

tions, I also lost group support and cut off
the encouragement I could offer my fellow
swimmers, two cherished advantages of participating in team sports. Fortunately, those
artificial barriers—which shut out more than
they let in—were to be broken early on, but
not without the help of a complete stranger.

At one meet, a friendly girl swimming in the lane next to Joan
smiled and reached out to her. Joan relates that the girl's charm and
warmth broke through her barriers of seclusion:

> . . . Even after such a lovely demonstration
> of genuine goodwill, the old and stereotypic
> ideas surrounding athletic competition did
> not fail to surface. This time, though, I
> looked at the principles a little different-
> ly, began to question the validity and value
> of having to always win, win, win, or of
> constantly viewing the opponents as "the
> enemy." For as much as I'm ashamed to say it,
> I'll admit that I blindly accepted those
> notions in concept, though I may not have had
> the guts or natural talent to put those
> "ideals" fully into practice. Of course, it
> was to the strange and wonderful girl next to
> me that I owed this gradual awakening, and
> exhausted though I was at the end of the race,
> I was still quite eager to talk to her. . . .

And they did talk, the girl being particularly complimentary of
Joan's skills, as Joan beat her, though only by a "hair's breadth." It
was unmistakable that this was a turning point in Joan's life, one
that set off a chain reaction of reexamination and transformation of
previous beliefs.

> Everyone deserves a measure of respect and
> trust, and the best way to keep an atmosphere
> of good faith in competition is while we're
> practicing and competing. Thus, all of a
> sudden, I also figured out that I was not
> alone, that I belonged on a team who put

```
sportsmanly ideals into action everyday by
supporting each other, building team cama-
raderie, developing good rapport—all things
which can be extended to the community at
large.
```

I heard from many girls like Joan that teamwork has changed their view of living in the world. The support and camaraderie they experience builds a sturdy foundation for relationships.

```
One learns to support a teammate like a
friend, a sister, a brother. Teammates lean
on one another for support and are always
there to back each other up. They pull
together to achieve a common goal. As a team,
we learned not only skills, but determina-
tion, intensity and desire to succeed. We
played with our bodies, our minds, our hearts
and our souls. We felt that as long as we
stayed together we could conquer the
world. . . . I pity my children because I have
this feeling that I'll talk about my high
school soccer team like old men do war
stories. . . .
```
                                    —*Heather Ehrman*

* * *

Throughout the Jocks' writings, I discovered another attribute that has changed many girls' points of view, like seventeen-year-old Anette Pham, from Colonia, New Jersey:

```
She said that we had to be strong—to assert
ourselves on the court. After all, basketball
is a contact sport and the most successful
team is the team that outhustles the other
team and remains aggressive throughout the
entire thirty-two minutes. Consequently,
being assertive on and off the court is my
key to success.
```

Yet is this quality just another pressure that is imposed on a girl? Fourteen-year-old Ronee Cochrane from Princeton, Idaho, seems to think so:

"BE AGGRESSIVE"

I would describe myself as a tall, quiet A student that is very easy-going and maybe even too nice. "What exactly do you mean?" you might ask. Well, put in more detail, I am a girl that may say "sorry" when she is tripped and just smiles when she is upset. A girl that lets people take advantage of her easy-going nature. . . .

Basketball is a sport that I have played and enjoyed since the fifth grade. I love the thrill of making a point, assisting in a great play, or getting compliments from the crowd, team, or coach. The one thing that I thoroughly hate about basketball is the phrase that I constantly hear: "be aggressive." I hear it from every coach I ever had, the crowd, team, and my family. When I come on and off of the court I hear the coach say, "You've got to get aggressive, get mean. Throw some elbows!" My only response is the nodding of my head and a short "O.K." This is my response on the outside, but in the inside I am shouting wildly, "I'm trying! What exactly do I have to do to fit 'aggressive'? Is there somewhere that I can get a set of instructions?"

The reason that "aggressive" is such a hateful word in my eyes, is because I don't feel that I will ever learn how. I don't believe that I will ever find it in me. I was born to be generous, giving, and nice, not aggressive and mean; not even on the court.

Perhaps the intention behind the idea of being aggressive is to experience one's power and alleviate fear. In Hannah's story, told through her hockey stick, she expands this notion:

> . . . On the outside she seems confident,
> ready, but on the inside she's unsure, terri-
> fied of making a mistake. Then the ball is
> passing the links, passing the halfbacks,
> heading straight for us. The tension is
> mounting, can she handle the pressure? She's
> frozen in place, fear emanating from her
> entire body. Her hands are slippery now. She
> shakes her head slightly, as if to shake off
> the fear, then runs towards the ball, all
> terror gone, because it has to be. We've
> worked too hard for this moment to let that
> little round ball go by. . . .

And coxswain Jessica Smith battles with fear and uncertainty
as well:

> . . . I made some excuse to my friend and
> went up to my room and burst into tears.
> Later that day we were leaving for Boston and
> what was I doing? Crying! Me, tell the big,
> mean rowers what to do? Me, motivate them and
> soothe their fears and tell them there was
> nothing to worry about and smile blithely
> when I was scared shitless? Me, steer us
> around a tricky race course with a number of
> turns, including one at the notorious Weeks
> Bridge where, if navigated incorrectly, one
> could either crash the boat into the bridge
> or run aground because the river made a
> ninety-degree turn? No way!

In the face of fear many girls, like seventeen-year-old Melani
Lowman from Sidney, Montana, push through with determination.
Her story is reminiscent of surfer Kelly who competed in Tahiti,
despite feeling quite sick and having her feet all cut up:

> . . . Having a fractured foot the last part
> of the track season, it was an accomplishment
> in itself to be competing at State. Fighting
> my pain and tears I set a new Montana State

record in the triple jump, but it was recorded as wind-aided (the jump was not my personal best so my goal is to break that record
with my personal best jump.) I also went on
to place in the long jump and the 1600m
relay. Even though I am still suffering from
a fractured bone and the doctors say it was
a mistake to compete, I wouldn't have had it
any other way. For myself it was a great
challenge because I knew I had enough courage
and pride to compete. . . .

* * *

The bravery displayed by the following group of girls is inspiring. Proficient in a variety of sports, these athletes refuse to let anything, including physical disability, stop them.

There are many sports organizations for the disabled. According to NHS (National Handicapped Sports), of the 60,000 who partic-ipate in sports programs, 20 percent are women.

As the recess bell rang, the large doors
burst open with shrieks of delight from the
school children. Children ran to the yellow
diamond in anticipation of the daily kick-
ball game. One by one the children were
picked by the two opposing sides, until only
two girls remained standing on the yellow
line; both wishing to be picked before the
other; but the little girl left over was the
one who had the brace. . . .

That girl was Julie Wolfe from Lafayette, Indiana, who, despite having to wear a brace from the effects of cerebral palsy and still having to endure periodic operations to correct the problems with her right leg, has gone on to become the athlete representative to the board of directors for the United Cerebral Palsy Athletic Association. She broke eight national records, winning eight gold medals, in various swimming events at the 1994 USCPAA National

Championship Games. Julie competed in the 1988 Paralympic
games in Seoul, South Korea, and the '92 Paralympics in
Barcelona.

```
    . . . I had never before realized the inten-
sity required of an Olympic athlete. I began
a rigorous training regimen full of many
challenges. I was training for victory. As
each day passed my focus was to stand on the
gold medal platform and hear the national
anthem as I felt the gold medal being placed
around my neck. Gone were the days of skip-
ping practice to be with my friends; I knew
I had taken on a responsibility—to win a gold
in Seoul for my country. . . . The day before
my trip began, I was surprised by a pep rally
in my honor. The day had finally arrived when
handicapped people were praised, not pitied.
My dreams had come true. . . .
```

Julie had the time of her life in Seoul, signing autographs, being
treated like a star, swimming in the same pool where world record
holders Matt Biondi and Janet Evans had won just two weeks earlier. To the Korean people, Julie was an American hero.

Yet at the last minute, her events were canceled. Paralympic rule
requires that at least four countries be represented in each event,
and in Julie's events, only three countries had competitors. Julie
never had the opportunity even to try to realize her dream of the
gold medal being placed around her neck. She came home disappointed, but not daunted:

```
    I gained the confidence I lost as a child.
I felt whole in Korea. Growing up I felt as
if a part of me was missing. The part that
needed to know if I was good athletically
compared to people with a similar degree of
disability. I had to prove to the world that
I don't have to be picked last. It made me
realize I was special . . . and it is not in a
negative way.
```

Julie finally was able to compete in the 1992 games in Barcelona, and placed sixth, eighth, tenth, and twelfth in various events. She is currently training for the world championships in Malta, and holds two world records: one in the 100 Freestyle and one in the 400 Freestyle.

Growing up with a rare congenital heart defect that nearly killed her, at the age of eleven Danielle Cafferata finally received a heart transplant. Shortly thereafter, due to a degenerative disease that was affecting her eyesight, Danielle lost her vision entirely, as well as a portion of her hearing. She now must wear hearing aids. With courage and determination, Danielle, now eighteen, has only grown stronger, and more accomplished:

> Since my heart transplant and knowing how close I was to not being here at all, I decided to try whatever I can in life. One month after my heart transplant, I competed in the Braille Olympics being able to run for the very first time in my life without getting tired. Since then, I've competed in other track and field events for the blind and visually impaired. . . . Another sport I recently tried was downhill skiing. Wow! What an experience, although I wasn't so sure at first that I would like it. But being the way that I am, I am always willing to give something a try! . . . I hope some of my life story can help other girls who might just be a little afraid of taking a chance to fulfill their dreams. Believe me I'm going to continue to fill mine.

* * *

Beating the odds and overcoming physical and other limitations, striving for and achieving goals, feeling camaraderie and forming friendships through teamwork, and simply experiencing the joy of competing and playing—these are reasons why girls play sports.

And despite the hardships many female athletes endure, it is clear that girls will continue to be "Willing to Dream":

```
The Dream: Conquer and Defeat
My hard work will carry me to my destination
while my determination will fight my battle
when I cry out, "I can't do it!"
I slowly begin to drown in that dreadful word:
                    self-doubt.
But, I must protect what I cherish
So, my hope will act as Superwoman
and throw me a life jacket before I drown.
I desperately grab for it
so I can keep my dream alive.
Whether I win or lose this scary battle
I don't think it really matters
what matters is that I was willing to dream.
```

—Danielle Purfey

And there are those who might not have survived if not for athletics—those who were nurtured and cared for by sports. Kelo R. Le'Igiro, age fifteen, from North Little Rock, Arkansas, is one such girl. Here is an excerpt from her piece "Yes, I've Felt All This":

```
. . . Some say I don't have a lot to be thank-
ful for. All my life people have come and gone
stripping parts of my heart away from me as
they chose new paths. Paths on which I would
not stand. But out of all these memories, all
the hate and unforgiving, all the sadness and
hurt, there was something. Something that
pulled me through each time. Then, I didn't
know exactly what it was or how much it meant
to me. But now I understand, grown up enough I
can grasp the idea.
     It wasn't voluntary. My mom got me started and
everytime made me finish. At first it was only
one lap around lake #3. Only .9 mile once
everyday. Then after a while it was three laps;
2.7 miles everyday. The family would pile in
```

the car, go to the lake and run, everyday. Some
faster than others, some even walking, but it
always got done. Everyday until my older brother, Brandon, moved out. Meredith and Brent quit
but I ran even more. It was because Brandon had
been accused of selling and using drugs.
Misunderstandings and anger were plentiful in
my thoughts.
Yes, I've felt all this.
I ran for help concentrating, trying to understand. I was too young, I didn't know. Mom and
I ran. We ran and ran. That was the only thing
we could do to escape: run and pretend it never
happened or was not happening. Mom understood,
but I couldn't. Brandon was my big brother, the
guy I was supposed to try to make myself be
like. I was supposed to grow into his life with
admiration, respect and adoration. Trying to
understand, I ran more. I ran my first half
marathon the day after I turned twelve in 2
hours and twenty minutes. Of course Mom ran with
me. Victory, accomplishment, relief.
Yes, I've felt all this. . . .

Kelo's challenges continued as her sister, whom she adored,
walked out, never to return. She describes her sister: "When my
siblings fought in such rages, she would hide me away under the
sink to protect me from their fury. She was my hiding place, my
first and last resort, my childhood Jesus."

Once again, running was an essential element in Kelo's finding
escape and solace.

. . . All my life I've turned to writing, to
running and to God to solve everything. Writing
changed my world to the way I wanted it,
running relieved me from my deepest pressures,
and God moved it all out of my way so I could
achieve my highest goals, to be all I could be.
Happiness, despair, victory, loss, fulfillment, emptiness, and the breath of God across
my face.
Yes, I have felt all this.

KRYSTLE MORTIMORE

ASHLEY TENDICK

BAY AREA METEORITES

Part Four

Insîders

"Sister" means so many things and
all of them are special.
For "sister" is the one who will always
care.... She's someone who is
a treasured part of all your
memories

Who's there each time you have something
to share.

She's someone who knows what you
need without your ever asking,
Who's there each time you reach out
for her hand.

"Sister" means so many things...
compassion and support,

And a bond of closeness
that will never end.
Someone who will share your dreams
and challenges alike,

But most important "sister" means

GOOD FRIEND.

Alpha Phi ♡ and mine,

ANONYMOUS

CHAPTER ELEVEN

Sorority Girls

They're secret societies. Rituals and ceremonies are held behind closed doors. Rush week, hell week, pledging and initiations—not to be spoken of, never to be written about, lest some trace, some proof, be caught on paper forever.

They're called sororities.

I found very few sorority girls willing to write about their experiences; those that did made sure they didn't reveal too much.

> Being in a sorority, I have found most of all that true friendship is based on sharing secrets. For two years, I have shared the secrets of Sigma Kappa with my sorority members only.

Kara Kocal is a tall, dark-haired young woman with a strong sense of herself. In a room full of girls, she stands out, leaving an impression of confidence and warmth. Kara, like the handful of others who were willing to express themselves, shares her feelings on the "Greek System," and in the process, seeks to dispel some of the stereotypes that are often connected to sorority girls:

> ...Some see sorority girls as giggly airheads who have no idea about anything other than clothes, matching ribbons for

```
their hair, and which fraternity has the best
looking members. This image is false. In my
house alone we have girls majoring in Nuclear
Engineering, Mechanical Engineering, Pre Med,
Pre Law, Computer Science, and many other
supposedly "difficult" majors. Being in a
sorority does not make you an instantaneous
airhead. . . .
```

In the next breath, Kara points out that "all work and no play makes a very dull lady." Sororities provide quite an opportunity to play—and, most importantly, close friends to play with.

Almost every sorority girl I heard from mentioned the significant bonds they have formed with their sisters.

```
I came here as an only child. Now I have 80
sisters.
```

—Jennifer Thuma

Jennifer, "pledge educator" of the Beta Chi Chapter of Sigma Kappa at the University of California at Santa Barbara, is an energetic young woman. Generous, supportive, a friend to all, she's quite intelligent and has to juggle her active sorority life with three jobs. To maintain her high grade-point average, there's also schoolwork:

```
I have always been the type of person to get
involved. I can't just go to class and be
happy. Also, being at a large university,
it's easy to get lost in the crowd. Joining
the Greek System allowed me to get involved
in a smaller community within the universi-
ty. . . .
    While in Sigma Kappa, I hope to be able to
give back half of what it has given me. It is
a wonderful feeling to be there for a sister
when she really needs someone to listen and
vent with her. The support system that we
have in Sigma Kappa is stronger than I ever
```

thought it could be. Sisterhood is probably the greatest part of being in a sorority. Through Sigma Kappa, as well as the Greek community as a whole, I have found <u>true</u> friends that will last forever, and I wouldn't trade my sorority experiences in for anything.

Kara agrees:

The bond between women is the most powerful, intoxicating element a friendship can possess. For who like better than women to sit for hours and gossip, share secrets, and receive support from your closest friends? Topics inevitably are about boys (only called "men" when they are behaving), sex, lack of sex, who went out with who last weekend, and the stress of who you will take to the next date party. . . .

The best part about sorority life is the friendships that are created when you live with thirty of your sisters. As ghastly as this may sound, it has been one of the best experiences of my life. I love these girls. Where else would I have thirty other wardrobes to choose from? There is always someone willing to go somewhere with you, whether it's down the street for yogurt or to LA to pick up some shoes that are necessary for that week's social function. We laugh together until our stomachs hurt and tears pour down our faces. We cry to each other because we know we are loved and will be understood. We drink beer together and go to the beach together. We visit the elderly and we take road trips. We share shampoo, and we share secrets. Patience, love, and understanding are abound in this house. We share a bond deeper than friendship: it's that of sisterhood.

In an anonymous poem from an Alpha Phi sorority member, the bond is further described:

```
          "Sister" means so many things and
             all of them are special.
        For "sister" is the one who will always
            care . . . she's someone who is
         a treasured part of all your memories,
        Who's there each time you have something
                      to share.
           She's someone who knows what you
             need without your ever asking,
          Who's there each time you reach out
                    for her hand.
          "Sister" means so many things . . .
              compassion and support,
             And a bond of closeness
                that will never end,
         someone who will share your dreams
              and challenges alike,
         But most important "sister" means
                   GOOD FRIEND.
```

Karin Daugherty turns to her sisterhood to calm self-doubts, and discovers herself in the process:

```
        . . . I'm sure many women suffer from the
      same ailment I do, not enough control of
      their emotions. It's very hard getting along
      in a world run by men when my emotions keep
      getting in the way. I suppose this is part of
      being a woman, and don't get me wrong, I love
      being a woman but sometimes long to be calm
      in tense situations.
        The comfort of other women always helps me
      to understand my own self and women as a
      whole. This is probably the main reason that
      I went through sorority Rush. . . .
```

The process of selecting, and then being accepted into, a sorority is called rush week. Hosted by the Panhellenic Society, the governing body of the entire sorority system, rush week begins with a rushee looking at all the sorority houses and meeting the members. She surveys them, and they evaluate her. Since there's only a short time to visit, first impressions are essential. A sorority usually looks for a girl with an outgoing personality, so shy girls can be at a disadvantage.

After two days of that process, the rushee then visits with the houses that invite her back. As the week progresses, both the sororities and the rushees narrow down their choices. There are then theme parties, which last longer and become more formal each night. These parties are the time for a sorority to "sell themselves" to the rushee. The rushee observes as the house acts out themes with costumes, decorations, skits, slide shows, etc. Themes include Dr. Seuss (where they speak only in rhyme), English Tea Party, and the very popular cartoon themes, including Aladdin and Cinderella. A rushee visits her top two houses on the last night and, finally, a decision is made.

Once a girl is chosen, and she accepts, she officially becomes a pledge. There is a pledge period, which can last from one and a half to three months. In this time, the pledge must learn the history of the sorority and attend only informal meetings—no rituals yet. Finally, after passing tests and proving she's ready, the pledge attends an initiation ceremony where she finally learns the sorority's secret rituals.

> I didn't understand what a sorority was before I rushed, and I still cannot exactly describe it. All of my good friends are in the sorority. I think we have a bond beyond the realms of friendship. I feel almost connected to many of these women. We attend meetings together, live together, attend sports events together, comfort each other. I know all of the sororities on this campus are not the same as ours. When I went through rush, I could sense that this is a place where I won't feel any pressure, there won't be any competition, and I could find true friendship.
>
> *—Karin Daugherty*

Karin is not the only one who thinks her sorority is different from others. Piper Appleby is in the Gamma Iota Chapter of Alpha Phi at Texas Tech University:

> When I pledged Alpha Phi, I wasn't sure what
> to expect and where I'd fit in. I was just a
> lonely freshman who spent her time between
> being homesick and lost between classes. Over
> time, my sisters at Alpha Phi showed me that
> they loved and supported me <u>no matter what</u>
> and that I could be myself—not fake and
> "showy" like most sororities. In Alpha Phi,
> we are all different individuals, yet we
> share a common bond—sisterhood!

When her sisters selected Piper to represent them in the Miss Fall Rush Pageant (held by Delta Sigma Phi to raise money for the March of Dimes), she felt their love, pride, and support.

She won, and the experience made her realize that "a sorority is not just fraternity parties and candlelight ceremonies, it is my 'home away from home'—somewhere I can always get love and support. I love my Alpha Phi sisters—each and every one—and am so blessed to have them in my life."

The "home away from home" feeling is shared by many. Alpha Kappa Alpha sorority member Tabitha Brogden is her chapter's (Eta Zeta Omega) 1992–93 Miss Cotillion, at Morris College in Sumter, South Carolina.

For Tabitha, her sorority has provided a family—literally. She is a foster child who has been taken care of by the mother of another chapter member.

While in high school, Tabitha wrote a poem that shows her inner state at the time. Though it ends with a sense of hope, it is filled with the pain of a young woman, "Alone":

> Left alone in this world
> Searching for a peace of mind.
> Comparing my life to the "other girls"
> While trying to leave the past behind.
>
> I've questioned why things are how they are;
> I've wondered why I feel so sad,
> And each night I pray upon a star
> For God to restore the happiness I once had.

```
      Bearing the hurt that I feel
   With teary eyes I try to move on,
 Telling myself that the pain isn't real;
   With hope, I face another dawn.

And as the sun rises to begin another day,
Like the dark night my problems fade away.
```

Tabitha's prayers were soon answered. Now that she belongs to a family, both at home as well as in the sorority, her writing takes on a new feel, one of pride and strength. Describing her poem "AN 'ALPHA KAPPA ALPHA' DEBUTANTE Means: 'Sprout, and Grow!,'" she writes:

```
Being an Alpha Kappa Alpha Debutante has
meant a lot to me as a growing college
student. It has given me fifteen characteris-
tics that have assisted me in becoming an
intelligent,   determined,   African-American
woman!
```

```
           I became an Aspirer,
     Able to rise, meet and tower my dreams.
           I became a Listener,
     Able to cooperate, and be a part of teams.

           I was always Prepared
     To accept the challenges of life.
           I was always a Helper,
     Assisting someone through their strifes.

 "Aspirer, Listener, Prepared to be a Helper:"
       An Alpha Kappa Alpha Debutante
           Means being an "Advisor."

        It means being Kindhearted
          To everyone around you
           It means being Able
     To be responsible for what you do.

       It means acting like a Princess,
     Even when you feel your worst.
```

It means to always "keep the Peace"
Even when you don't come in first.

"Kindhearted and Able to be a Princess of Peace:"
An Alpha Kappa Alpha Debutante
Is "Angelic" to say the least!

Some call me an Antagonist,
Because I strive for what is right.
Some call me a Leader,
Because I chief the "good fight."

Some call me a Proclaimer.
They hear my voice, and take heed.
But others call me Headstrong,
Because I seldom follow—but lead.

Well, I'll be that "Antagonistic Leader who's a
Proclaimer that's Headstrong:"
For I'm the seed of an Alpha Kappa Alpha Debutante
Again I'll sprout, and grow!!

* * *

One of the sisters of Julee Gordon, the vice president of the Sigma Kappa house at the University of California at Santa Barbara, describes her as "an incredibly organized person who gets things done." Like the fifteen characteristics of being in a sorority that have enriched Tabitha's life, Julee has a list of reasons why she is in a sorority. Along with "friends for life," Julee writes:

1. Leadership opportunities
2. The chance to dress up for formals and theme parties. At college you don't have many opportunities, especially in UCSB, so it's something to look forward to.
3. A base—a place where when you walk through the doors you have 100 friends & a place where you will always feel welcome.
4. I like the opportunity of experiencing living in a sorority house—

```
      —late night chats
      —borrowing everyone's clothes
      —Always someone to go out w/ or talk to
      —family style dinners
   5. There is a lot of support.
```

Not included in Julee's list is another sorority "plus" some of the girls mentioned: the community service they all participate in. Each house works for an individual "philanthropy." Julee's sorority's philanthropic interests are gerontology and Alzheimer's. The girls not only visit seniors in nursing homes, they also put on fund-raising events, giving the proceeds to their cause.

Albeit few, Julee openly admits some "bad points" about sorority life:

```
      1. Competitive—even though we may not like
      to admit it
            —body          —to be popular
            —elections     —how much to drink
```

Jennifer Thuma also refers to drinking in her writing:

```
      When I mention the fact that I am in a
      sorority, people automatically put a label on
      me and think they know exactly what kind of
      person I am. The reason I joined a sorority
      was not to "buy me friends," or acquire a set
      of "drinking buddies."
```

Jennifer shares how she had plenty of friends before she decided to join, and since she attends a university known for its parties, she didn't need a sorority to find people to drink with:

```
      . . . Yeah, we party and do crazy things, but
      that's all part of being in college—not just
      the Greek System.
```

Although it is an old stereotype that fraternities and sororities support, or even encourage, heavy drinking, it is a legitimate concern. Through the years, many members have died from excessive alcohol intake. As a result, tough laws and rules have been imposed. By 1986, some eighteen states had passed laws forbidding "hazing," a dangerous and demeaning ritual where pledges are forced to prove themselves "worthy" of becoming a member, which usually involves alcohol. On some campuses the time of hazing, once known as "hell week," is now called "inspiration week."

Due to increased liability, parties at the Greek houses may no longer supply liquor, like the kegs and shots of the past. What were once called "happy hour" parties are now alcohol-free and referred to as "mixers."

Sororities often socialize with fraternities through these mixers, as well as "theme" parties, "exchange" parties, and "TG's" (shortened from TGIF, Thank God It's Friday). They also participate in traditional rivalries: "serenading" (a mock courting ritual where girls sing to a fraternity house and vice versa), "composite stealing" (sneaking into a house and taking the large, framed piece that contains pictures of all the members, then holding it for ransom), and "stenciling" (where houses spray-paint their letters on another house's sidewalk—this act is now virtually banned, due to vandalism laws, but every so often still occurs).

Date rape is a crime certainly not limited to, but unfortunately often prevalent on, college campuses. In 1986, Neil Malamuth, a researcher from UCLA, conducted a survey and found that 30 percent of college men said they'd commit rape if they were certain they'd get away with it. When the word *rape* was replaced with *force a woman into having sex*, a shocking 58 percent said they would do so.

In an untitled piece from a trilogy of poems, Kara depicts the terror and powerlessness a girl can feel through this kind of violation:

```
        Although you cannot feel me
        I am always there
        With you, in you, on you
        For your beauty is so fair.
        I watch you from behind the trees
```

As you walk on home
My arms long to feel you
Possess you as my own.

The night is drawing nearer now
The light is dwindling fast
You better hope that your good luck
Will forever last.
Because once I get a hold of you
Press your porcelain face to mine
You will become one with me
I am the Creator, the Divine

Although your eyes allude me
I can see it in your walk
You want me to take you
Keep you with key and lock
So come with me, already mine
The night is hurrying on
I leap out from behind the trees
And grasp my startled pawn.

You start to fight and begin to cry
You twist and turn to free
But don't you know, you stupid bitch
That you belong to me?
With a hand over your mouth
I pull you to the alley
Where the mice scurry about
Here's one more for the tally.

Your screams are drowned out by my tongue
Your limbs held down by mine
You know so much you want this
Why else dress so fine?
You are all mine now
Every move I make
I can tell by your screams of pain
It's your virginity I take.

I leave you in the alley
Your clothes all torn to shreds
Your underwear, though, I will keep
So my ego will be fed

```
You know you want to fuck me
Why'd you deny it for so long?
Walking home the same old route
I knew it wasn't wrong.

All along you send signals
You're young and pretty and sweet
Putting my hand over your mouth
I can feel your breath's heat.
It's women like you
Who make me itch
Why do you call it rape?
You know you wanted it, bitch.
```

And in the next untitled poem, Kara writes about dealing with the subsequent damage:

```
You can't wash off your beauty
By washing off your face
You can't go to a magician
To have your soul replaced.
You can't hide from the flash
That rapes you in the room
You can't expect your trusting smile
To return anytime soon.
You can't expect to shake
The shadow that follows you around
You can't lose the fear
That keeps your senses bound.
You can't expect the world to stop
For you and your choking pain
You can't wash all your troubles away
With a little autumn rain.
You can't expect them to understand
For they will never know
You can't expect them to sympathize
With the pain that your eyes show.
You can't expect to hide
From the demon living within
You can't hide behind the armor
Made for you from tin.
```

What you can expect is the lump in your throat
To shrink as days go past
And for your perfect memory
To falter and forget—fast.

Kara's third poem was written for her boyfriend. It reveals a newfound glimmer of trust. Kara is finally feeling safe enough to explore passionate feelings again:

TO THE MAN I LOVE WITH THE PASSION
OF THE SKY

Like Zeus, you stand before me
Green eyes the color of a dyed egg
Easter egg, wet with dew
From being laid in the roses
The night before.

Your smile, too much for words
Too wonderful to look at
Much like the sun
It shows the joy, the love, the knowledge
That you, O Prophet, possess.

Your chest puts David to shame
Were that I worthy enough
To press my mouth to it
To gaze up at you
From my position of reverence.

O Cathedral!
O Eiffel Tower!
To me you are the summit
Of wondrous black bottom night
Like cake.

Words of spun candy
Pour from your lips
Like shooting stars
Te amo, mi amor
Para siempre, mi corazon es tuyo.

* * *

And perhaps a part of healing comes from the power of a collective that has a common purpose. Certainly, this is a recurring theme amongst Riot Grrrls, and is evident in the tribal community of Native American girls. It is obvious how important it is for girls to feel a sense of belonging, receiving love and support from those they've aligned themselves with.

These connections and relationships empower girls to move into their future with confidence and pride. Karin writes:

> My sorority helps its members to feel as if they can make a contribution. You can serve the sorority in an executive or cabinet position and gain experience while guiding your sorority.
>
> One of the girls in our house is abroad in England. She says that it is difficult to describe Greek life to those in England. I too find it hard to describe to anyone who hasn't had experience with it, but my sorority is something that has enriched my life greatly and has helped me to become the woman I am.

And thanks to her sisters, Jennifer Thuma also has seen positive changes in herself:

> I have been able to challenge myself and grow as a person during my two years in Sigma Kappa. If I decide to put myself out on a limb and present new ideas, I know that no one in my house will judge me or shoot me down. I have recently been elected to the position of pledge educator which is probably one of my greatest challenges. I have yet to know what is in store for me, but I do know that when things get tough—all of my sisters will be there to support me and push me to do my best.

Jennifer Beck is a dedicated Sigma Kappa member and friend:

> Being a sorority girl is anything <u>but</u> being a girl: I have learned <u>here</u>, through my sorority, that I am a woman. My confidence has grown so much over the last 2 years that I have been a Sigma Kappa. My friends from high school even remarked about my higher level of self-esteem. One friend in particular, Leon, said "Jenny, you are <u>not</u> the same person I knew in high school."
>
> In fact, I am the same person, but better. I have learned my strengths: strong leadership capabilities, listening and empathy skills, an ability to think quickly and rationally on my feet, even strong organizing abilities. It is because of this sorority that I have learned these strengths. When we see wonderful traits in our sisters, we tell them!
>
> A recent example of Sigma Kappa's confidence in my leadership skills was my recent election as President for the 1994–1995 school year. Had I never joined, I may never have had the opportunity to find these qualities in myself. This is truly the one place I can depend upon for complete support, love and understanding. In fact, it is <u>here</u> that we are "really ourselves," as one sister, Beth, said once.

Jennifer describes a personal revelation she had recently. She was baby-sitting a one-year-old baby and a five-year-old child, and as she put them to bed, reading them a story, the youngest snuggled up close to her and fell asleep. The five-year-old grabbed her hand and asked her to stay, even though the child was rolling over and closing her eyes. She assured Jennifer she was still listening to the story, as she held her hand tightly, cuddled up close, then fell asleep.

Having such small children depend on me that
way hit me as being so incredible. It was so
innocent, pure and trusting to fall asleep
with a sitter that way. That they fell asleep
in my arms still moves me. Especially lately,
I have felt that marriage and children would
never be a part of my life. I have seen myself
as not "nurturing" or patient enough for
children. Yet it was something that has
always made me sad. I only wanted to take
care of myself—not children who I could "mess
up."

Later, when I was telling this to my
sisters, I said, "For the first time I felt
that I might really be a good mother—I might
really be <u>needed</u>, after all."

One of my sisters said, "Jenny, you <u>are</u>
needed. Now. Of course you'll be needed in
the future."

And perhaps sororities will be needed in the future as well.
Although the internal issues for girls have remained constant
through the years, the outer challenges change. Sororities, like their
members, seem to be evolving to reflect the concerns of each generation.

JENNIFER THUMA

SIGMA KAPPA SORORITY GIRLS

FHA—

Since you asked specifely for FHA experiences, I can tell you only positive things about this program.

FHA has given me so many opportunities with my writing. My wonderful Home Ec teacher, Mary Ann Hanson, has sent my poems to the two FHA magazines and newspaper. All of whom have published them. I am also given the chance to use Search/Star to give speeches on topics concerning me.

FHA gives young people the chance to change things that frustrate you about society. It gives you a voice. I feel FHA deals with important issues, like the need for multicultural education. It also is not just for girls anymore. It's now including boys in a big way, which I think is good because women alone do not make a home.

FHA is one of the best programs I've been involved in and I'm proud to be an officer in my chapter. The experiences I've had in FHA will really help me in the future I have planned. It teaches values to carry with you in life. (Ginger Lewis)

CHAPTER TWELVE

Homemakers

"A woman's place is in the home and her work is never done," has been the cry of past generations, handed down with family recipes and child-rearing tips.

Current generations are finding themselves caught somewhere between these old notions and the more recent dramatic, and necessary, increase of women in the work force.

There are, however, females who, at an early age, feel it is their calling to be, first and foremost, a wife and mother.

Evidence of this is the fact that there have been over 8 million youth involved with Future Homemakers of America since its founding in 1945.

As described on their information sheet, FHA/HERO (Home Economics Related Occupations was added in 1971) is a "nonprofit national vocational student organization for young men and women in home economics in public and private schools through grade 12."

This might conjure up images of girls learning how to get rid of waxy yellow buildup on their kitchen floors, how to bake cakes rivaling Betty Crocker's, the best way to pack a child's lunch box, and tips on ironing their husband's shirt; while the boys' participation may seem a bit more enigmatic.

Actually, as the Homemakers who wrote indicated, the organization encourages leadership, community service, and the development of life skills for the workplace as well as at home—including planning, goal setting, and problem solving.

Ginger Lewis is a sophomore at a high school in the small town of Doniphan, Nebraska (population 1,000). She gives some idea of what the organization offers:

> FHA gives young people the chance to change things that frustrate you about society. It gives you a voice. I feel FHA deals with important issues, like the need for multicultural education. It also is not just for girls anymore. It is now including boys in a big way, which I think is good because women alone do not make a home.

As the definitions of "home" are changing in our society now that dual incomes are more the norm and what we know as traditional family structures are becoming more alternative, FHA is also exhibiting signs of new thought. As Ginger points out, it "now includes boys."

Although the organization was always open to males, in the early days their involvement was minimal. FHA/HERO now boasts a comparatively high 16 percent male membership.

Still, as much as boys are involved, taking on new roles in the home, many of the girls who wrote feel that there is still a majority of boys who see things in a more "traditional" manner.

A fourteen-year-old girl from Bettsville, Ohio, who is involved with Home Economics, because "it teaches you how to do things on your own" and "gives you a head start in society" prefers to remain anonymous as she writes about the opposite sex:

> It's hard being a girl in this world. Some men think women are so easy. They try to pressure women into doing things they don't want to do. So men also expect you to do everything (housework, cooking, etc.)....A man should help the wife and not believe that a job is just for a man or a woman.

* * *

"Music is my lifeline," declares seventeen-year-old Angie Pearman, an exuberant young woman who lives in the tiny town of Arnold, Nebraska (population 679). In describing herself further, she writes: "I don't have a clue what I'm going to do with the rest of my life—I've considered everything. Right now, it's either business management, criminal law, or astronomy. I also like to go to heavy metal concerts, when I get the chance."

However "clueless" Angie feels about her future life, participating in FHA seems to have provided some valuable leads to solving this mystery:

> Throughout the last four years, FHA/HERO has proven to be a very fun and educational experience for me. I have helped plan or have chaired the annual turtle races, Sweethearts dance, and float for the Fall Festival parade. I have seen the buddy system in action, pairing underprivileged children with high school buddies. I have participated in STAR/SEARCH, educating people about various concerns, and learning many things from watching other presentations. I have completed five Power of One modules that have been a boost to my confidence, as well as contributing to personal growth. These are just a few examples of the many, many projects and opportunities that FHA/HERO offers.

Angie has served as vice president in her district and was chosen to represent that district as a state officer candidate. She attended a Cluster meeting in Omaha where she found value in social issue sessions, which educated teens on various concerns including teen pregnancy, AIDS, and drug abuse. After that, Angie prepared for the State Leadership Conference:

> Obtaining a position on the FHA/HERO State Executive Council had been a goal of mine for three years. I knew that I must work hard to

> merit such an honor. I began studying FHA/HERO
> facts, such as membership, history, purposes
> and programs. . . . I studied public speaking
> skills, practiced quick thinking and public
> relations strategies, and sharpened my lead-
> ership skills by executing my duties as
> Chapter President. I finally felt that I was
> ready for the big Conference.

The first step was taking a written test. Shortly after, Angie was
grateful to see her name on the list of finalists.

> The next morning consisted of the general
> opening session. A few moments before the
> session began, I was given a dustpan and
> broom, and I was told to go onstage and tell
> four thousand people how those objects relat-
> ed to FHA/HERO. The adrenaline of nervous
> excitement brought the words to mind and
> helped me get through it.

Angie passed the next several steps: giving a prepared speech,
answering four impromptu questions posed by the voting delegates,
and being "interrogated" by a panel of advisers, members of the
existing State Executive Council, and members of the Adult
Advisory Board. Finally, after waiting an "extremely nerve-wrack-
ing" twenty-four hours, there was the moment of truth, the instal-
lation ceremony:

> As I heard them start to announce the new
> state officers, my hands started shaking, my
> palms got sweaty, and my heart was thumping
> loudly in my chest. Finally, the moment came.
> "The new Region D Vice President is . . . Angie
> Pearman." A feeling of relief and joy flood-
> ed over me as I could feel the tears of happi-
> ness start to fall. My dream had come true!

Being chosen for office not only gave Angie the excitement and
fulfillment of her wishes, but also provided many growth opportu-

nities through extensive leadership training, traveling, and the formation of strong alliances with like-minded friends. What emerged was a more confident, self-assured young woman:

> FHA/HERO has been the source of many outstanding events in my life. The organization has provided me with countless opportunities to make use of my full potential, and it has encouraged me to do all that I can. For that I am grateful. I am honored to hold such a prominent position, and I will continue to work hard to show it justice. I want to give back to FHA/HERO as it has offered to me.

* * *

It is not only the organization and their events that support a young woman's desire to be a "Future Homemaker." There are some who simply enjoy home economics, like Kate Hill, age thirteen, from San Luis Obispo, California.

Kate describes herself as being into "regular teen stuff. Friends, fun, and boys. (Well, I don't have a boyfriend, but crushes are perfectly safe, I mean, there's boys everywhere I look, why not?) My fave food is chicken and red is the color for me." She continues:

> When I took Home Ec., I really enjoyed it. I then joined FHA-HERO Club at my school which is like the Home Ec. club. . . . We help the community, hold fundraisers, and get together with other school chapters around the nation and discuss what the club is all about. We also have FUN! I think becoming a homemaker is just part of life! Even if you're a college student living in a dorm. If you're ready to live right, then learn how to start a family and/or just keep your life & house organized. I think a man's role in the house is equal to the woman's role, basically. (Except producing the kids and carrying them around for 9 months, of course!) They should all share the cooking, cleaning, ect. and be

```
helpful with anything that needs to be done! When I get
married, I'll look for love, care, and willingness to
help with anything!
     I'm happy I'm here to enjoy life . . . and Home Ec.!!!!!
```

Eighteen-year-old Cindy Bowerman has been named sophomore of the year, junior of the year, and outstanding senior at her high school in Cloverdale, California, because of her achievements through FHA/HERO. She has contributed her time and efforts to many community service activities such as public awareness projects on abusive relationships and date rape, as well as global warming and its effects. She is very involved with helping educate students, from kindergarten through seventh grade, and will be going to the University of California at Santa Barbara to major in chemical engineering not only because of her love for mathematics and chemistry, but also because "not many women are in it."

Like other future Homemakers, as well as most girls today, Cindy has concerns about the world:

```
          The river flowing by, clouds in the sky.
          A peaceful day to just get away.
          I think to myself, why?
          Why is this world in such unrest?
          Innocent people being put to death,
          and people afraid to go out after dark.
          Why won't someone take the step to
          end all this violence?
          To gain what we want, we need to give.
          We, as teens, need to give of ourselves.
          If we show the public we care about
          peace, then maybe they will care.
          What this world needs is a river of
          people who really care, and peace, all
          mixed together.
```

Cindy comes from a family with a strong foundation. Their love and support, as well as her faith, contribute to who she is:

```
          I am proud to say that I am a Christian who
          has Christian friends that truly care. . . .
```

I have been blessed by being in a wonderful church who see their youth as the future leaders, the future generation. The church has shown me that 1 Timothy 4:12 is true, which says: "Do not let ANYONE look down on you because you are young, but set an example for the believers in speech, in life, in love, and in purity." Some people say that teenage years are their worst time in their life, I really don't think this is true. My teenage years have been a true blessing. The Lord has shown me how to live my life in order to glorify Him and others. My love for the Lord is so strong that I have felt the need to fulfill a call He has laid on my life. I have chosen to be a missionary this summer in the state of California. I feel that this will lead me to a greater understanding of my love for Christ and it will also prepare me for college, and my life on my own.

My testimony is that I have not been burdened by the temptations of youth. I have been able to "flee the evil desires of youth" because of my Christian friends and faith in the Lord. My teenage years have not hindered my faith, but enhanced it. I have fought the good fight as a teenager, and am now pressing on to new experiences. The Lord will lead and guide me in the right direction, just like He always has.

* * *

A poet in combat boots. An ex-drug user who listens to Pearl Jam. Strong in her opinions, and stubborn in her beliefs, a Future Homemaker of America? You bet. Meet Ginger Lewis:

. . . I'm into some different things than a lot of people here, like the music I listen to and the way I dress. I listen to Pearl Jam and Alice in Chains, but I also like country music because a lot of it really says something. I own combat boots and cowboy boots,

wranglers and flannels. It just all depends
on what I feel like that day.
I'm also different from most people here
because I'm drug-free and extremely proud of
it. I haven't always been, but I made a
choice three years ago to be and have stuck
to it.
I got into writing poetry when I was about
11 years old. It is my way of venting anger,
frustration, happiness or sadness. It's my
release! Poetry is my way of expressing what
I think is wrong with society, what I think
about certain issues, and maybe just to give
my opinion. Which is often, according to my
friends. I'm a rather opinionated person. If
I feel strongly about something, I will stick
to it.

And Ginger does feel strongly about many issues: drugs is one
major concern, considering her past experience with them; another
is racism. She writes: "Prejudice is ignorance.... Racism is the
most idiotic concept I can think of. It's based on the pigmentation
of your skin and I believe it to be absurd."

Another matter that is vital to Ginger is AIDS prevention. Her
poem "Mistake," written about a girl who got AIDS after a one-
night stand when she was drunk, has been printed in the national
FHA magazine *Teen Times*. Ginger believes:

. . . education and being aware are the only
keys to prevention. A lot of my friends could
very easily end up with AIDS even though they
do not realize it. They think you can't get
AIDS in Doniphan, NE, but they're wrong.
"Mistake" is a blunt "wake-up" call to anyone
who believes AIDS can't affect them.

Today or tomorrow, I'll never know
The hands on the clocks run so slow

I lie here thinking, "Why, why me?"
I just don't understand how this can be.

```
One stupid, unloving night
And now for my life, I have to fight

Thinking of this fatal mistake I've made
All of the good times seem to fade

I long to turn back the hands of time
But the choice I made was all mine

I weep alone for the future that I've lost
Before doing the same, look at the cost.
```

As Ginger uses writing to express her opinions and release and vent her feelings, FHA/HERO has given her an audience for her speeches and her poems.

Cindy, the Christian girl from Cloverdale, also believes that the opportunities and support FHA has given her have changed her life:

```
I have never really been encouraged about
my writing until this year, and only because
of FHA-HERO. My teachers, except one in third
grade, did not take a liking to my writing.
I never thought that I was a "good" writer.
But, because of Alisha Montecalvo (the
National FHA-HERO person in charge of a
national magazine) I have found a new mean-
ing in my writing. My high school teachers
seemed to not be impressed with anything that
I wrote. I rarely got an "A" on any essays.
This proves that anything you do can effect
someone else. . . .
```

The writing that Cindy judged negatively, because others "didn't take a liking" to it, was, like Ginger's, published in the national FHA/HERO magazine. She describes further gains:

```
I was a shy, introverted girl lacking self-
confidence when I joined and now I am an
extroverted young woman with enough self-
esteem to share with others. (No, I am not
```

big headed!) . . . If someone would have told
me when I was a shy, little freshman that I
would be a region officer, a chapter president, a state officer, talk in front of one
thousand teens, compete at state and national level, and talk in front of numerous
service clubs, I would have thought them to
be crazy. I had virtually no self-confidence,
at least not enough to stand up and do public
speaking. Through FHA-HERO I have gained
numerous leadership capabilities that I will
take with me throughout my life.

* * *

Seventeen-year-old Janna Paschal, national vice president of
membership at New Hampton School in Meredith, New Hampshire,
describes the transformation in her life due to the impact of her
homemaking involvement:

I wish I could tell every young person in
this country how important the Future
Homemakers of America have been to me. I want
to tell you about the "Janna of old." I want
to tell you about some of the things I went
through growing up in New Hampshire. My
family is the only black family in town. My
first day at school was not only memorable,
it instilled a fighting spirit in me. I
remember going to buy my special lunchbox, my
new clothes, and my other school supplies. My
mom had spent hours doing my hair. My parents
took me to the bus. I was so excited as I
waved good-bye to my parents. I felt sure
that everyone would love me. Everyone always
had! I still remember at the end of the school
day, a day I had awaited eagerly, my mom
picking me up. She hugged me and said, "How
did my big girl like her first day at
school?" I tried to smile, through trembling
lips, I tried to say it was fine. Instead, I
burst into tears. My mom hugged me and said

"let's talk." As she led me to the car, I
thought she'll never make me come back here
again! We went out to have a hamburger. I told
how I had been spit on by high school boys on
the bus. I told her how they had said they
didn't need a little "nigger." Her eyes
filled with tears and she said that is terrible. Then she did the most amazing thing, she
said "never forget today, it will be your
strength." She said that she and my dad would
take care of the bus, I had to take care of
me. I had to be the best!

The next morning, Janna's parents got on the school bus with her,
and her father told all the students that if there was any more of that
kind of behavior, they would have to deal with him personally.

Janna basically grew up around FHA/HERO; her mother was an
adviser and she'd accompany her to every meeting. "I'm sure that
the term 'FHA brat' applied to me," she writes.

But it was one particular Cluster meeting that had a profound
effect on Janna's life. She felt "sort of adopted" by the Maryland
state president:

He was a black guy who spent time telling
me what all I could accomplish. He probably
doesn't remember me, but I'll never forget
him. He took time out to talk to me and in
the process helped me to stay on the right
path.

FHA has helped me find my strength. I
believe that if we could give every young
person a shot of self-esteem, many of our
nations problems would be solved. I believe
that is exactly what FHA can do, give a shot
of self-confidence.

I ran for state junior high vice president
as a seventh grader. I found I loved running
and especially winning. I also ran for vice
president of my junior high student council.
I would never have attempted it without my
FHA experience.

Janna found that "the more I dared to dream dreams of success, the more successful I became." She competed in speech contests, became varsity cheerleader, then a varsity basketball player. She's the president-elect for New Hampshire State Student Councils, as well as president of the New Hampshire High School Democratic Party, and was elected national FHA vice president of membership. She has spread word of the value of FHA through all media, and has even carried the message to the President of the United States, whom she got to meet.

> I have a wish list I want to share. I wish that all babies could be born with equal prenatal care. I wish that all preconceived expectations due to gender or race could be dropped. I wish that every little child could have all the self-esteem needed. I wish that governments would spend as much on the advancement of their children as they do on their military. I wish the peoples of the world could unite as one. Now, I know at seventeen that this is a WISH list. Wishing, hoping, and hard work will make it happen. . . .
>
> I want to be able to sit with my grandchildren and talk about the old days when people were not equal. My grandchildren will smile and say, "How could people have believed that?" I'll explain that someone had to hold the light so everyone could see their way. I will be holding the light! I will always remember fha gave me the light.

And as these young women move into the future to "light the way," they will give thanks to FHA/HERO, and home economics in general, for helping prepare them perhaps to make the world a better home for everyone.

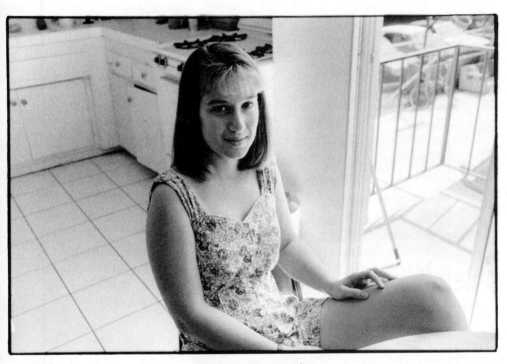

CINDY BOWERMAN

PAGEANT: <u>The Pageant</u>

Backstage, my stomach takes on that uneasy feeling
And before I go on, you'll see me there kneeling.
Dear God, give me the courage to stand before the crowd
Give me the strength to stand tall and speak loud.
So I step up, and assume my position
The blinding stagelights are the extent of my vision.
My ears can hear the audience applaud
As I remember to stand straight, with my shoulders broad
Then as soon as it came, that memorable moment is gone
Now they announce the lucky girl, who's head the crown lies on.

Jaime Maggio

CHAPTER THIRTEEN

Teen Queens

```
BURYING THE BARBIES

All my life
I have felt confused
Torn between the desire to braid Barbie's hair
And the desire to pull her arms off.
I have watched Miss America Pageants
With a sick fascination,
Wondering how anyone could inflict such
objectification upon themselves.
I have watched friends flirt mindlessly,
Giggling
Tossing their hair.
Torn between my friendship with them
And the absurdity of their behavior.
But I think I have made my decision now,
To bury the Barbies
Turn off the beauty pageants
And be myself.
```

—Ann-Marie Larson, age 16
Northfield, Minnesota

Pageants have often been a controversial subject amongst women and girls. While many, such as Ann-Marie Larson, see them as detrimental—degrading and derogatory, perpetuating the treat-

ment of females as objects, and encouraging competition and jealousies between women and girls—those who compete in them, like
fifteen-year-old Stacey Sprenkle, maintain that they are valuable,
empowering, and instill confidence and self-esteem, especially in
teenage girls.

As Stacey, aka Miss Pleasant Hill, pursues her dreams on the
pageant circuit, she also considers herself a feminist. Stacey shares
her unique viewpoint in her piece entitled "A Feminist Opinion on
Pageants":

> I am a feminist, or a supporter of women's
> claims to be given rights equal to those of
> men. I participate in Pageants. Many feel that
> pageants are a direct contradiction to the
> beliefs of a feminist. I disagree entirely.
>
> I am going to be a lawyer, defending women's
> rights. I do pageants for many reasons. Among
> those reasons are the following. I love the
> opportunity to travel and meet new people. In
> addition, pageants are a great way for me to
> express my feminist views. Pageants give
> young women a chance to get recognition for
> their achievements, and compete for college
> scholarships.
>
> I believe in equal rights and opportunities
> for women, but I don't see many women getting
> football or wrestling scholarships for
> Universities. As our gender progresses in
> society, we have to take it upon ourselves to
> pursue a career. As we strive towards equal-
> ity, we need to further educate ourselves. In
> many cases, this means going to college,
> which can be very expensive.
>
> The main concern of a feminist should be
> letting women have the opportunity to pursue
> their goals. This is exactly what pageants
> do. They help young women follow their
> dreams.

Today, more pageants seem to be focused on girls' achievements,
personality, and presence. But there still exist the more traditional
beauty competitions, based primarily on appearance.

Kimberly June Allin, age sixteen, has placed in several pageants including runner-up position in Miss Hawaii National Teenager. In 1992, she won the title of Miss Hawaii American Teen. She writes:

> . . . I have been careful in choosing pageants without swimsuit contests because I feel they are derogatory to the whole concept of pageants. Standing on a stage in a bathing suit and uncomfortable high heels just isn't my idea of fun. I want to be proud of what I do, and advocate the benefits of pageants. In general, other teen-age girls I have spoken with are against swimsuit competitions. The "best" criteria for judging in a teen pageant includes academic achievements, leadership, talent, personality, poise, attitude, and overall general appearance.

Many girls, like Kimberly, feel that beauty comes from within, and find that it's important to pick the pageant systems, agencies, and sponsors that promote the celebration of inner beauty.

Carrie Ann Simpson, age sixteen, was named third runner-up in her first local pageant in Clarion, Pennsylvania, the Miss Teen Autumn Leaf Festival 1993:

> . . . After my first pageant, I realized that there is more to competing than smiling and trying to walk gracefully in three-inch heels! To be a pageant winner, you have to possess more than grace and a winning smile— that someone has to be a caring, compassionate person with intelligence, a great personality, and the will to always help others. That person represents and speaks for whatever she's won her title for.

Yet there are still many girls whose self-satisfaction is determined through appearance.

When asked "What makes you happy?" April Brackner, age seventeen, from Birmingham, Alabama, answered, "The love and excitement I feel from dressing up and looking pretty."

Sixteen-year-old Natalie Kowal from Malvern, Ohio, began participating in preteen pageants:

> Competing made me feel nervous but so excit-
> ed! Here I was just barely eleven and walk-
> ing down this runway, with this beautiful,
> pink, lacy dress, just like a model. It was
> a great feeling.

* * *

While there are, perhaps, other ways to feel beautiful and glamorous, participating in pageants provides a key element that attracts many teenage girls: validation through competition.

Natalie continues:

> Pageants are an important tradition because
> there will always be competition between
> people and what better way to compete than in
> a pageant.

Seventeen-year-old Heather Lyons, Miss Texas Teen All American, agrees:

> . . . Competition, to me, is the key to
> success. Being a varsity soccer player, if
> you do not maintain a competitive edge, you
> will not survive on the soccer field. As in
> job interviews, without a competitive edge,
> who will get the job? In pageantry, competi-
> tion can be vicious.

Although systematically pageants are based on competition, blatant rivalry is not supported. As a matter of fact, many promoters encourage camaraderie and even give awards for congeniality.

Seventeen-year-old Elizabeth Peisner, aka Miss Woodland Hills, is a vivacious girl with energy and drive. When asked to provide additional material displaying her accomplishments on her application for the Miss Teenage California Pageant, Elizabeth included a powerful, moving, and sensitive play she wrote about her best friend dying of AIDS.

Her take on competition, as experienced in this particular pageant, is positive and uplifting:

> . . . Competing. That's such a negative word. It wasn't really some blood thirsty battle to the death. There were no catfights or girls feeling resentment for another girl, maybe because she was prettier in some way.
>
> . . . This group of girls would dance together, eat together, get ready for the competitions together, and spend hours together, just laughing and talking. I was thinking one night, is this a beauty pageant, or a sorority? These girls were my sister contestants, but also my <u>sisters</u>. We were all there for the same reason, to win the crown. Of the 257 competing, only one would win. Going into this pageant, I knew I had a chance, but was smart enough not to think of myself as the winner. I had come this far, and I had a chance. To even be in this pageant, not to mention an opportunity at the fun and the friends and the memories that would last a lifetime.
>
> Forget about how ruthless pageants can be. It's nothing like you'd ever expect. Don't judge what you haven't done.

* * *

Assigned roommates are commonplace in pageants. Often, by the end of a week, or even a weekend, the competitor who shares a girl's room is transformed into much more.

When I first met my roommate, I knew that we would become great friends. But I never imagined that we would become best friends.

—Courtney A. Keller, age 14
Miss Teen Delta Cities

Besides the actual competition, I think the nights were the most fun. My roommate and I would stay up late watching movies while eating pizza, candy, and all that other healthy stuff. Before going to bed each night, my roommate and I would soak our feet together. We used that time to talk and really get to know each other.

—Jennifer Coleman, age 16
Miss Teen North San Diego County

. . . You get lots of wonderful things from a pageant. . . . The friends there will be a friendship that will last forever. Those friends will always be different because you did something unique together.

—Joann Gonzales, age 14
Miss Imperial, California

* * *

Where does the desire to compete against other girls in such a manner begin? Often from childhood fantasies. From years of growing up watching Miss America be crowned, just like Cinderella and all those fairy-tale princesses. A tear slipping from her eye, smiling victoriously as she waves to those who "made it all possible" for her to parade down the runway with an armful of roses to the familiar strains, sung worshipfully: "There she is, Miss America, There she is, our ideal. . . ."

> What first attracted me to pageants was the
> thought of being one of those glamorous young
> girls who are every little girl's dream—
> hoping that one day they would be one of
> them.

—Carrie Ann Simpson

And Heather Lyons was another girl who was often tucked into bed with this childhood dream:

> As a little girl I grew up watching the
> pageants on television, in hopes of fulfill-
> ing a dream as they were doing. . . . I was
> inspired by the women who had the gusto to
> participate in such a challenge, and fulfill
> their dream. Having the confidence those
> women portrayed as they spoke their views and
> showed their poise is more than you could ask
> of a role model. I remember in grammar
> school, we had to select someone we admired
> for Black History Month, and I of course
> chose the first African-American to win Miss
> America, Vanessa Williams. I will always
> cherish those wonderful childhood memories.
> I feel that pageants provide a way for girls
> to meet a diverse group of people that other-
> wise they would never have met. Pageantry
> also provides a way for girls to speak up for
> their views on different issues. With the
> confidence you gain from pageantry, there is
> no reason to believe that you can not succeed
> at anything you want. . . . Personally, I have
> retrieved the confidence I was beginning to
> lack, and once again I am able to hold my head
> up high and smile at the world.

As for Heather, for Miss East Contra Costa County, sixteen-year-old Kim Croteau, pageants have been no less than inspirational:

> In the last year of my life, I have grown
> so much. I know so many people in my town now,

I feel I belong in so many places throughout
my community. I have a retail job, I teach my
very own catechism class, I am involved with
student government, I am <u>very</u> active in my
church's youth group and liturgical committee
and I am currently enrolled in a Speech class
at my school which I love! All this, I never
would've imagined happening to me a couple of
years ago. I never would've had the <u>GUTS</u> to
do any of this, without my outstanding
pageant experiences.
    I entered my first pageant because it
offered a scholarship for the winner. Never
would I've thought that I'd be a "pageant
girl." But when I got on that stage . . . I
didn't want to get off! I loved the glamorous
feeling of the lights and cameras on me—and
all the cheering. Hard to believe for someone who turns red and gets sweaty when I have
to get up in front of my class at school! But,
yes, it was great! I honestly believe that
one of the main reasons I have the confidence
in myself that I do now is because of my experiences in the pageants I've been in. The
pageant productions I have worked with have
done such a great job of calming nerves and
reassuring the contestants of their importance.

Transformed, Kim is presently able to make speeches at school in
front of 2,000 people with ease. Not only has she gained confidence
in presenting herself, but also:

        . . . I love being heard! . . . Never would I
    have believed that I would be doing these
    things but I am, and I am so proud of myself!

* * *

Being proud of oneself is also reveling in one's individuality.
Rather than trying so hard simply to fit in, it's discovering what's

uniquely special about oneself and putting that forward. This is a healthy approach to life, one that seems to fit in with what many pageants promote.

> In pageants, it is usually the most unique, individualistic, well-balanced woman that wins, not the one almost exactly like all of the others.

> —*Carla Jo Snyder, age 15*
> *Texarkana, Texas*

Many Teen Queens, such as fifteen-year-old Sarah Milford from Burkburnett, Texas, thrive on individuality:

> Competing with other girls my age makes me feel confident about myself. It also makes me self-aware in the fact that I have to find something different about myself that's not like the other girls. Competing makes me believe in myself more than I would without competing. (Lots of people close to me tell me there is no use in competing because when I don't win I'll feel less about myself, but, in fact, it makes me try even harder the next time.)

Marlease Fleumer, age fourteen, from San Rafael, California, looks beyond the surface:

> To be happy with who I am
> is the key to being happy with what I am
> I should accept myself
> so that others can accept me
> instead of wishing and striving
> to be something I am not
> I should make the best of what I have. . . .
> It is possible for me to go on diets
> and place borders and strict rules
> to give my appearance a better angle

```
but instead of concentrating on how others see me
I should concentrate on how I see myself.
```

Some girls don't yet have the insight Marlease has and feel extremely pressured to appear a certain way to gain acceptance and fit in.

```
   . . . Growing up as a teenage girl is also a
very challenging experience. The 90's gener-
ation is very materialistic and the visual
impression that you give seems to be your
best asset for success. In the strive to be
beautiful, teen girls go through pains that
are generally unnecessary. From dieting to
lose weight to plastic surgery, the pressure
to look good is on the shoulders of every
teenage girl.
```

—Carrie Ann Simpson

And what is looking good? Magazines, television, movies, music videos, billboards, commercials, and ads dictate a "look" that's deemed acceptable, that most girls and women aren't even close to achieving. Fashions are primarily designed for, and modeled by, tall, stick-thin women; makeup and hair products are geared to make all females—no matter their features—fit into an agreed-upon definition of beauty. Even televised pageants dictate what our culture perceives as beautiful. This perpetuates judgment and disdain for one's appearance, especially at an age when a girl feels less self-confident as it is.

Consumerism is being pushed on adolescents, promoting items like nail polish, makeup, and other beauty products. It is estimated that each year, teenage girls spend over $32 billion, $10 million more than boys, and have been outspending boys for each of the past forty years.

There's Slim-Fast, Weight Watchers, Jenny Craig, and Nutri System; Revlon, Maybelline, Clairol, and Cover Girl; and if none of that works, there's always plastic surgery and the "ultimate diet":

. . . Unlike my friends, I am not skinny, I am not pretty, and my clothing is far less than perfect. . . . I thought that if I could just lose weight and get down to 110 then I could be like my friends. The only problem is that unlike my 5'4" friends, I am 5'10". This kinda caused a problem. I stopped eating and lost 15 pounds. I felt really hungry at first but then it was ok and I wasn't hungry anymore. After 2 weeks of eating nothing I got really shaky and I went to my volleyball coach and she helped me to start eating again. I know a lot of girls who have done the same thing. I have always had low self esteem and I still do. This was just one of my weird ways to try to make myself feel better. I know that if I could just raise my self esteem then I wouldn't look at myself in such a bad way. I just don't know how to do it. I look in the mirror and see a plain ugly girl who is overweight. Who would want to be friends with that person?

I entered the pageant because I wanted to be special, I wanted to be noticed. I thought that by being successful people would look at me the way they look at my friends. I wanted people to admire me. . . .

I don't want to lie and say that I entered the pageant to make the world a brighter place. No one would invest that amount of time and effort if they didn't think that they would gain something from it. Like I said before, I was selfish, but people need to be selfish every once in a while. The one important thing that I would like to stress is that the girls in the pageant are not perfect they have their flaws. They have just worked hard and have been able to reach their goals.

—Amber Ellsworth, age 16
Issaquah, Washington

Piper Appleby, the sorority girl from Alpha Phi, was both Miss
Texas Teen All American in 1993 and Miss Fall Rush 1993. Self-
destructive behavior emerged while she tried to cope with a negative self-image and the tensions of preparing for her first pageant:

> . . . It is most important that you are
> emotionally capable to deal with this stress.
> Unfortunately, I was not.
>
> For months before the big weekend, I worried
> about every detail of my body: "Would the
> judges think I was fat?", "Would my tummy
> stick out in the swimsuit competition?"—
> These were questions that bothered me. After
> all, I would be in front of hundreds of people
> who would be judging me on my appearance. I
> mean, I was by no means fat, but there were
> just some areas from the top of my head to my
> feet that could use some improvement. I
> decided to take off 5 pounds, and I knew this
> would be really hard since I just loved to
> eat! But unfortunately I found an "easy way
> out" that many teenage girls find as well
> today—throwing up anything and everything
> fattening I put into my body. This constant
> bingeing and purging (otherwise known as
> bulimia) went on for close to three months,
> and combined with taking aerobic classes 5
> times a week, I was in pretty good shape. As
> a matter of fact, along with those 5 pounds,
> I lost another 5 more. I was really ready for
> the big weekend in Dallas, even though I was
> still nervous and felt awful—I had very
> little energy, a quick temper, and every time
> I looked in the mirror all I saw were yellow-
> ing teeth.
>
> During the required meals at the hotel, I
> was careful not to overdo it like some girls.
> All I needed was to put all my hard work to
> waste on the night of the pageant. All of my
> close friends and family were there to
> support me. The result? Very good—I came out
> First-runner-up to the crown! For my very
> first pageant, I had done quite well. Back

```
home in San Antonio, my self-esteem was
higher than ever and I felt as if I could
conquer the world! But, my eating disorder
did not improve—I came to the scary conclu-
sion that I had bulimia. For the first time
in my life, I felt out of control! My life
revolved around my eating and I felt so
alone. No one knew—not even my parents.
Bingeing and purging sometimes three times in
one day I realized I needed help and could
not stop on my own.
```

Piper finally told her boyfriend, who threatened to tell her parents if she didn't do it herself. She broke down and told them, and was quite surprised by their support and eagerness to help her. She had expected anger and disappointment. They assured her they would all get through it together and, after nearly four months of psychotherapy, Piper's bulimia subsided.

```
    . . . And in August of 1993, I received a
phone call from pageant headquarters telling
me that the winner had handed her title down
to me! This meant I was now the winner! I do
believe it was fate that I had to first win
First-Runner-Up and not the title, in order
to be able to recover from my bulimia.
    One year later, I sometimes wonder if it was
the stress of pageantry that caused my bulim-
ia. I'll never know. To this day I have to
watch my weight and eating habits to keep
from suffering a relapse.
```

Piper now feels she was destined to have the experience she did, because it led her to what she believes is her life's work: helping others in similar circumstances.

She is currently majoring in psychology with a minor in nutrition, and plans to become a psychologist specializing in eating disorders. She is also heavily involved with an eating disorders support group on campus. She continues:

> ...Maybe I am a strong believer in fate
> but I do believe that God gave me bulimia for
> a reason—so that I may be able to help and
> to understand others and touch their lives in
> letting them know that they are not alone.

Jennifer Datlik, age seventeen, won the title of Miss Napa County, was crowned Napa County Fair Queen in 1993, achieved first runner-up to Miss Teen San Francisco 1992, second runner-up to Young Woman of the Year for 1994, was selected first runner-up to Miss Teenage California for 1994, and is the recipient of the Teen Image Award for 1994. This is a long, impressive list of wins for a young woman who just a few short years ago barely felt comfortable being in her body.

> It is amazing to me how one can see a person
> not for who she is, but how she looks. Until
> the age of fifteen, I was severely overweight
> and pretty unhappy. Stricken with asthma, I
> thought there wasn't much that could be done
> to improve my state of health or appearance.
> I was at that awkward age where kids teased
> me because of my weight. Something inside
> began to ache. I wanted to change, I knew that
> I had to. . . .
> I decided to take control. I was tired of
> being unhappy and I was unhappy about being
> tired. . . .
> I refer to it as "my courageous summer." I
> lost 60 lbs and 11 sizes in clothing.

Jennifer lost weight with sensible and balanced eating, as well as exercise. However, her personal transformation was not all about losing. After her "courageous summer," she also gained a great deal: self-confidence and a new insight and wisdom she feels she can share with others.

For the past two years Jennifer has been selected nationally to represent the United States as a student ambassador to Russia. She was also selected as one of 2 percent of the nation's teens to attend the Congressional Youth Summit in Washington, D.C. She

acknowledges that pageants have played a significant role in helping her to attain many other accomplishments as well:

> My experiences in pageantry have been an
> important aspect of my growth and develop-
> ment. And although sometimes I am disappoint-
> ed by the outcome, I remember what I am
> really here for. I am participating so that
> I can represent my hometown, my views, and
> most of all—my commitment to be a positive
> role model for all girls.

She defines a real winner as one who helps others, and believes
she was put on this earth to make a difference.

Jennifer shares that another motivation for her commitment to
helping and educating teens is that she comes from an alcoholic
family and has "seen the violent effects of substance abuse firsthand." This has led her to speak out on such matters.

Many girls attribute their weight issues to family problems. Some,
feeling neglected, turn to food for comfort and solace; others blame
the overly high expectations of their parents.

Elizabeth Peisner felt that competing in the Miss Teenage
California Pageant was "the most wonderful three days of my life."
However, she confides that her experience was flawed by only one
thing: "a handful of cruel mothers."

> I saw so many stage mothers chastise their
> daughters, calling them failures and making
> them go into hysterics. How dare they, I
> thought. These girls, all of them, worked
> long and hard, enjoying themselves, and feel-
> ing beautiful. How dare these hags call their
> daughters ugly, blaming their appearance for
> not winning, or ask "What the hell did you do
> wrong?" Nothing. They didn't do anything
> wrong. It wasn't the girls. It was the moth-
> ers. They were trying to live vicariously
> through their daughters. When a girl enters a
> pageant, it should be for themselves, not for

```
their mothers. When these girls stand on
stage, they should stand tall and proud for
what accomplishments THEY have made, not
worried whether they're pleasing their mother
in the audience. These pageants are for the
girls, not the parents. My parents made sure
that I was doing this for what I wanted to
do. They were proud that I had the confidence
to take on such a task.
```

Kimberly Allin has witnessed similar situations:

```
. . . Some of their mothers were very force-
ful, and the girls themselves did not want to
be in the pageant. This was especially true
of the Southerners. The mothers did all the
work; they found sponsors, clothing, did
their makeup and hair, told them how to act
and what to eat, and wouldn't allow them to
associate with other competition, which
included all the other contestants.
```

But there are, of course, many parents who support and encourage their daughters; some who even *inspire.*

Rinita Helene Mueller and her mother, Helene Sharon Mueller, have competed together in many pageants. As individuals, they were both state finalists, Rinita in the Miss North Carolina/Miss U.S.A./Miss Universe Pageant, and Helene in the Mrs. North Carolina/Mrs. U.S.A./Mrs. Universe Pageant.

Dancing since the age of two, with her mother as her instructor, Rinita also created, along with her mother, a "dance ministry" known as the Dancing Disciples to, in their words, "bring the Good News and add to His glorification through the art of dance." The mother-daughter duo performs jazz, tap, ballet, and modern dances to religious songs such as "The King is Coming." The Muellers have received countless awards, and have been contacted by many dignitaries, including the pope and the president of the United States.

When asked what makes her happy, Rinita remarks, "Of course when you win! Meeting new friends and also all the fun that took place at the pageants." In addition:

> . . . Most of all—the support I received from my family
> throughout all the preparation. . . .
> We are all so close—a father that was always there for
> me—and my mother—my best friend. Who could have a more
> perfect set of parents.

A supportive family can come in an unexpected fashion. Eighteen-year-old Georgezetta "Terri" Rogers, Miss Foster City, California, has had quite a challenging life:

> In a short period of time I suffered many
> losses. I had been ostracized from my 6th
> home in a three year period. I was literally
> homeless on the street.

Terri went to stay with her biological father, who lived in a studio apartment with one bathroom and one bed, in a senior citizens' complex. She wrote that oftentimes, three to four people would live in that very small space:

> . . . I felt trapped emotionally and physical-
> ly because I didn't have any space of my own.

At that time, Terri also experienced the loss of her older brother, who was murdered in a drive-by shooting:

> . . . The pain from his death could never be
> measured from tears alone because his death
> took a piece of me with him.
> During this time in my life I felt a blan-
> ket of comfort in my life. I felt God's grace
> carrying me through with His love and the
> greatest blessings that I had received from
> Him was my "Earth Angel."

Terri's "angel" is a compassionate woman who saw Terri's anguish and took her under her wing. She was her teacher.

> . . . Because I was so unhappy during this
> time I was closed, shut-down and unreceptive.

> My behavior had changed in ways which made me
> uncomfortable to be around. As a result of
> being a teacher for so long she could see my
> behavior was connected to my emotional pain.
> Through the vision that she had she exchanged
> some kind words with me that lit the fuse of
> the bomb. . . . The bombshell exploded with
> pieces of love, communication and attention
> falling from the ceiling.

This student-teacher relationship blossomed into a friendship, then a "big sister" kind of closeness, finally leading to a legal adoption:

> . . . She not only provided me with a home
> (my own room fully furnished) but she gave me
> a "gift of hope" something that no one had
> ever given to me before. My "gift of hope"
> turned into a light that reflects my ability
> to dream once again.

Realizing such a unique relationship, Terri asks: "Can the most influential person in your life be white in a black person's life?" Of course, her answer is yes:

> As we focus on our relationships between
> friends and family who influence us, these
> concepts appear to be color-blind. . . . I do
> not want you to think of who I am writing
> about as being just a "white woman," but as
> my "Earth Angel" who is also my "mommy!"
> Our opportunity to become a family was a
> dream come true for me and "my mommy" because
> I always wanted a "mommy" and "my mommy"
> always wanted a daughter. I am the proud
> daughter of my "Earth Angel" who represents a
> "mommy," teacher, big sister, and above all
> the person who gave me the spirit of life
> which is recognizable today.

This newfound spirit led Terri to compete in a state pageant, representing her town as Miss Foster City. She reflects:

```
     After my "Nobel Prize" winning speech in
front of about 2,000 people, my whole family
(my mommy and daddy, my dad and sister and I)
went to the finest restaurant in the hotel
(because I couldn't leave the hotel during
the weekend) and had dinner together. It
brought tears to my eyes to see the people
who mean so much to me sharing in one of the
happiest moments in my life. If I had to say
"What was the best part of my weekend?" it
would have been all the joy and peace I felt
in my heart during our dinner time.
```

                          * * *

I learned from my contact with Teen Queens that those who have
the encouragement and support of their parents often also receive
much-needed help from them in a vital part of pageantry: preparation. Piper describes its importance:

```
     . . . It would be very easy to say that a
pageant is just "a walk in the park" but
unfortunately it is not. There is so much
preparation necessary. Besides knowing the
proper stage presence, how to do both your
make-up and hair for both on-stage and your
interview, and the knowledge of answers to
the possible interview questions, it is very
important that you have the proper clothing
requirements (interview outfit, evening gown
and swimsuit) and the body to put in
them. . . .
```

And once the week or weekend of a pageant begins, there is much
on-the-spot preparation as well. Many pageant systems encourage
girls to work together behind the scenes despite the onstage competition. However, encouraged or not, it is in most girls' nature to
come together and be there for each other, especially under such
demanding circumstances:

. . . The first rehearsal was very hectic.
From the second we arrived until the second
we left, we were on our feet practicing our
walk, and our dance for the opening number.
When we were finished, we were allowed to
return to our rooms to prepare for the
preliminary   pageant   in   about   2
hours. . . . About 6 people came to our room
asking us to do their hair. . . . 2 o'clock we
went down backstage and practiced our speech
for the show. . . .

The next morning after breakfast Rosie and
I went straight to rehearsal. This one was
the most active one yet. I don't think I sat
down once through the whole thing. It seemed
as though it lasted forever. . . .

—*Courtney A. Keller*

They've spent months preparing and hours rehearsing. Finally
the time comes when the lights shine brightly, the audience cheers
wildly, and the pageant begins.

Sarah Milford gives us a peek from backstage:

. . . There were so many people out there and
in a matter of seconds, they would all be
looking at me! I was so nervous that when
they opened the curtains I could feel my legs
shaking! Then they started calling out our
numbers. When they got to mine, 18, I walked
out to the middle of the stage and stated my
name and age and did my turns.

* * *

RUNWAY JITTERS

TRY AND STOP SHAKING.
IT'S YOUR TURN.
"Oh my gosh, I forgot my speech!"

RELAX, IT WILL COME TO YOU.
You're on!
THIS IS YOUR MOMENT, MAKE IT LAST.
READY?
STAND UP STRAIGHT, SHOULDERS BACK
Don't forget to breathe!
SMILE. **HAVE FUN.**
FEET AT ELEVEN AND TWO.
WAIT. DON'T GO YET.
OKAY, NOW GO.
HEAD UP, LOOK AROUND. SMILE.
FINGERS GENTLY BRUSH YOUR DRESS,
But don't hold on!
EYE CONTACT, SMILE, LOOK AT THE JUDGES.
BREATHE!!!
SPEAK CLEARLY AND LOUD.
"I can't do it."
RELAX, DEEP BREATH, RECOVER.
GOOD GIRL.
DEEP BREATH, NOW WALK.
Watch out for the center bar!
REMEMBER YOUR POSTURE,
SHOULDERS BACK.
SMILE!
HERE'S THE JUDGES, EYE CONTACT. THEY DON'T BITE.
CAMERA MAN, **Say cheese!**
LAST CHANCE, **stand out!**
DEEP BREATH, YOU DID GREAT,
UP THE STAIR.
DON'T TRIP!
OFF STAGE, SIGH OF RELIEF.
BIG SMILE IT'S OVER.

"Can I do it again?"

—*Marisa Mendoza, age 16*
Miss Stanton

Through the competition, the pressure builds as the judges narrow down contestants to semifinalists, then finalists. Those who remain have fewer girls to compete with. As they get even closer to winning the coveted crown, butterflies turn into nervous tension:

. . . After I was chosen as one of the Top Ten
Contestants in the 1993 Miss Teen San
Francisco Pageant, I was sent to a soundproof
room along with the other nine girls. We were
all so excited—"We're eligible to go to the
finals now!" But I was more nervous then
ever! Next, we had to answer a spontaneous
question on stage. I didn't know what to
expect. When I got out there, I was confident, but SHAKY! I didn't know quite how to
answer my question, so I stumbled a bit. It
was so hard to think rationally with lights
and cameras and a thousand eyes on you! When
it was over, I hadn't even remembered what I
said. But I knew I pretty much blew my chance
at placing. Oh well! I now have a GREAT
respect for all of the pageant finalists who
belt out those spontaneous answers. I know
what it feels like—it's not easy!"

—Kim Croteau

Marlease Fleumer, in her insightful way, has a positive approach
to dealing with nerves:

THE Question

Many would think that the pressure of a
pageant would be overwhelming. I think that
the pride I feel when sharing myself and my
accomplishments with others overcomes most of
the pressure. It does not matter what kinds
of goals you have in life, it is a mentality
you need to succeed. That mentality is to be
proud of everything you do, no matter what.
When you are in the spotlight and you have
hundreds of minds listening to you, just
remember an experience you have had. Then
incorporate it into your answer. By sharing
yourself and being the true you, people will
see that and notice. Your telling them you
are proud of who YOU are. Be proud of everything you do, no matter what.

* * *

April M. Myers, age thirteen, from Yukon, Ohio, describes herself: "I love to do all the kid things I can do. I love to jump on our trampoline with my brother and friends. I love to swim, to go fly kites and to roller skate. I love to blow bubbles outside and draw with chalk on the driveway, and I love to play with my hamster 'Biscuit.' And I love to do pageants."

Although she sounds like an ordinary young teenage girl, April is anything but that. At an age where confidence usually begins to waver in girls, April possesses a strong sense of herself, and has accomplished this against odds:

I have some of the same hopes and fears as most of the girls whom I do pageants against, but most of those girls and judges do not know how much harder the interview or talent portion is for me because I can't hear. I have worn hearing aides since I was 5 years old. I have continued to lose my hearing over the years and have a very substantial loss. But I have always told my mother before we do any pageant that I want to go up against these other girls on my ability to speak and perform and not win because judge one has a soft spot because they know I'm hearing impaired. Neither Mom or I tell them I am hearing impaired. Fair or unfair I have been taught I have to learn to survive in this world against odds that most kids my age won't have to face yet, but I know I will be a stronger person in the end. . . .

I love life and everything in it. Don't get me wrong I get mad because I can't understand everybody when I'm at the mall with my friends or at an amusement park. And I have to work a lot harder to catch all of someone's conversation by reading their lips or having to ask them to repeat what they said, but I am strong and healthy otherwise and thank God for that. I know sign language and

```
when I'm just tired of it all sometimes it's
easier to sign, like when I'm at home but most
of my friends don't know sign language so I
do  not  depend  on  that  for  my  first
language. . . .
   Because I have had to grow up with a hear-
ing impairment I have had other kids and
sometimes even adults tell me I couldn't do
something or keep up with a group because I
always had to ask people to repeat themselves
or I just didn't get what was being said. My
parents have at times had to fight our local
public  schools  to  let  me  stay  in  public
school with all my friends . . . but at no time,
even when we all wanted to, did we give up or
give in.
```

Miss Pacifica, Danielle Cafferata, age eighteen, the accomplished
skier and runner from the "Jocks" chapter, exhibits extraordinary
pride and love for life. Having undergone a heart transplant at age
eleven, Danielle is partially deaf and totally blind. In the Miss
Teenage California Pageant, she won a special Queen of Hearts
award. Like April, her resolve in the presence of great challenge
crowns her Queen of Courage.

                                   * * *

Many pageants seem to be inclusive, giving girls of varied circumstances an opportunity to compete despite different physical abili-
ties, economic standing, and cultural background.

Miss Teen USA 1993 was a sixteen-year-old girl who had lived in
placement centers and six foster homes since she was three years
old, and the triumphant 1994 winner of the Miss America title was
a hearing-impaired woman who captured the nation's heart.

Pageants provide a chance for those who have grown up in sheltered communities to expand their horizons and be with girls with
whom they might never associate otherwise.

By the same token, it is apparent that some contestants continue to perpetuate separation.

Kimberly Allin was dismayed by her experience at a national pageant:

> ...I was surprised by the prejudice against non-Caucasian contestants. I am Caucasian, but live in the culturally diverse state of Hawaii, and I am actually a minority. About 23% of Hawaii residents are white, but that statistic has never bothered me. At school, I am friends with people who are Japanese, Chinese, Filipino, Spanish, Native American, Hawaiian, and a variety of other races. Skin color has never been important to me. I was appalled when some of the girls at the National Pageant would only speak with members of their own race. I found that to be old fashioned, disappointing, immature, and without reason.

As demonstrated in their writing, as well as their speeches at the Miss Teenage California Pageant, racism is only one of many issues that the girls are concerned with.

In a troubled teenage world, a good friend becomes more than a "pal" to hang out with at the mall. Just ask Amber Ellsworth:

> ...teenagers have tough lives. Most of the time they hide it, but there are so many pressures. I have helped two of my friends stop doing drugs, I have convinced one of my friends not to commit suicide. It's tough, most people just want to be loved, by friends and family. Kids just need someone to show that they care, and that they will always be there. There are so many things to worry about. One of my friends was raped just walking home from a neighbor's house. Some of my friends have made a career out of shoplifting. My ex-boyfriend sold drugs (I didn't know). I have made new friends of course, actually I changed schools because I didn't

want to be around the bad influences. I have
seen people go from straight A students to
dropping out of school. I have a friend who
at 16 had to get an abortion. I want to do
more with my life. I wish there was a place
that was free of all of these problems, but
problems are all around. I am lucky, I have
avoided all of the really bad things, instead
I changed schools, became active in student
government and the community.

. . . My friends might have their faults, but
they are fantastic people. They might have
gotten off track, but I am sure that with a
little push they will be on the right road
again. I just don't want to push them down
before they have a chance to get on their feet
again. My friends are wonderful people. They
were all there for me, through everything that
happened to me. When I wouldn't eat, when I
wanted to die, when my hair got chopped off
and I looked like a mushroom, when I really
needed to raise my grades drastically. They
were always there. At one time in your life
or another you do something wrong. Their
faults make them no different from anyone
else. I will always hold the highest amount
of respect for my friends. Please do not
diminish them for what I have said. They are
no better nor no worse than you and I. . . .

People are out there, people who just need
to be loved. Who is going to step up and help
them?

I guess that I just want you to know one
thing life is tough and there are lots of
people who can't get through it alone. I want
to be there for them. I think that pageants
are there for me. They give me hope that I can
be the best person possible. When all else is
gone, hope and dreams will still be here.

Amber found renewed hope through her participation in pageants
and they have clearly contributed to her desire and willingness to
be there for other people.

Heather Lyons gets the same value out of pageantry, which allows her to speak out on concerns such as underage drinking, drinking and driving, drugs, violence, and other issues:

> . . . I feel that carrying the title, Miss Texas Teen All American, has given me an opportunity to fulfill a dream, and go the extra mile with it. I have been able to speak to many elementary, junior high, and high school students about confidence and self-esteem.

Fifteen-year-old Stacie Sorenson, Miss Teen Palmdale, California, also acknowledges how pageantry provided her with a forum to speak out:

> I entered this pageant because from my standpoint I could not make my dream come true. If you stand in an empty field and scream from the top of your lungs no one will hear you, but in a room with eager listening people things can be done. Lives can be changed. Love can be shared by everyone. My goal is to make this dream into a reality. By entering this pageant, I have a right and a way to express my feelings and opinions. I WANT A CHANGE.

Kim Croteau writes:

> I really would like to win the title of a pageant queen. I know most teens would. But I want to be heard! I have so much to say and I don't know who to address! I feel my generation is so full of life—we are ready for changes to instill hope in our nation for our children. . . .
> My pageant experiences have been great and I am so thankful for that, but I do hope some changes will be made in the future. Girls are getting to be heard more and more these days, and that is wonderful.

Kim is one of the many girls who see pageants as an opportunity to build inner strength in participants, as well as provide a vehicle for expression. She concludes:

```
    . . . Some people, I believe, don't get the
true meaning of pageantry. Pageants are not
here to solicit us, but to give us an oppor-
tunity to be heard, and to shine for a while!
I don't believe girls need to model a bikini
to get their message across. I also think
that girls should not feel that they aren't
pretty enough or skinny enough to be a
pageant contestant. Every girl is worthy of a
moment to shine!
```

MISS TEENAGE CALIFORNIA PAGEANT CONTESTANTS

AMANDA AARDSMA—WINNER OF MISS TEENAGE CALIFORNIA 1994

DANIELLE CAFFERATA

OUTRO

One of the most significant things I discovered while working on *Girl Power* is that while I set out to get a broad cross-section of experiences, the writing I received from every single group revealed that all girls are basically grappling with the same issues.

Certainly, lives are different due to opportunities, class, upbringing, and environment. But the thread that weaves these young women's lives together is one that ties us all together. From the beginning of our days, from the core of our beings, we all share the universal desire for love, acceptance, and a sense of belonging.

These girls are creating their own families and communities. Whether it be in a gang or sorority, a sports team or a tribe, they are bonding in companionship and uniting through a shared vision.

I've led a fairly bohemian lifestyle as a writer and artist, and nothing I've ever done has been very "traditional." I think because of this, it was easy for me to slip in the door as "one of the girls."

But when a Riot Grrrl called me "ma'am," and a Homegirl called me "lady," I realized that age does set us apart, especially considering the fact that I'm old enough to be their mother. So, if I must surrender to that, then I will also indulge in "when I was your age . . ." because, indeed, times really have changed.

During my preteens, I hung out on the streets—with other neighborhood kids—playing games, making up songs, riding bikes, exploring, and adventuring. Aside from the average parental warning "Don't take candy from strangers," we had no real concern that one of us would actually be lured away. Kidnapping was not a common occurrence and milk cartons had no missing child's face staring at us by our cereal. Now children are kept on leashes at malls and most kids aren't allowed to play outside; even a family's suburban yard is no longer a safe haven.

When I was fourteen, I spent my summer days hitchhiking through Los Angeles canyons on the hunt to track down two of the strongest female musicians of the time: Joni Mitchell and Carole

King; then at night I'd hitch to the clubs to watch them, and others, play. Today, just walking to your parents' car unattended can be risky.

In my high school years, I was part of a young women's consciousness-raising group where one of the things we did was attempt to set up an abortion and birth-control counseling center on the campus. We wanted to educate girls and provide resources. Yet, although unwanted pregnancy was a concern, the teenage pregnancy rate was far lower than today, and even though we set out to inform girls of the dangers of sexually transmitted diseases, there was not yet the threat of AIDS.

The school dress code said our miniskirts couldn't be too short (the principal actually measured suspect hemlines!) and for a while, it was mandatory that girls wear bras, but we fought that absurd rule and won. Today, the imposed dress code in many high schools forbids students to wear oversized, baggy clothing—to help prevent the concealment of weapons.

There's so much violence in movies and on television (not to mention video games, music videos, and song lyrics) that the government is considering imposing guidelines and regulations, fearing that the dramatic increase in violent crimes is directly related.

Creativity seems an indulgent luxury when one is more concerned with her very survival.

The onslaught of the "information superhighway" is also taking its toll on society and the girls in it.

Although the advancements we've made are phenomenal, adding a vast wealth of information and resources, I feel they also can take us out of balance with our own personal, and creative, spirit.

It's an amazing statement of our times that children are learning to use computers in the first grade. However, sometimes the radical reliance on faster-paced technology prevents them from ever learning of the richness of picking up a pen and handwriting a letter.

Museums are closing, but no problem—even art now is on CD-ROM, where one can call up paintings from masters and view them on a computer screen. Synthesized drum tracks have replaced the ancient art form and ritual of drumming with a stick on a surface of animal skin, quashing the sensual experience of creating art and music through human expression. Many old, finely crafted buildings with intricate artistic detail and architectural style are being demolished in favor of strip malls whose design is based on cost-effectiveness and speed, reflecting the businesses there: fast-food restaurants and one-hour dry cleaners.

Efficiency often robs us of our inclination to go to a more primal, spiritual place, full of emotion and human essence.

In all the girls I met in person and through writing, I have witnessed a desire, whether conscious or not, to make some sort of return to a simpler and more meaningful way of living. Ritual is a way of providing meaning. Many of the groups of girls included in *Girl Power* participate in some sort of ritual: sorority girls with their secret customs; gang girls who are "jumped in"; Native American girls who practice tribal traditions of ceremony. These initiations establish membership and reinforce a sense of belonging.

Creative self-expression can also give meaning to confusing times. Through writing, a girl can examine her own feelings and beliefs, providing a catalyst for revelation. When a feeling is internalized, not spoken, it expands and can become overwhelming. As emotions are released onto paper, it often leads to healing.

Writing is a tool of transformation and can shine the light on the inside, dispelling the darkness, taking us through external layers, bringing us closer to our souls.

> Sometimes paper is the only thing that will listen to you.

When I first read Jennifer's quote, I felt moved to answer her call, showing her, and all the other young women yearning to have a voice, that someone wanted to listen.

Whether they have written of their passion in whispers, or screamed of their rage and pain, you, the reader, complete the circle as one more person willing to listen.

* * *

RESOURCE AND REFERRAL LIST

HOMEGIRLS:

Transitional Living Programs:

Queens
76–23 47th Ave.
Elmhurst, New York 11373
(718) 424-6156

For females ages seventeen to twenty for a period of up to one year. You may call on your own to set up an appointment.

Pride Site
371 East 10th St.
New York, New York 10009
(212) 533-2470

Males and females age fifteen and up for twelve to eighteen months. Functions as a therapeutic community.

Organizations:

We Care for Youth
P.O. Box 10399
Glendale, California 91506
(818) 279-3124

A multiservice youth organization that builds bridges between youth and adult communities with intervention and prevention programs. Their focuses include getting and keeping girls out of gangs, providing job training seminars, and self-esteem work.

National Network of Runaway and Youth Services
1319 F Street N.W., Suite #401
Washington, D.C. 20004
(202) 783-7949

Guides the development of programs and services that aim to ensure *that all young people can be safe and lead healthy, productive lives.* Represents over 1,000 agencies that serve runaways, homeless children, and other youth in high-risk situations and their families. Has fact sheets, publications, including *Sounds from the Streets: A Collection of Poems, Stories and Art Work,* from youth living on the streets, in foster homes, detention centers, and runaway and homeless shelters. Also other publications, resource lists, fact sheets, reports, and training manuals for those who work with youth.

National Runaway Switchboard
(800) 621-4000

Publications:

Foster Care Youth United
144 W. 27th St., Suite #8R
New York, New York 10001

A monthly newspaper/magazine written by and for young people in foster care.

RIOT GRRRLS:

Publications:

Riot Grrrl Press
1573 N. Milwaukee Avenue #473
Chicago, Illinois 60622

Gerll
656 West Albine #3
Chicago, Illinois 60657

Both are all-girl fanzine distributors. Send self-addressed stamped envelope for information.

Factsheet Five
P.O. Box 170099
San Francisco,
California 94117-0099

A guide featuring hundreds of zines (including *Grrrls*), descriptions, where and how to get them. Also available at many newsstands.

TEEN MOTHERS:

Organizations:

New Chance (**MDRC**)
3 Park Avenue, 32nd Floor
New York, New York 10016
(212) 532-3200

Provides services for young mothers and their children: education, employment, health, and personal development; enhancing the development of participant's children; case management. List available of national sites of schools/educational programs.

Early Childhood Center
Cedars-Sinai Medical Center
8730 Alden Drive
Los Angeles, California 90048
(310) 855-5377
Day-Care "Warm Line"
(310) 855-3500

A nonprofit nationally recognized organization dedicated to the healthy emotional development of children, featuring teen parent community outreach services. Offers a Day-Care "Warm Line" —a free telephone consultation service for parents of children in day care and for day-care providers where they can discuss issues and problems and receive practical suggestions. Also offers special programs at selected sites serving low-income families at risk, including parenting classes and workshops, alternative education and child-care techniques, crisis intervention, and community referrals.

California Alliance Concerned
with School Age Parents
(CACSAP)
900 Fulton Ave., Suite #200
Sacramento, California 95825
(916) 974-7812

Can refer teen mothers to school
programs, health care professionals, social workers, and other
resources throughout California.

Los Angeles County
Department of Education
Pregnant Minor Program
9300 Imperial Highway
Downey, California 90242-2890
(310) 940-1812

Coordinates pregnant minor
programs for Los Angeles City
schools; has list of school
programs/contacts.

QUEER AND BI GIRLS:

Organizations:

Lambda Youth Network
P.O. Box 7911
Culver City, California 90233

A very comprehensive quarterly
list (with monthly and sometimes
bimonthly updates!) of national
and local resources and referrals.
Listings of gay, lesbian, bisexual,
and transgender youth help-lines,
pen pal programs, newsletters and

publications, student groups,
AIDS education and information,
P-FLAG (Parents and Friends of
Lesbians and Gays) chapters, and
a wide variety of ethnic, profes-
sional, and cultural organizations.

Send a self-addressed stamped
envelope, include your age and
$1.00.

Publications:

Inside Out
P.O. Box 460268
San Francisco, California 94146

Produced by and for gay and
lesbian youth. Welcomes readers'
submissions. Local resources and
some out-of-state resources available. Pen pals too. Write for free
sample issue.

Outyouth
Youth Enrichment Services
/BiGLYNY
Lesbian and Gay Community
Service Center
208 West 13th Street
New York, NY 10011

Free; published by and for youth.

Lesbian News
P.O. Box 1430
Twenty-nine Palms,
California 92277

National monthly magazine.

COWGIRLS:

Organizations:

Women's Professional Rodeo Association (WPRA)
Rt. 5 Box 698
Blanchard, Oklahoma 73010
(405) 485-2277

Service organization for women in professional rodeo; sanctions events at rodeos, publishes monthly newspaper and reference book.

National High School Rodeo Association (NHSRA)
11178 Huron #7
Denver, Colorado 80234
(800) 466-4772

Promotes development of sportsmanship, horsemanship, and character in youth. Offers scholarships.

National Little Britches Rodeo Association
1045 W. Rio Grande
Colorado Springs, Colorado 80906
(719) 389-0333

Membership of boys and girls ages eight to eighteen with rodeos coast-to-coast and Canada. Also publishes newspaper.

Bill Pickett Invitational Rodeo
P.O. Box 39163
Denver, Colorado 80239
(303) 373-1246

"A salute to the Black Cowboy"; an African-American traveling rodeo for all ages.

NATIVE AMERICAN GIRLS:

Organizations:

National Indian Youth Leadership Project
650 Vandenbosch Parkway
Gallup, New Mexico 87301
(505) 722-9176
Director: McClellan Hall

To instill cultural values and provide Native youth with opportunities in developing skills for becoming productive citizens, role models, and meeting expectations as culture bearers.

Association of Community Tribal Schools
616 4th Avenue West
Sisseton, South Dakota 57262
(605) 698-3112

Resource for national schools and Indian education. To help tribes and tribal organizations prepare children to be tribal leaders.

American Indian Resource Center
(Los Angeles County Public Library)

6518 Miles Avenue
Huntington Park,
California 90255
(213) 583-1461

Serves the Native American population and those interested in it.
Many resources, including
comprehensive list of national
Native American schools and
organizations.

Publications:

Prairie Winds
208 East Colorado Blvd.
Spearfish, South Dakota 57783
(605) 642-8286

Project of Black Hills Special
Services Cooperative. Literary
and visual arts publications
aimed toward youth; resource
guides developed by South
Dakota teachers and artists;
sponsors young writers' confer-
ences; staff development for
teachers (how to teach writing);
anthologies available.

The Circle
1530 E. Franklin Avenue
Minneapolis, Minnesota 55404
(612) 879-1760

Monthly publication of national
and local events and concerns of
Native American people and
those interested in Native

Americans. Includes youth pages,
written and designed by and for
youth.

FARM CHICKS:

Organizations:

**National Future Farmers
of America**
5632 Mt. Vernon Memorial
Highway
P.O. Box 15160 Alexandria,
Virginia 22309-0160
(703) 360-3600

National 4-H Council
7100 Connecticut Avenue
Chevy Chase, Maryland
20815-4999
(301) 961-2800

National Farmers Union
10065 East Harvard Avenue
Denver, Colorado 80231
(303) 337-5500

A general farm organization
representing 250,000 families
through its legislative, cooperative, and educational efforts.
Offers specific youth programs
and publications.

Publications:

National Grange
1616 H Street N.W.
Washington, D.C. 20006

Publications for farmers, farm families, women, and youth.

RAPPERS AND SISTAS:

Organizations:

Youth for Positive Alternatives
(310) 219-7512

Designs employment, educational, and recreational opportunities for young people in Los Angeles, including rapping and graffiti art events; sponsors open mike night for rappers at the Good Life Cafe and offers "Sounds of Good Life" compilation tape.

Publications:

The Fly Paper
1573 A. North Milwaukee Avenue
Chicago, Illinois 60622

Rap Pages
9171 Wilshire Blvd., Suite #300
Beverly Hills, California 90210

Flavor
20112 18th Avenue N.W.
Seattle, Washington 98177-2210

Urb
1680 N. Vine Street, Suite #1012
Hollywood, California 90028

SURFERS AND SK8ERS:

Organizations:

Association of Women Bodyboarders
P.O. Box 8, Haleiwa,
Hawaii 96712

Promotes international contests for women; quarterly newsletter.

United States Surfing Federation
(Western Region)
P.O. Box 512, San Juan
Capistrano, California 92693
(714) 493-2591

West Coast competition program to qualify competitors for United States Amateur Championships and United States World Team; also offers Los Angeles summer surf camp.

National Scholastic Surfing Association
P.O. Box 495 Huntington Beach,
California 92648
(714) 536-0445

Nationwide amateur surfing and bodyboarding competitions for all ages; scholarships available.

United Skateboard Federation
(also California Amateur Skateboard League and

Professional Skateboard League)
P.O. Box 30004
San Bernardino, California 92413
(909) 883-6176
FAX: (909) 883-8036

For young skateboarders and their
communities. To promote the
sport of skateboarding as both a
recreational and a serious athletic
endeavor with emphasis focusing
on communities providing skaters
with safe skating environments.
Sponsors series of amateur and
professional competitions; publishes monthly newsletter, yearly book
of information, and offers a list of
national skate parks.

Publications:

Surf Report
P.O. Box 1028
Dana Point, California 92629

Monthly journal of international
surfing destinations. Write for
subscriptions and back issues.

Pool Dust
P.O. Box 85664
Seattle, Washington 98145

Send $1.50 for sk8 zine.

Gunk
16 Lord Stirling Road
Basking Ridge, New Jersey 07920

Send $2.00 for sk8 zine.

JOCKS:

Organizations:

National Association for Girls and Women in Sports
1900 Association Drive
Reston, Virginia 22091
(800) 709-6636

Committed to the professional
development of women in sports,
advancement of female sports
knowledge, and the development
of sport programs and increased
leadership roles for women in
sports. Provides opportunities for
girls and women in sports-related
careers. Sponsors conventions and
championships; offers educational
materials and many publications
and books.

Women's Sports Foundation
Eisenhower Park, East Meadow,
New York 11554
(800) 227-3988

A nonprofit educational organization dedicated to promoting sports
and fitness opportunities through
educational resources, grants, and
scholarships for girls and women.
Has youth membership and offers
publications for youth.

Melpomene Institute
1010 University Avenue
St. Paul, Minnesota 55104
(612) 642-1951

A nonprofit organization that helps girls and women of all ages link physical activity and health through research, education, and publication. Available: journal, published three times a year; books and videos.

National Handicapped Sports
451 Hungerford Drive, Suite 100
Rockville, Maryland 20850
(301) 217-0960

Referral service for year-round sports for people with physical disabilities; chapters all around the country.

Wheelchair Sports USA
3595 East Fountain Blvd.,
Suite L-1 Colorado Springs,
Colorado 80910
(719) 574-1150

Provides competitive opportunities in sports at the local, national, and international levels for persons with physical disabilities who use wheelchairs in competitions.

Publications:

Sports 'n' Spokes
2111 E. Highland, Suite #180
Phoenix, Arizona 85016

Magazine of sports and recreation for wheelchair users.

SORORITY GIRLS:

Check with campus Panhellenic Association, Office of Greek Life, or Student Activities Office.

HOMEMAKERS:

Organizations:

Future Homemakers of America/HERO
1910 Association Drive
Reston, Virginia 22091
(703) 476-4900

American Association of Family and Consumer Sciences (formerly American Home Economics Association)
1555 King Street
Alexandria, Virginia 22314
(703) 706-4600

Newsletters, journals, and information.

Publications:

Scholastic Choices
555 Broadway
New York, New York 10012
(212) 343-6100

Magazine for pupils in junior high and high school home economics classes.

TEEN QUEENS:

Organizations:

**International Pageant
Association (IPA)**
P.O. Box 93402
Los Angeles, California 90093
(213) 896-5437

Produces 35,000 events in the
United States with over 3 million
participants. Publishes quarterly
journal with information, articles,
tips, interviews, pageant listings,
and pageant publication
listings/related publications.

Publications:

**International Directory of
Pageants**
World Pageants, Inc.
18781 W. Dixie Highway,
Suite #285 North Miami Beach,
Florida 33180
(305) 933-2993

A book of listings of thousands of
local, national, and international
pageants. $50.

Pageant Life Magazine
Vivienne La Cour
P.O. Box 2732, Citrus Heights,
California 95611-2732

Pageant Consultant Magazine
Patricia Cruz

P.O. Box 20689
Cranston, Rhode Island 01910

Pageant Scene Magazine
6747 Muddy Creek Road
Archdale, North Carolina 27263

MISCELLANEOUS
REFERRAL NUMBERS:

Sexual Abuse Hotline
(800) 4 A CHILD
National line with local referrals.

**Los Angeles County Child
Abuse Hotline**
(800) 540-4000

Protects, investigates, and offers
options for emotionally, physically,
and sexually abused children and
those who have been generally or
severely neglected.

National HIV/AIDS Info Center
(800) 342-AIDS

MISCELLANEOUS
PUBLICATIONS:

Teen Voices
P.O. Box 6009 JFK Post Office
Boston, Massachusetts 02114

A national magazine committed to
encouraging teenage and young

adult women's expression and empowerment. Written by and for young women.

New Moon
P.O. Box 3587
Duluth, Minnesota 55803-3587

"The magazine for girls and their dreams." For girls ages eight to fourteen. Also offers *New Moon Parenting*, "for adults who care about girls."

Here are several youth-oriented magazines and newspapers from various cities. These specific city-wide publications are written by and for teenagers about the issues affecting their lives. Anyone can order copies or subscriptions, but you must live in the specific city to have your writing published.

United Youth
100 Massachusetts Avenue
Boston, Massachusetts 02115

New Youth Connections
144 W. 27th Street, Suite #8R
New York, New York 10001

New Expressions
70 E. Lake Street, Suite #815
Chicago, Illinois 60601

Young D.C.
P.O. Box 65057
Washington, D.C. 20035
(Also offers youth news on-line service.)

L.A. Youth
6030 Wilshire Blvd., Suite #400
Los Angeles, California 90036

Yo! Youth Outlook
450 Mission Street #506
San Francisco, California 94105